# KING LEAR

# KING LEAR

## William Shakespeare

a *Broadview Anthology of British Literature* edition

General Editors,
*The Broadview Anthology of British Literature*:
Joseph Black, University of Massachusetts, Amherst
Leonard Conolly, Trent University
Kate Flint, Rutgers University
Isobel Grundy, University of Alberta
Don LePan, Broadview Press
Roy Liuzza, University of Tennessee
Jerome J. McGann, University of Virginia
Anne Lake Prescott, Barnard College
Barry V. Qualls, Rutgers University
Claire Waters, University of California, Davis

Contributing Editor, *King Lear*:
Craig Walker

broadview press

**Library and Archives Canada Cataloguing in Publication**

Shakespeare, William, 1564-1616
     King Lear / William Shakespeare ; contributing editor Craig Walker.

(A Broadview anthology of British literature edition)
Includes bibliographical references.
ISBN 978-1-55111-967-0

     I. Walker, Craig Stewart, 1960- II. Title. III. Series: Broadview anthology of British literature

PR2819.A2W35 2010       822.3'3      C2010-907404-1

Broadview Press is an independent, international publishing house, incorporated in 1985.

We welcome comments and suggestions regarding any aspect of our publications—please feel free to contact us at the addresses below or at -broadview@broadviewpress.com.

*North America*          PO Box 1243, Peterborough, Ontario, Canada K9J 7H5
                      2215 Kenmore Ave., Buffalo, New York, USA 14207
                      Tel: (705) 743-8990; Fax: (705) 743-8353
                      email: customerservice@broadviewpress.com

*UK, Europe, Central Asia,*    Eurospan Group, 3 Henrietta St., London WC2E 8LU, UK
*Middle East, Africa, India,*    Tel: 44 (0) 1767 604972; Fax: 44 (0) 1767 601640
*and Southeast Asia*        email: eurospan@turpin-distribution.com

*Australia and New Zealand*   NewSouth Books, c/o TL Distribution
                      15-23 Helles Ave., Moorebank, NSW, Australia 2170
                      Tel: (02) 8778 9999; Fax: (02) 8778 9944
                      email: orders@tldistribution.com.au

www.broadviewpress.com

Broadview Press acknowledges the financial support of the Government of Canada through the Canada Book Fund for our publishing activities.

Developmental Editor: Jennifer McCue
Editorial Assistant, In Context materials: Laura Buzzard

# Contents

*Introduction*

# William Shakespeare
# 1564–1616

The plays of Shakespeare are foundational works of Western culture; in the English-speaking world they have influenced subsequent literary culture more broadly and more deeply than any other group of texts except the books of the Bible. The language and imagery of the plays; their ways of telling stories; their innovative dramatic qualities; the characters that populate them (and the ways in which these characters are created); the issues and ideas the plays explore (and the ways in which they explore them)—all these have powerfully shaped English literature and culture over the past four centuries. And this shaping influence has continually touched popular culture as well as more "elevated" literary and academic worlds. From the eighteenth century on Shakespeare's plays have held the stage with far greater frequency than those of any other playwright, and in the twentieth century many have been made into popular films (some of the best of which are films in Japanese and in Russian). Even outside the English-speaking world the plays of Shakespeare receive unparalleled exposure; in the Netherlands, for example, his plays have been performed in the late twentieth and early twenty-first centuries more than twice as often as those of any other playwright. In 2000 he headed the list both on the BBC "person of the millennium" poll and on the *World Almanac's* poll listing the 10 "most influential people of the second millennium." The fact that a playwright, a member of the popular entertainment industry, has continued to enjoy this kind of cultural status—ranked above the likes of Newton, Churchill, Galileo, and Einstein—is worth pausing over. Why are these plays still performed, read, watched, filmed, studied, and appropriated four centuries after they were written? What is the source of his ongoing cultural currency?

There are many ways to answer this question. One is surely that the plays tell great stories. Fundamental, psychologically sophisticated stories, about love, death, growing up, families, communities, guilt, revenge, jealousy, order and disorder, self-knowledge and identity. Another, just as surely, is that they tell them with extraordinary verbal facility in almost all respects: Shakespeare is generally regarded as unsurpassed in his choice of individual words and his inventiveness in conjuring up striking images; in his structuring of the rhythm of poetic lines; in balancing sentences rhetorically; in shaping long speeches; and in crafting sparkling dialogue. A third is that the characters within the stories are uniquely engaging and memorable. In large part this can be attributed to Shakespeare's ingenuity: within the English literary tradition he more or less invented the psychologically realistic literary character; within the European literary tradition he more or less also invented the strong, independent female character. The bare bones of his characters are typically provided by other sources, but the flesh and blood is of Shakespeare's making. Fourth, and perhaps most important of all, Shakespeare's plays tell their stories in ways that are open-ended emotionally and intellectually: no matter how neatly the threads of story may be knitted together at the end, the threads of idea and of emotion in Shakespeare's plays are never tied off. It is this openness of the plays, their availability for reinterpretation, that enables them to be endlessly re-staged, rewritten, and re-interpreted—and to yield fresh ideas and fresh feelings time and time again.

Given the centrality of Shakespeare to Western culture, the wish of many readers to know far more than we do about his life is understandable. In fact we do know a fair amount about the facts of his life—given late sixteenth- and early seventeenth-century norms, perhaps more than we might expect to know of someone of his class and background. But we know a good deal less of Shakespeare than we do of some other leading writers of his era—Ben Jonson, for example, or John Donne. And, perhaps most frustrating of all, we know almost nothing of an intimate or personal nature about Shakespeare.

Shakespeare (whose surname also appears on various documents as Shakespear, Shakspere, Shaxpere, and Shagspere) was baptized in Stratford-upon-Avon on 26 April 1564. Reasonable conjecture, given the customs of the time, suggests that he was born two-to-four days earlier; the date that has been most frequently advanced is 23

April (the same day of the year on which he died in 1616, and also the day on which St. George, England's patron saint, is traditionally honored). His father, John, was a glove-maker and also a local politician: first an alderman and then bailiff, a position equivalent to mayor. Some scholars have argued that he had remained a Catholic in newly-Protestant England, and that Shakespeare thus grew up in a clandestinely Catholic home; though the evidence for this is suggestive, it is not conclusive. (If Shakespeare had grown up Catholic, that background might lead readers to see some of his history plays in a different perspective, and might lend even greater poignancy to images such as that of the "bare ruined choirs" of Sonnet 73, with its allusion to the monasteries destroyed by Henry VIII following the break with Rome.)

Stratford-upon-Avon had a good grammar school, which is generally presumed to have provided William's early education, though no records exist to confirm this. Not surprisingly, he did not go on to university, which at the time would have been unusual for a person from the middle class. (Even Ben Jonson, one of the finest classicists of the period, did not attend university.) Shakespeare's first exposure to theater was probably through the troupes of traveling players that regularly toured the country at that time.

On 28 November 1562, when Shakespeare was eighteen, he was married to Anne Hathaway, who was eight years his senior. Six months later, in May of 1583, Anne gave birth to their first daughter, Susanna; given the timing, it seems reasonable to speculate that an unexpected pregnancy may have prompted a sudden marriage. In February 1585, twins, named Hamnet (Shakespeare's only son, who was to die at the age of eleven) and Judith, were born. Some time later, probably within the next three years, Shakespeare moved to London, leaving his young family behind. There has been considerable speculation as to his reasons for leaving Stratford-upon-Avon, but no solid evidence has been found to support any of the numerous theories. Certainly London was then (as now) a magnet for ambitious young men, and in the late 1580s it was effectively the only English city conducive to the pursuit of a career as a writer or in the theater.

It is not known exactly when Shakespeare joined the professional theater in London, but by 1592 several of his plays had reached the stage—the three parts of *Henry VI*, probably *The Comedy of Errors* and

*Titus Andronicus*, and possibly others. The earliest extant mention of him in print occurs in 1592: a sarcastic jibe by an embittered older playwright, Robert Greene. Greene calls Shakespeare "an upstart crow beautified with our feathers," probably referring to Shakespeare's work on the series of *Henry VI* plays, which may well have involved the revision of material by other writers who had originally worked on the play. In any case, from 1594 on, Will Shakespeare is listed as a member of the company called The Lord Chamberlain's Men (later called The King's Men, when James I became their patron).

Professional theater in London did not become firmly established until 1576, when the first permanent playhouses opened. By the late 1580s four theaters were in operation—an unprecedented level of activity, and one that in all probability helped to nurture greater sophistication on the part of audiences. Certainly it was a hothouse that nurtured an extraordinary growth of theatrical agility on the part of Elizabethan playwrights. Shakespeare, as both playwright and actor in The Lord Chamberlain's Men, was afforded opportunities of forging, testing, and reworking his written work in the heat of rehearsals and performances—opportunities that were not open to other playwrights.[1] And in Christopher Marlowe he had a rival playwright of a most extraordinary sort. It seems safe to conjecture that the two learned a good deal about play construction from each other. In the late 1580s and early 1590s they both adopt virtually simultaneously the practice of having their characters express their intentions in advance of the unfolding action, thereby encouraging the formation of audience expectations; they also begin to make it a practice to interpose some other action between the exit and the re-entry of any character, thereby further fostering the creation of a sense of temporal and spatial illusion of a sort quite new to the English stage.

---

[1] From the nineteenth century onwards (though, perhaps tellingly, never before that), the suggestion has occasionally been put forward that Shakespeare never wrote the plays attributed to him, and that someone else—perhaps Francis Bacon, perhaps Edward de Vere, 17th Earl of Oxford—was actually the author. These conspiracy theories have sometimes gained popular currency, but scholars have never found any reason whatsoever to credit any of them. One of the many reasons such theories lack credibility follows from our sure knowledge that Shakespeare was an actor in many of the plays that bear his name as author. If Shakespeare had not written the plays himself it would surely have been impossibly difficult to conceal that fact from the rest of the company, in rehearsal as well as in performance, over the course of many, many years.

In his early years in London Shakespeare also established himself as a non-dramatic poet—and sought aristocratic patronage in doing so. In the late sixteenth century the writing of poetry was accorded considerable respect, the writing of plays a good deal less. It was conventional for those not of aristocratic birth themselves to seek a patron for their writing—as Shakespeare evidently did with the Earl of Southampton, a young noble to whom he dedicated two substantial poems of mythological narrative, *Venus and Adonis* (1593) and *The Rape of Lucrece* (1594). (It is a measure of the enormity of Shakespeare's achievement that these poems, which would be regarded as major works of almost any other writer of the period, are an afterthought in most considerations of Shakespeare's work.) Before the end of the century Shakespeare was also circulating his sonnets, as we know from the praise of Francis Meres, who wrote in 1598 that the "sweet, witty soul" of the classical poet of love, Ovid, "lives in mellifluous and honey-tongued Shakespeare, witness his Venus and Adonis, his Lucrece, his sugared sonnets among his private friends, etc." Such circulation among "private friends" was common practice at the time, and was not necessarily followed by publication. When Shakespeare's sonnets were finally published, in 1609, the dedication was from the printer rather than the author, suggesting that Shakespeare may not have authorized their publication.

There are thirty-eight extant plays by Shakespeare (if *Two Noble Kinsmen* is included in the total). Unlike most other playwrights of the age, he wrote in every major dramatic genre. His history plays (most of them written in the 1590s) include *Richard III*; *Henry IV, Part 1 and Part 2*; and *Henry V*. He wrote comedies throughout his playwriting years; the succession of comedies that date from the years 1595–1601, including *Much Ado About Nothing*, *As You Like It*, and *Twelfth Night*, may represent his most successful work in this genre, though some have argued that *The Merchant of Venice* (c. 1596) and the "dark comedies" which date from between 1601 and 1604 (including *All's Well That Ends Well* and *Measure for Measure*) resonate even more deeply. The period of the "dark comedies" substantially overlaps with the period in which Shakespeare wrote a succession of great tragedies. *Hamlet* may have been written as early as 1598–99, but *Othello, King Lear*, and *Macbeth* were written in succession between 1601 and 1606. Several of his last plays are romance-comedies—notably *Cymbeline*,

*The Winter's Tale*, and *The Tempest* (all of which date from the period 1608–11).

Shakespeare was a shareholder in The Lord Chamberlain's Men, and it was in that capacity rather than as a playwright or actor that he made a good deal of money. There was at the time no equivalent to modern laws of copyright, or to modern conventions of payment to the authors of published works. Nineteen of Shakespeare's plays were printed individually during Shakespeare's lifetime, but it is clear that many of these publications did not secure his co-operation. It has often been hypothesized that some of the printers of the most obviously defective texts (referred to by scholars as "bad quartos") are pirated editions dictated from memory to publishers by actors; there is some evidence to support this theory, though even if correct it leaves many textual issues unresolved.

The first publication of Shakespeare's collected works did not occur until 1623, several years after his death, when two of his fellow actors, John Heminges and Henry Condell, arranged to have printed the First Folio, a carefully prepared volume (by the standards of the time) that included thirty-six of Shakespeare's plays. Eighteen of these were appearing for the first time, and four others for the first time in a reliable edition. (*Two Noble Kinsmen*, which was written in collaboration with a younger playwright, John Fletcher, and *Pericles*, of which it appears Shakespeare was not the sole author, were both excluded, although the editors did include *Henry VIII*, which is now generally believed to have been another work in which Fletcher had a hand.)

A vital characteristic of Shakespeare's plays is their extraordinary richness of language. After several centuries of forging a new tongue out of its polyglot sources, the English language in the sixteenth century had entered a period of steady growth in its range, as vocabulary expanded to meet the needs of an increasingly complex society. Yet its structure over this same time (no doubt in connection with the spread of print culture) was becoming increasingly stable. When we compare the enormous difference between the language of Chaucer, who was writing in the late fourteenth century, and that of Shakespeare, writing in the late sixteenth century, it is remarkable to see how greatly the language changed over those two centuries—considerably more than it has changed in the four centuries from Shakespeare's time to our own. English was still effectively a new language in his time, with immense and largely unexplored possibilities for conveying subtleties of meaning. More than any other, Shakespeare embarked on that exploration; his reading was clearly very wide,[1] as was his working vocabulary. But he expanded the language as well as absorbing it; a surprising number of the words Shakespeare used are first recorded as having been used in his work.

The popular image of Shakespeare's last few years is that first expressed by Nicholas Rowe in 1709:

> The latter part of his life was spent, as all men of good sense wish theirs may be, in ease, retirement, and the conversation of his friends. He had the good fortune to gather together an estate equal to his occasion, and, in that, to his wish; and is said to have spent some years before his death at his native Stratford.

We know for a fact that around 1610 Shakespeare moved from London to Stratford, where his family had continued to live throughout the years he had spent in London, and the move has often been referred to as a "retirement." Shakespeare did not immediately give up playwriting, however: *The Tempest* (1611), *Henry VIII* (c. 1612), and *Two Noble Kinsmen* (c. 1613) all date from after his move to Stratford. By the time he left London Shakespeare was indeed a relatively wealthy man, with substantial investments both in real estate and in the tithes of the town (an arrangement that would be comparable to buying government bonds today).

After 1613 we have no record of any further writing; he died on 23 April 1616, aged 52. In his will, Shakespeare left his extensive property to the sons of his daughter, Susanna (described in her epitaph as

---

1    In his early years in London Shakespeare may well have acquired much of his reading material from Richard Field, a man from Stratford-upon-Avon of about Shakespeare's age who was in the book trade. Field printed Shakespeare's early poems, *Venus and Adonis* and *The Rape of Lucrece*, and it is certainly possible that the two men had some understanding by which Shakespeare borrowed some of the books he read, which otherwise might have been prohibitively expensive. (Among the works printed by Field was a multi-volume Thomas North translation of *Plutarch's Lives*, of which Shakespeare made extensive use.) Shakespeare also lodged for a time in London with a French Huguenot family named Montjoy, whose home may have been the source for some of the French books that his plays demonstrate a familiarity with. And he may also have had the use of the libraries of one or more of his aristocratic patrons.

"witty above her sex"). To his wife, he left his "second-best bed"—a bequest which many have found both puzzling and provocative. He was buried as a respectable citizen in the chancel of the parish church, where his gravestone is marked not with a name, but a simple poem:

> Good friend, for Jesus' sake forbear
> To dig the dust enclosed here.
> Blest be the man that spares these stones,
> And curst be he that moves my bones.

Shakespeare's work appears to have been extremely well regarded in his lifetime; soon after his death a consensus developed that his work—his plays in particular—constitute the highest achievement in English literature. In some generations he has been praised most highly for the depth of his characterization, in others for the dense brilliance of his imagery, in others for the extraordinary intellectual suggestiveness of the ideas that his characters express (and occasionally embody). But in every generation since the mid-seventeenth century a consensus has remained that Shakespeare stands without peer among English authors.

In most generations the study of Shakespeare has also helped to shape the development of literary criticism and theory. From John Dryden and Samuel Johnson to Samuel Taylor Coleridge to Northrop Frye, works central to the development of literary theory and criticism have had Shakespeare as their subject. And in the past 50 years Shakespeare has been a vital test case in the development of feminist literary theory, of post-colonial theory, and of political, cultural, and new historicist criticism: just as with each generation people of the theater develop new ways of playing Shakespeare that yield fresh insight, so too do scholars develop new ways of reading texts through reading Shakespeare.

❧❀❧

# King Lear

Most scholars and critics of the past century or so would agree that *King Lear* is Shakespeare's greatest play. That doesn't make it his most popular play: *King Lear* is difficult to stage, hard to film, and intimidating to read. With its reputation as the greatest work by the greatest writer in English, it bears the weight of great expectations.

*King Lear* was probably written in 1605, which makes it one of Shakespeare's later plays, from about four-fifths of the way through his career. The story of Lear had been around since at least the twelfth century, when it appeared in Geoffrey of Monmouth's *Historia regum Britanniae* (c. 1135–39), and had been retold in Holinshed's *Chronicles* (1577), in the multiple-authored *The Mirror for Magistrates* (1574–87), in Book II, Canto X of Spenser's *The Fairie Queene* (1589), and, most relevantly, in an anonymous play, *King Leir*, which had been first performed in 1594 and was published in 1605, the same year Shakespeare's play was first performed. Today, Lear is regarded by historians as based more upon legend than upon fact (he appears to have been derived from the Celtic god, Llyr); but Shakespeare's audience believed Lear to have been a historical figure. That fact makes Shakespeare's alterations to the story seem strikingly audacious—most notably, his changing of the ending; in earlier versions the main protagonists all survive.

Assertions of *King Lear*'s supremacy among Shakespeare's works chiefly begin to appear within the twentieth century; for most of the eighteenth and nineteenth centuries *Hamlet* held pride of place, with *Lear* ranked somewhat below it as literature, and rated a good deal below it as drama. Indeed, for much of the more than four hundred years of its history, *King Lear* was regarded as being virtually unplayable in its unaltered form—unplayable less on the conventional grounds of its being difficult to stage convincingly (though it surely is that), than on the grounds of its tragic ending embodying too massive an assault on our sensibilities and our belief in a just universe. In 1681—seventy-five years after Shakespeare's version was first published—the poet laureate, Nahum Tate, published a radically revised version of *King Lear* that would hold the stage until well into the nineteenth century. In Tate's version, the Fool has been eliminated, and there is a happy ending: neither Lear nor Cordelia dies, and Gloucester is blinded but spared death. Cordelia loves not the King of France but Edgar, whom she marries at the end of the play, the pair becoming the new monarchs of Britain while Lear goes off into a happy retirement with his friends Gloucester and Kent. Tate's revised text of *Lear* has become a favorite *bête noir* among historians of drama, but we should beware of jeering; a reluctance to embrace tragic endings is widespread in many eras, including our own, and in Tate's day many demanded "poetic justice" in drama. Moreover, in sparing the lives of the main protagonists and eliminating the Fool Tate was essentially returning the story to its original pattern.

In the preface to his 1681 revision of *King Lear*, Tate explained some of his reasons for undertaking an alteration of Shakespeare's play, describing the original as

> a Heap of Jewels, unstrung and unpolisht; yet so dazling in their Disorder, that I soon perceiv'd I had seiz'd a Treasure. 'Twas my good Fortune to light on one Expedient to rectifie what was wanting in the Regularity and Probability of the Tale, which was to run through the whole A Love betwixt Edgar and Cordelia, that never chang'd word with each other in the Original. This renders Cordelia's Indifference and her Father's Passion in the first Scene probable. It likewise gives Countenance to Edgar's Disguise, making that a generous Design that was before a poor Shift to save his Life.

In large part, then, Tate's revision was his attempt to rationalize the play, to tie up some of what he regarded as its loose ends. It is indeed a play that leaves a number of outstanding questions of this kind. Why does Cordelia not find a gentler way of answering Lear while still avoiding the hypocrisy of her sisters? Why does Edgar keep up his Poor Tom disguise with the mad Lear, and in the presence of his blinded and remorseful father? Why does Kent maintain his disguise until the last scene of the play? Why does the Fool appear only at the beginning of Lear's trials and then disappear in Act Three? Interestingly, in the old anonymous play, *King Leir*—so much cruder a work in many respects—far greater care is taken to give apprehensible motives to the characters in many of these instances. Shakespeare seems to have deliberately stripped these from his play; it is as if the characters were saying to us, as Edmund (or, in the Quarto, Gonorill) says, near the end of the play, "Ask me not what I know."

If *King Lear* leaves a number of small questions unanswered, far more so does it leave unanswered the many large questions it raises. What is the play about? At one level, it tells a very simple story, almost like a folktale. Once upon a time there was a foolish king, who decided to divide his kingdom into three parts, and give one part to each of his three daughters. At this level, as George Orwell observed, "*Lear* is one of the minority of Shakespeare's plays that are unmistakably *about* something. For example, *Macbeth* is about ambition, *Othello* is about jealousy, and *Timon of Athens* is about money. The subject of *Lear* is renunciation." But from its simple beginning the play expands in resonance to become a work about life, about the universe, about everything. *King Lear* is a play about growing old, and about death; about the relations between parents and children; about power, and rule, and justice; about the bonds of human love; about the depths of human despair, and the depths of human cruelty and evil of which humans are capable; about the difficulty of achieving knowledge of other humans, and perhaps even more the difficulty of achieving knowledge of oneself. It explores what it means to be human, and it asks what remains when everything that gives us identity is taken away. Above all, *King Lear* asks: does life have meaning? Is humanity ultimately the victim of a cruel, indifferent, or meaningless universe? Are we defined only by suffering?

The story of Gloucester, Edmund, and Edgar (which is based on that of the King of Paphlagonia and his sons, Plexirtus and Leonatus, in Philip Sidney's *Arcadia*) was added by Shakespeare to the plot of *King Leir*. It is the most highly developed subplot in Shakespearean drama, and opens up a variety of thematic and theatrical parallels with the main story—parallels that substantially broaden and deepen the impact of the play as a whole. On the practical plane the interweaving of the two stories and the oscillation between settings it entails help Shakespeare to add scope to a story that otherwise (as it does in the anonymous *King Leir*) might unfold with undue rapidity. But the addition of a story that in large part parallels that of Lear also considerably expands the play's intellectual and emotional range. The story of filial betrayal and loyalty in Gloucester's case, for example, adds to our understanding of Lear's. Gloucester's loss of sight and Lear's loss of reason each gain in force for being juxtaposed with one another. The bleak vision that Lear gives voice to is echoed by that of the more innocent Gloucester; it is through Gloucester rather than Lear that perhaps the bleakest vision is presented: "as flies to wanton boys are we to the gods: they kill us for their sport." And elements in one line of story sometimes cast a different and surprising light on both narrative and thematic narrative elements in the other. Edmund's worship of nature, for example, may lead us to question the degree to which the selfishness of Lear's two eldest daughters really should be considered "unnatural," as Lear calls it. Is goodness natural, or is it merely part of a veneer of civilization that we have been taught? That is one more of the large questions that this play, perhaps more than any other work of English literature, spins off in rich profusion.

### The Text

Every modern edition of *King Lear* depends to varying degrees on the two first published texts, the Quarto edition of 1608 and the First Folio of 1623. These words, "Quarto" and "Folio," refer to how a book's paper was folded. A standard sized sheet of paper folded once to make two pages would be a folio; if it were folded twice to make four pages, it would be a quarto. Quarto books were used in the publication of single plays. The folio format was generally used for large, authoritative works (works of theology, editions of classical literature, certain sorts of Bibles); Ben Jonson set a precedent for playwrights by publishing his collected plays in a folio edition in 1616.

There are often substantial differences between the Quarto and the Folio texts of Shakespeare's plays; *King Lear* is an extreme case. To begin with, there are 300 lines which appear in the Quarto but not in the Folio, and there are 100 lines which appear in the Folio, but not in the Quarto. There are also many smaller differences;

some are negligible (it hardly matters, for instance, whether one spells the expletive "Oh" or "O"), but others may be important to the interpretation of the play. There are a number of cases in which a difference in a particular word or phrase alters the meaning of a speech; and on several occasions a particular speech is assigned to different characters in the two editions. An early instance of this is the assignment of a line in the first scene: "Here's France and Burgundy, my noble Lord." In the Quarto edition this line is assigned to Gloucester, but in the Folio it is assigned to Cordelia. Whoever says the line, the same information is given to Lear, but it makes a difference to the way in which we may interpret the character of Cordelia whether the announcement is made by Gloucester or by Cordelia (whom Lear has at this point banished). Most editors have preferred the Quarto's assignment in this instance, but the Folio offers a provocative dramatic possibility.

For many years editors generally assumed that each of the two editions represented an imperfect version of Shakespeare's intended text. Accordingly, the usual practice was to blend the two editions into one slightly longer play, choosing between the specific variations by using one's judgement as to which was the stronger text in any given instance, and attempting to include all or nearly all the lines that Shakespeare had written. However, scholarly opinion is now largely in agreement that the two editions represent two different versions of the play, each of which is legitimate (although each does include some obvious errors). Most probably the Quarto was printed from an early version of Shakespeare's uncorrected papers, and the Folio was an attempt to revise the Quarto edition, with reference to an altered and shortened version in a prompt book that had been prepared for performance.

The Folio edition has usually been preferred to the Quarto, quite simply because it contains a number of clear improvements. This anthology, too, presents the Folio text in the first instance, but with substantial reference made to the Quarto throughout. The notes indicate all instances where the Quarto contains important differences, and for three scenes where the Folio and Quarto are markedly different both versions are presented side by side, enabling readers conveniently to explore issues of text and meaning.

In declaring that the Folio edition is preferable, it is important to exercise considerable caution, in large part because we cannot be sure that all the revisions found in the Folio were indeed the work of Shakespeare himself. While it seems that many of these were made for performance (including additional passages which are certainly of the same quality as the rest of what Shakespeare had written), others are clearly editorial attempts to clarify and normalize certain passages for publication. In the former case, it is likely that Shakespeare himself made the revisions, so as to improve the play in performance. But in the case of those revisions which seem to have been made for publication, there are a number of reasons to suspect a hand other than Shakespeare's. First, we know that Shakespeare was dead by the time that the First Folio was prepared, and it seems unlikely that he would have concerned himself with the preparation of one of his plays for publication on a speculative basis. And there is also some evidence that some person or persons—perhaps Heminge and Condell—exercised personal judgement over many of the revisions.

❧❦❧

## King Lear[1]

DRAMATIS PERSONAE
  Lear, *King of Britain*
  King of France
  Gonerill, *Lear's eldest daughter*
  Duke of Albany, *Gonerill's husband*
  Regan, *Lear's second daughter*
  Duke of Cornwall, *Regan's husband*
  Cordelia, *Lear's youngest daughter*
  Duke of Burgundy

---

1  *King Lear* The present text was originally prepared for *The Broadview Anthology of British Literature* by Craig Walker. The first Folio edition is used as the copy text; the more significant differences between the Folio and Quarto texts are detailed in the notes, and for the scenes in which the degree of divergence between the two is greatest both versions are provided on facing pages.

Earl of Kent
Earl of Gloucester
Edgar, *Gloucester's elder son, later disguised as Tom o' Bedlam*
Edmund, *Gloucester's younger, bastard son*
Oswald, *Gonerill's steward*
Old Man, *Gloucester's tenant*
Curan, *Gloucester's servant*
Fool, *attending on Lear*
Doctor
Servants, Captains, Herald, Knight, Messenger, Gentlemen,
    Soldiers, etc.

## ACT 1, SCENE 1

(*Enter Kent, Gloucester*[1] *and Edmund.*[2])

KENT.   I thought the King had more affected[3] the Duke of
Albany than Cornwall.

GLOUCESTER.   It did always seem so to us, but now, in the
division of the kingdoms, it appears not which of the Dukes
he values most, for equalities are so weighed, that curiosity in     5
neither can make choice of either's moiety.[4]

KENT.   Is not this your son, my Lord?

GLOUCESTER.   His breeding, Sir, hath been at my charge.[5] I have
so often blushed to acknowledge him, that now I am brazed[6]
to it.     10

KENT.   I cannot conceive[7] you.

---

1   *Gloucester*   Occasionally in the first Folio edition (hereafter F) and throughout the
    first Quarto edition (hereafter Q), the name is spelled phonetically as "Gloster."

2   *Bastard/Edmund*   In Q, the stage directions and tag-lines begin by referring to the
    character as "Bastard" (or "Bast."), and then maintain this practice throughout most
    of the rest of the play. F begins by using the character's name, at first spelling it
    "Edmond," then "Edmund," but then also uses "Bastard" for much of the play.

3   *affected*   Favored.

4   *equalities ... moiety*   Their shares have been apportioned so equally that close ex-
    amination of one or the other cannot show that either has a preferable share.

5   *breeding ... charge*   A pun: I have been charged with having begotten him / he has
    been raised at my expense.

6   *brazed*   Brazened.

7   *conceive*   Understand; Gloucester then puns on the word in the sense of "become
    pregnant by."

GLOUCESTER. Sir, this young fellow's mother could; whereupon she grew round wombed; and had indeed, Sir, a son for her cradle, ere she had a husband for her bed. Do you smell a fault?

15 KENT. I cannot wish the fault undone, the issue of it being so proper.

GLOUCESTER. But I have a son, Sir, by order of law,[1] some year elder then this—who yet is no dearer in my account. Though this knave came something saucily to the world before he was sent

20 for, yet was his mother fair; there was good sport at his making; and the whoreson[2] must be acknowledged. (*To Edmund.*)[3] Do you know this noble gentleman, Edmund?

EDMUND. No, my Lord.

GLOUCESTER. (*To Edmund.*) My Lord of Kent. Remember him

25 hereafter, as my honourable friend.

EDMUND. (*To Kent.*) My services to your Lordship.

KENT. (*To Edmund.*) I must love you, and sue to know you better.

EDMUND. Sir, I shall study deserving.[4]

30 GLOUCESTER. (*To Kent.*) He hath been out[5] nine years, and away he shall again. The King is coming.

(*Sennet.*[6] *Enter King Lear, Cornwall, Albany, Gonerill,*[7] *Regan, Cordelia, and attendants.*)

LEAR. Attend the Lords of France and Burgundy, Gloucester.

GLOUCESTER. I shall, my Lord.

(*Exit.*)

---

1 *by order of law* Legitimately born.

2 *whoreson* Bastard (jocular).

3 *(To Edmund.)* All stage directions or parts of stage directions appearing in square brackets have been inserted by the current editor; those appearing in round parentheses are derived from the source text.

4 *study deserving* Attempt to prove worthy of your kindness.

5 *out* Away from home (presumably at school or some similar arrangement).

6 *Sennet* Notes played on trumpet or cornet to signal a royal entrance.

7 *Gonerill* While it has become common to spell this character's name "Goneril" (with an e and one l), apparently that was not the spelling used by Shakespeare. In F, the name is consistently spelt "Gonerill"; in Q it is usually spelt "Gonorill."

LEAR.    Meantime we shall express our darker purpose.[1]      35
Give me the map there. Know that we have divided
In three our kingdom; and 'tis our fast° intent,      *firm*
To shake all cares and business from our age,
Conferring them on younger strengths, while we
Unburdened crawl toward death. Our son of Cornwall,      40
And you, our no less loving son of Albany:
We have this hour a constant will to publish[2]
Our daughters' several[3] dowers, that future strife
May be prevented now. The Princes, France and Burgundy,
Great rivals in our youngest daughter's love,      45
Long in our court, have made their amorous sojourn,[4]
And here are to be answered. Tell me, my daughters—
Since now we will divest us both of rule,
Interest° of territory, cares of state—      *ownership*
Which of you shall we say doth love us most,      50
That we, our largest bounty may extend
Where nature doth with merit challenge.[5] Gonerill,
Our eldest born, speak first.
GONERILL.    Sir, I love you more than word can wield°      *convey*
the matter;
Dearer than eye-sight, space, and liberty;      55
Beyond what can be valued, rich or rare;
No less than life, with grace, health, beauty, honour;
As much as child e'er loved, or father found;°      *experienced*
A love that makes breath poor, and speech unable;
Beyond all manner of so much, I love you.      60
CORDELIA.    What shall Cordelia speak? Love, and be silent.

---

1  *darker purpose* Hidden intention. The equivalent speech in the Quarto version
   is substantially shorter. It reads as follows: "Meantime we will express our darker
   purposes. / The map there; know we have divided / In three, our kingdom; and 'tis
   our first intent, / To shake all cares and business of our state, / Confirming them on
   younger years. / The two great Princes France and Burgundy, / Great rivals in our
   youngest daughter's love, / Long in our Court have made their amorous sojourn, /
   And here are to be answered. Tell me my daughters, / Which of you shall we say doth
   love us most, / That we our largest bounty may extend, / Where merit doth most
   challenge it. / Gonorill, our eldest born, speak first."
2  *constant ... publish* Resolute intention to announce.
3  *several* Separate, individual.
4  *amorous sojourn* Visit for the purpose of courtship.
5  *Where nature ... challenge* Where natural affection is equal to merit.

LEAR.  Of all these bounds even from this line, to this,
  With shadowy forests, and with champains°          *open plains*
    riched
  With plenteous rivers, and wide-skirted meads,¹
65  We make thee Lady. To thine and Albany's
      issues°                                        *descendants*
  Be this perpetual. What says our second daughter?
  Our dearest Regan, wife of Cornwall?
REGAN.    I am made of that self-mettle² as my sister,
  And prize me³ at her worth. In my true heart,
70  I find she names my very deed⁴ of love;
  Only she comes too short, that I profess⁵
  Myself an enemy to all other joys,
  Which the most precious square of sense⁶ professes,
  And find I am alone felicitate°                    *made happy*
75  In your dear Highness' love.
CORDELIA.                          Then poor Cordelia!
  And yet not so, since I am sure my love's
  More ponderous than my tongue.
LEAR.   To thee, and thine hereditary ever,
80  Remain this ample third of our fair kingdom;
  No less in space, validity, and pleasure
  Than that conferred on Gonerill.⁷ Now our joy,
  Although our last and least; to whose young love,
  The vines of France, and milk of Burgundy,
85  Strive to be interest. What can you say, to draw
  A third more opulent than your sisters'? Speak.
CORDELIA.  Nothing my Lord.
LEAR.  Nothing?
CORDELIA.  Nothing.

---

1  *wide-skirted meads*  Widely spread meadows.
2  *self-mettle*  Same spirit (with perhaps a pun on "metal").
3  *And prize me*  I.e., and I do prize myself.
4  *deed*  Pun on action and document of real estate ownership.
5  *that I profess*  In that I recognize.
6  *most precious square of sense*  Invaluable state of the well-balanced mind.
7  The following lines are substantially different in the Quarto text. The Quarto reads
   as follows: "Than that confirmed on Gonorill. But now our joy, / Although the last,
   not least in our dear love, / What can you say to win a third more opulent / Than
   your sisters'?"

LEAR.  Nothing will come of nothing; speak again.                    90
CORDELIA.   Unhappy that I am, I cannot heave
  My heart into my mouth. I love your Majesty
  According to my bond,[1] no more nor less.
LEAR.  How, how Cordelia? Mend your speech a little,
  Lest you may mar your fortunes.                                    95
CORDELIA.                          Good my Lord,
  You have begot me, bred me, loved me.
  I return those duties back as are right fit:
  Obey you, love you, and most honour you.
  Why have my sisters husbands, if they say                         100
  They love you all? Happily, when I shall wed,
  That Lord, whose hand must take my plight,[2] shall carry
  Half my love with him, half my care, and duty.
  Sure I shall never marry like my sisters.
LEAR.  But goes thy heart with this?                                 105
CORDELIA.                          Aye, my good Lord.
LEAR.  So young, and so untender?
CORDELIA.   So young, my Lord, and true.
LEAR.  Let it be so: thy truth then be thy dower;
  For by the sacred radiance of the sun,                            110
  The mysteries of Hecate[3] and the night;
  By all the operation of the orbs,[4]
  From whom we do exist, and cease to be:
  Here I disclaim all my paternal care,
  Propinquity and property of blood,[5]                             115
  And as a stranger to my heart and me,
  Hold thee from this forever. The barbarous Scythian,[6]
  Or he that makes his generation messes[7]
  To gorge his appetite, shall to my bosom

---

1  *bond*  Bond between daughter and father, but also carrying the implication of legal
   obligation.
2  *plight*  Oath of marriage.
3  *mysteries of Hecate*  Rites of the goddess of witchcraft and crossroads (F reads "miseries," clearly an error).
4  *operation ... orbs*  Movement of the planetary spheres (i.e., astrological influence).
5  *Propinquity ... blood*  Relationship and shared blood.
6  *Scythian*  Literally, an inhabitant of what is now Russia, but established by Roman
   poets as a byword for savage.
7  *makes ... messes*  Makes meals of his parents or children.

120       Be as well neighboured, pitied, and relieved,
          As thou my sometime° daughter.                      *former*
       KENT.    Good my Liege—
       LEAR.   Peace, Kent!
          Come not between the dragon[1] and his wrath.
125       I loved her most, and thought to set my rest[2]
          On her kind nursery. Hence, and avoid my sight!
          So be my grave, my peace, as here I give
          Her father's heart from her. Call France! Who stirs?[3]
          Call Burgundy! (*To his sons-in law.*) Cornwall, and Albany:
130       With my two daughters' dowers, digest[4] the third.
          Let pride, which she calls plainness, marry her![5]
          I do invest you jointly with my power,
          Preeminence, and all the large effects
          That troop with majesty.[6] Ourself, by monthly course,
135       With reservation of[7] an hundred knights,
          By you to be sustained, shall our abode
          Make with you by due turn. Only we shall retain
          The name, and all th'addition[8] to a king. The
            sway,°                             *management*
          Revenue, execution of the rest,
140       Belovèd sons, be yours; which to confirm,
          This coronet part between you.[9]
       KENT.                    Royal Lear,
          Whom I have ever honoured as my King,
          Loved as my father, as my master followed,
145       As my great patron thought on in my prayers—
       LEAR.   The bow is bent and drawn; make from the shaft.[10]

---

1   *dragon*   Heraldic emblem of Britain.
2   *set my rest*   Pun: build my retiring years; stake everything (a term drawn from *prim-ero*, a card game).
3   *Who stirs?*   Move it!
4   *digest*   Swallow (i.e. split the third between the first two).
5   *Let pride … her*   Let her pridefulness, which she insists is merely plain speaking, stand as her dowry and find her a husband.
6   *large effects … majesty*   Splendid retinues and display of pomp.
7   *with reservation of*   Reserving the privilege of having.
8   *addition*   Additional honors.
9   *This coronet … you*   This crown be split between you.
10   *The bow … shaft*   Lear suggests that he is figuratively an archer who has drawn his bow, so Kent should get out of the arrow's way.

KENT.   Let it fall rather, though the fork° invade      *arrow-head*
The region of my heart. Be Kent unmannerly,
When Lear is mad.[1] What wouldest thou do, old man?
Think'st thou that duty shall have dread to speak,                    150
When power to flattery bows?
To plainness honour's bound,
When Majesty falls to folly. Reserve thy state;[2]
And in thy best consideration check°                          *stop*
This hideous rashness. Answer my life, my judgement:[3]              155
Thy youngest daughter does not love thee least;
Nor are those empty hearted, whose low sounds
Reverb no hollowness.[4]

LEAR.                    Kent, on thy life no more!

KENT.   My life I never held but as pawn[5]                          160
To wage against thine enemies, ne'er feared to lose it,
Thy safety being motive.

LEAR.                    Out of my sight!

KENT.   See better Lear, and let me still remain
The true blank of thine eye.                                       165

LEAR.   Now by Apollo—[6]

KENT.                    Now by Apollo, King
Thou swear'st thy gods in vain.

LEAR.   O, Vassal! Miscreant!

ALBANY and CORDELIA.   Dear sir, forbear.[7]                        170

---

1   *Be Kent ... mad*   When you behave insanely, it calls for a breach of manners on my
    part.
2   *Reserve thy state*   Hold on to your power.
3   *Answer ... judgement*   I'll answer with my life if I am wrong in this judgement.
4   *Nor ... hollowness*   Nor does the lack of a loud rhetorical expression of emotion
    from someone suggest that she has nothing in her heart.
5   *pawn*   Least valuable piece in a chess game.
6   *Apollo*   God associated not only with clear sight, but also with archery (the world
    of the play is nominally pagan).
7   *Dear Sir, forbear*   Many editors follow Nicholas Rowe (1709) in inserting, prior
    to this line, the stage direction for Lear: "laying his hand on his sword." It is pos-
    sible, however, that they would suggest Lear restrain himself from violent outbursts,
    without his having made any threat of actual violence. It is also possible that Kent's
    continued defiance of the King could provide sufficient motivation for Albany and
    Cordelia to address the line to him.

KENT. Kill thy physician, and thy fee bestow
    Upon the foul disease![1] Revoke thy gift,
    Or whil'st I can vent clamour[2] from my throat,
    I'll tell thee thou dost evil.

175 LEAR. Hear me, recreant°; on thine allegiance, hear me!   *apostate*
    That thou hast sought to make us break our vows,
    Which we durst° never yet; and with           *dared*
      strained° pride,                      *forced*
    To come betwixt our sentences, and our power,
    Which, nor our nature, nor our place can bear;
180   Our potency made good,[3] take thy reward.
    Five days we do allot thee for provision,
    To shield thee from disasters of the world,
    And on the sixth to turn thy hated back
    Upon our kingdom; if on the tenth day following,
185   Thy banished trunk° be found in our <u>dominions</u>,     *body*
    The moment is thy death. Away! By Jupiter,[4]
    This shall not be revoked.

KENT. Fare thee well King; sith° thus thou wilt appear,   *since*
    Freedom lives hence, and banishment is here.

(*To Cordelia.*)

190 The gods to their dear shelter take thee maid,
    That justly think'st, and hast most rightly said.

(*To Gonerill and Regan.*)

And your large speeches, may your deeds approve,
That good effects may spring from words of love.

(*To Albany and Cornwall and the others.*)

Thus Kent, O Princes, bids you all adieu,
195 He'll shape his old course,[5] in a country new.

(*Exit.*)

---

1  *Kill ... disease*  Sarcastic reference to the way Lear is punishing those who are loyal
   to him and rewarding those who are disloyal.
2  *vent clamour*  Cry out.
3  *Our ... good*  My royal authority now having been asserted.
4  *Jupiter*  Supreme Roman god.
5  *shape his old course*  Resume his accustomed (truthful) behavior.

*(Flourish.[1] Enter Gloucester with [the King of] France, and [the Duke of] Burgundy, Attendants.)*

CORDELIA.  Here's France and Burgundy, my noble Lord.[2]
LEAR.  My Lord of Burgundy,
  We first address toward you, who with this King
  Hath rivalled for our daughter. What, in the least,
  Will you require in present dower with her,            200
  Or cease your quest of love?
BURGUNDY.                Most Royal Majesty,
  I crave no more than hath your Highness offered—
  Nor will you tender less?
LEAR.               Right noble Burgundy,        205
  When she was dear to us, we did hold her so,
  But now her price is fallen. Sir, there she stands;
  If aught within that little seeming substance—
  Or all of it, with our displeasure pieced
  And nothing more[3]—may fitly like your Grace,      210
  She's there, and she is yours.
BURGUNDY.              I know no answer.
LEAR.  Will you, with those infirmities she owes,°     *owns*
  Unfriended, new adopted to our hate,
  Dow'rd with our curse, and strangered[4] with our oath,   215
  Take her or, leave her?
BURGUNDY.          Pardon me, Royal Sir,
  Election makes not up in such conditions.[5]
LEAR.  Then leave her, Sir, for by the power that made me,
  I tell you all her wealth. (*To France.*) For you, great King,   220
  I would not from your love make such a stray,
  To match you where I hate; therefore, beseech you
  T'avert your liking a more worthier way,

---

1  *Flourish*  Fanfare to mark the entrance of important persons.
2  *Here's France ... Lord*  Most editors regard the assignment of this line to Cordelia as an error, and assign it either to Gloucester, as the Quarto does, or to Cornwall. But to have Cordelia helpfully speak to her father in a moment when he is upset and distracted is far from implausible, and could have dramatic force.
3  *with our ... nothing more*  With the addition of my displeasure and nothing else (i.e., without any dowry).
4  *strangered*  Made a stranger, disowned.
5  *Election ... conditions*  One cannot make a choice in such circumstances.

Than on a wretch whom Nature is ashamed
225 Almost t'acknowledge hers.

FRANCE.                              This is most strange,
That she—whom even but now, was your object,
The argument of your praise,[1] balm of your age,
The best, the dearest—should in this trice of time
230 Commit a thing so monstrous to dismantle
So many folds of favour. Sure her offence
Must be of such unnatural degree
That monsters it[2]—or your fore-vouched affection
Fall into taint[3]—which to believe of her
235 Must be a faith that reason without miracle
Should never plant in me.[4]

CORDELIA.    I yet beseech your Majesty—
If, for I want that glib and oily art,
To speak and purpose not; since what I will intend,
240 I'll do't before I speak—that you make known
It is no vicious blot, murder, or foulness,
No unchaste action or dishonoured step
That hath deprived me of your grace and favour,
But even for want of that for which I am richer:
245 A still soliciting eye,[5] and such a tongue,
That I am glad I have not, though not to have it,
Hath lost me in your liking.

LEAR.                              Better thou had'st
Not been born, than not t'have pleased me better.

250 FRANCE.    Is it but this? A tardiness in nature,[6]
Which often leaves the history unspoke
That it intends to do. My Lord of Burgundy,
What say you to the lady? Love's not love
When it is mingled with regards that stands

---

1  *object ... praise*  Both the object of your praise and the example of how it should be bestowed.
2  *Must ... monsters it*  Must be so outlandish as to be monstrous.
3  *or your ... taint*  Either that or your previously expressed affection must be suspected.
4  *faith ... in me*  A belief that I could never arrive at rationally without some miracle to prove it.
5  *still soliciting eye*  Eye that is always looking for advantage.
6  *tardiness in nature*  Reserved character.

Aloof from th'entire point;[1] will you have her?          255
She is herself a dowry.[2]
BURGUNDY.                    Royal King,
  Give but that portion which your self proposed,
  And here I take Cordelia by the hand,
  Duchess of Burgundy.                                     260
LEAR.  Nothing, I have sworn. I am firm.
BURGUNDY.   (*To Cordelia.*) I am sorry then you have so lost a
    father,
  That you must lose a husband.
CORDELIA.   Peace be with Burgundy,
  Since that respect and fortunes are his love,            265
  I shall not be his wife.
FRANCE.   Fairest Cordelia, that art most rich being poor,   *Sonnet 116*
  Most choice forsaken, and most loved despised,
  Thee and <u>thy virtues</u> here I seize upon,  *Loves her virtue*
  Be it lawful I take up what's cast away.                 270
  Gods, Gods! 'Tis strange, that from their cold'st neglect
  My love should kindle to inflamed respect.
  (*To Lear.*)  *They like their father when he's powerful and rich*

  Thy dowerless daughter, King, thrown to my chance,
  Is Queen of us, of ours, and our fair France.
  Not all the Dukes of wat'rish Burgundy,[3]              275
  Can buy this unprized precious maid of me.
  Bid them farewell Cordelia; though unkind,
  Thou losest here, a better where to find.
LEAR.   Thou hast her France; let her be thine, for we
  Have no such daughter, nor shall ever see                280
  That face of hers again. Therefore be gone,
  Without our grace, our love, our benison.°       *blessing*
  Come, noble Burgundy.

(*Flourish. Exeunt [all but France, Cordelia, Regan, and Gonerill].*)

---

1   *with regards ... point*  With matters, such as a dowry, that have nothing to do with
    love.
2   *she ... dowry*  Her own person is a great treasure.
3   *wat'rish Burgundy*  The insult is meant to suggest that Burgundy is weak in charac-
    ter, like watered down Burgundy wine.

FRANCE.    Bid farewell to your sisters.

285 CORDELIA.    The jewels of our father, with
            washed° eyes                                          *tearful*
        Cordelia leaves you. I know you what you are,
        And like a sister am most loath to call
        Your faults as they are named.¹ Love well our father:
        To your professèd bosoms² I commit him.
290     But yet alas, stood I within his grace,
        I would prefer° him to a better place.                  *recommend*
        So farewell to you both.

REGAN.    Prescribe not us our duty.

GONERILL.                              Let your study
295     Be to content your Lord, who hath received you
        At Fortune's alms.³ You have obedience scanted,
        And well are worth the want that you have wanted.⁴

CORDELIA.    Time shall unfold what plighted cunning⁵ hides.
        Who covers faults, at last with shame derides.⁶
300     Well may you prosper!

FRANCE.                        Come, my fair Cordelia.

*(Exit France and Cordelia.)*

GONERILL.    Sister, it is not little I have to say, of what most nearly
        appertains to us both. I think our father will hence tonight.

REGAN.    That's most certain, and with you; next month with
305     us.

GONERILL.    You see how full of changes his age is; the observation
        we have made of it hath been little.⁷ He always loved our sister
        most, and with what poor judgement he hath now cast her off,
        appears too grossly.⁸

---

1   *as ... named*   By their proper (ugly) names.
2   *professèd bosoms*   Hearts that claim to love him.
3   *at Fortune's alms*   As a charity case.
4   *are worth ... wanted*   Have deserved the lack of affection which you yourself
    lacked.
5   *plighted cunning*   Manipulative oath-taking (with a pun on "pleated," folded).
6   *Who covers ... derides*   Time conceals faults at first, but eventually exposes the sin-
    ner to scorn.
7   *the observation ... little*   We hadn't much noticed [how far his mind had slipped].
8   *grossly*   Obviously.

REGAN.   'Tis the infirmity of his age; yet he hath ever but    310
slenderly known himself.

GONERILL.   The best and soundest of his time hath been but
rash.[1] Then must we look from his age to receive not alone the
imperfections of long ingrafted condition, but therewithal the
unruly waywardness that infirm and choleric years bring with    315
them.[2]

REGAN.   Such unconstant starts[3] are we like to have from him, as
this of Kent's banishment.

GONERILL.   There is further complement of leave-taking[4] between France and him. Pray you, let us sit together;[5] if our    320
father carry authority with such disposition as he bears, this last
surrender of his will but offend us.[6]

REGAN.   We shall further think of it.

GONERILL.   We must do something, and i'th' heat.°          *quickly*

(*Exeunt.*)

## ACT 1, SCENE 2

(*Enter Edmund.*)

EDMUND.   Thou, Nature,[7] art my goddess; to thy law
My services are bound. Wherefore should I
Stand in the plague of custom,[8] and permit
The curiosity of nations[9] to deprive me?
For that I am some twelve, or fourteen moonshines°    *months*    5

---

1   *The best … rash*   At even his best moments, he's been imprudent.
2   *Then must … them*   So, with his advancing years, we should expect not merely the
    faults that have always been in his character, but also the difficulties that are associ-
    ated with troublesome old age.
3   *unconstant starts*   Sudden jerks, impulsive acts.
4   *further … leave-taking*   More diplomatic ceremonies connected with the King of
    France's departure.
5   *sit together*   I.e., during the leave-taking ceremony to follow.
6   *if our … but offend us*   If our father attempts to act officially in the mood he is in,
    his leaving us his property and authority is going to be nothing but trouble (e.g., if
    Lear should declare war on France).
7   *Nature*   The material world, as distinct not only from the spiritual realm, but also
    from civilized order (a realm in which Edmund, being "illegitimately born," is le-
    gally disenfranchised).
8   *stand … custom*   Accept a deplorable convention.
9   *curiosity of nations*   Arbitrary distinctions established by law.

Lag of <sup>1</sup> a brother? Why bastard? Wherefore base?
When my dimensions are as well compact,°                    *formed*
My mind as generous, and my shape as true
As honest madam's issue? Why brand they us
10  With base? With baseness, bastardy? Base, base?
Who in the lusty stealth of Nature, take
More composition, and fierce quality,
Than doth within a dull, stale, tired bed²
Go to th' creating a whole tribe of fops³
15  Got⁴ 'tween a sleep, and wake? Well then,
Legitimate Edgar, I must have your land.
Our father's love is to the bastard Edmund,
As to th' legitimate. Fine word: legitimate.
Well, my legitimate, if this letter speed,°                  *prosper*
20  And my invention° thrive, Edmund the base               *plan*
Shall to'th' legitimate.⁵ I grow, I prosper.
Now gods, stand up for bastards.

(*Enter Gloucester.*)

GLOUCESTER.   Kent banished thus? And France in choler parted?
And the King gone tonight? Prescribed⁶ his power,
25  Confined to exhibition?⁷ All this done
Upon the gad?⁸ Edmund, how now? What news?
EDMUND.   (*Conspicuously hiding a letter.*) So please your Lord-
ship, none.
GLOUCESTER.   Why so earnestly seek you to put up⁹ the letter?
30  EDMUND.   I know no news, my Lord.
GLOUCESTER.   What paper were you reading?
EDMUND.   Nothing my Lord.

---

1   *lag of*   Behind, born later than.
2   *dull, stale, tired bed*   Bed of a married couple who have grown sexually bored with
    each other through long familiarity.
3   *fops*   Affected aristocratic fools.
4   *Got*   Begotten.
5   *Shall to th' legitimate*   Will become legitimate; usually emended to "shall top."
6   *Prescribed*   Limited.
7   *exhibition*   Pension.
8   *Upon the gad*   On the spur of the moment, impulsively.
9   *put up*   Put away.

GLOUCESTER.   No? What needed then that terrible dispatch of
it into your pocket? The quality of nothing hath not such need
to hide itself. Let's see; come, if it be nothing, I shall not need      35
spectacles.

EDMUND.   I beseech you Sir, pardon me; it is a letter from my
brother, that I have not all o'er-read; and for so much as I have
perused, I find it not fit for your o'er-looking.

GLOUCESTER.   Give me the letter, Sir.      40

EDMUND.   I shall offend, either to detain or give it. The contents,
as in part I understand them, are to blame.

GLOUCESTER.   Let's see, let's see.

EDMUND.   I hope, for my brother's justification, he wrote this
but as an essay, or taste[1] of my virtue.

GLOUCESTER.   (*Reads.*)      45
"This policy and reverence of age makes the world bitter to the
best of our times:[2] keeps our fortunes from us, till our oldness
cannot relish them. I begin to find an idle and fond bondage in
the oppression of aged tyranny, who sways not as it hath power,
but as it is suffered.[3] Come to me, that of this I may speak more.      50
If our father would sleep till I waked him,[4] you should enjoy
half his revenue for ever, and live the beloved of your brother.
Edgar."

Hum? Conspiracy? "... sleep till I wake him ... you should
enjoy half his revenue ..." My son Edgar—had he a hand to      55
write this? A heart and brain to breed it in? When came you to
this? Who brought it?

EDMUND.   It was not brought me, my Lord; there's the cunning
of it. I found it thrown in at the casement of my closet.[5]

GLOUCESTER.   You know the character[6] to be your brother's?      60

---

1   *as an essay ... taste*   As a trial, or test.
2   *This policy ... times*   This custom of deferring to old age makes life unpleasant when
we are in the prime of our life.
3   *sways ... suffered*   Is influential not because of any inherent power, but because it is
indulged by those who suffer under it.
4   *If our father ... I waked him*   Were it up to me when he should awake (i.e., never,
from death).
5   *casement of my closet*   Window of my bedroom.
6   *character*   Handwriting.

EDMUND. If the matter[1] were good my Lord, I durst swear it were his; but in respect of that,[2] I would fain[3] think it were not.

GLOUCESTER. It is his.

EDMUND. It is his hand, my Lord; but I hope his heart is not in the contents.

GLOUCESTER. Has he never before sounded you in this business?

EDMUND. Never my Lord. But I have heard him oft maintain it to be fit, that sons at perfect age, and fathers declined, the father should be as ward to the son, and the son manage his revenue.

GLOUCESTER. O villain, villain! His very opinion in the letter! Abhorred villain; unnatural, detested, brutish villain—worse than brutish! Go, sirrah, seek him! I'll apprehend him. Abominable villain! Where is he?

EDMUND. I do not well know my Lord. If it shall please you to suspend your indignation against my brother, til you can derive from him better testimony of his intent, you should run a certain course: where, if you violently proceed against him, mistaking his purpose, it would make a great gap in your own honour, and shake in pieces, the heart of his obedience. I dare pawn down[4] my life for him, that he hath writ this to feel my[5] affection to your Honour, and to no other pretence of danger.[6]

GLOUCESTER. Think you so?

EDMUND. If your Honour judge it meet,[7] I will place you where you shall hear us confer of this, and by an auricular assurance[8] have your satisfaction, and that without any further delay, than this very evening.

GLOUCESTER. He cannot be such a monster. Edmund, seek him out; wind me into him,[9] I pray you. Frame the business

---

1  *matter*   Content.
2  *in respect of that*   In view of the content, such as it is.
3  *fain*   Prefer to.
4  *pawn down*   Stake.
5  *feel my*   Feel out my.
6  *pretence of danger*   Dangerous possibility.
7  *meet*   Appropriate.
8  *auricular assurance*   Audible proof.
9  *wind me into him*   Worm your (and my) way into his confidence.

after your own wisdom. I would unstate my self to be in a due resolution.[1]

EDMUND.   I will seek him, Sir, presently; convey the business as I shall find means;[2] and acquaint you withal.

GLOUCESTER.   These late[3] eclipses in the sun and moon portend    95 no good to us. Though the wisdom of Nature[4] can reason it thus and thus; yet Nature finds itself scourged by the sequent effects.[5] Love cools, friendship falls off, brothers divide. In cities, mutinies; in countries, discord; in palaces, treason; and the bond cracked 'twixt son and father. This villain of mine comes under    100 the prediction:[6] there's son against father; the King falls from bias of Nature: there's father against child. We have seen the best of our time. Machinations, hollowness,[7] treachery, and all ruinous disorders follow us disquietly[8] to our graves. Find out this villain, Edmund; it shall lose thee nothing. Do it carefully.    105 And the noble and true-hearted Kent banished; his offence, honesty. 'Tis strange.

(*Exit.*)

EDMUND.   This is the excellent foppery[9] of the world, that when we are sick in Fortune,[10] often the surfeits of our own behaviour,[11] we make guilty of our disasters the sun, the moon,    110 and stars, as if we were villains on necessity; fools by heavenly compulsion; knaves, thieves, and treachers by spherical predominance;[12] drunkards, liars and adulterers by an enforced obedience of planetary influence; and all that we are evil in, by

---

1   *unstate ... resolution*   Give up my earldom to be resolved of all doubt.
2   *convey ... means*   Manage the business as best as I can.
3   *late*   Recent.
4   *wisdom of Nature*   Natural science (as opposed to astrology).
5   *yet ... effects*   The natural world nevertheless suffers the subsequent effects (of the eclipses).
6   *This villain ... prediction*   The behavior of this villainous son of mine was predicted by the astrological portents.
7   *hollowness*   Insincerity.
8   *disquietly*   Disturbingly.
9   *excellent foppery*   Splendid foolishness.
10   *sick in Fortune*   Having bad luck.
11   *the surfeits ... behaviour*   Caused by our own excesses.
12   *treachers ... predominance*   Traitors because a certain planet was in ascendancy at our birth.

a divine thrusting on. An admirable evasion of whoremaster man, to lay his goatish disposition on the charge of a star.[1] (*Sarcastically.*) "My father compounded with my mother under the dragon's tail; and my nativity was under Ursa major, so that it follows, I am rough and lecherous." I should have been that I

120 am, had the maidenliest star in the firmament twinkled on my bastardizing.[2]

(*Enter Edgar.*)

(*Aside.*) Pat[3] he comes, like the catastrophe of the old comedy.[4] My cue[5] is villainous melancholy, with a sigh like Tom o' Bedlam.[6] (*Aloud.*) O, these eclipses do portend these divisions.

125 (*Sings.*) Fa, Sol, La, Mi![7]

EDGAR. How now, brother Edmund, what serious contemplation are you in?

EDMUND. I am thinking, brother, of a prediction I read this other day, what should follow these eclipses.

130 EDGAR. Do you busy your self with that?

EDMUND. I promise you, the effects he writes of succeed unhappily. When saw you my Father last?

EDGAR. The night gone by.

EDMUND. Spake you with him?

135 EDGAR. Aye, two hours together.[8]

---

1  *An admirable ... of a star*  It is impressive that men evade responsibility for their lecherous natures by blaming astrology.

2  *I should ... bastardizing*  I'd be who I am if the most virginal star in the heavens had presided over my conception.

3  *Pat*  Right on time.

4  *like ... comedy*  As the climax of an old comedy might be contrived to arrive coincidentally at the perfect moment.

5  *My cue*  The part I must play.

6  *Tom o' Bedlam*  Archetypal madman, named from the Bethlehem (pronounced and often written "Bedlam") Hospital in London.

7  *Fa ... Mi*  Edmund appears to be mocking the neo-Pythagorean notion of a connection between music and the order of the cosmos. Several critics have attempted to show special significance to these notes, but this seems out of keeping with anything the character might be attempting.

8  *I promise you ... two hours together*  The equivalent passage in the Quarto version is longer, and substantially different: "BASTARD. I promise you the effects he writ of succeed unhappily: as of unnaturalness between the child and the parent;

EDMUND.   Parted you in good terms? Found you no displeasure in him, by word, nor countenance?

EDGAR.   None at all.

EDMUND.   Bethink your self wherein you may have offended him; and at my entreaty forbear his presence, until some little     140
time hath qualified the heat of his displeasure; which at this instant so rageth in him, that with the mischief of your person, it would scarcely allay.[1]

EDGAR.   Some villain hath done me wrong.

EDMUND.   That's my fear. I pray you have a continent forbearance[2]     145
till the speed of his rage goes slower; and as I say, retire with me to my lodging, from whence I will fitly bring you to hear my Lord speak. Pray ye, go. (*Hands him a key.*) There's my key. If you do stir abroad, go armed.

EDGAR.   Armed, brother?     150

EDMUND.   Brother,[3] I advise you to the best. I am no honest man, if there be any good meaning toward you. I have told you what I have seen, and heard but faintly: nothing like the image, and horror of it. Pray you, away!

EDGAR.   Shall I hear from you anon?     155

EDMUND.   I do serve you in this business.

(*Exit [Edgar].*)

A credulous father, and a brother noble,
Whose nature is so far from doing harms,
That he suspects none; on whose foolish honesty
My practises° ride easy: I see the business.          *schemes*     160

---

death, dearth; dissolutions of ancient amities; divisions in state; menaces and maledictions against King and nobles; needless diffidences; banishment of friends; dissipation of cohorts; nuptial breaches; and I know not what.
    EDGAR.   How long have you been a sectary astronomical?
    BASTARD.   Come, come, when saw you my father last ?
    EDGAR.   Why, the night gone by.
    BASTARD.   Spake you with him?
    EDGAR.   Two hours together."
1   *with the mischief ... allay*   With the additional provocation of your physical presence, his displeasure would be unlikely to ease.
2   *have a continent forbearance*   Control your feelings and keep your distance.
3   *Pray ye ... Brother*   These lines do not appear in the Quarto version.

Let me, if not by birth, have lands by wit,°        *intelligence*
All with me's meet, that I can fashion fit.¹

(*Exit.*)

## ACT 1, SCENE 3

(*Enter Gonerill, and [Oswald, her] Steward.*²)

GONERILL.   Did my father strike my gentleman for chiding of
his fool?

OSWALD.   Aye, Madam.

GONERILL.   By day and night, he wrongs me; every hour
5     He flashes into one gross crime, or other,
That sets us all at odds. I'll not endure it.
His knights grow riotous, and himself upbraids us
On every trifle. When he returns from hunting,
I will not speak with him. Say I am sick.
10   If you come slack of former services,³
You shall do well. The fault of it,⁴ I'll answer.

OSWALD.   He's coming Madam, I hear him.

GONERILL.   Put on what weary negligence you please,
You and your fellows; I'd have it come to question.
15   If he distaste it, let him to my sister,
Whose mind and mine, I know, in that are one.⁵
Remember what I have said.

OSWALD.   Well Madam.

GONERILL.   And let his Knights have colder looks among you.
20   What grows of it, no matter; advise your fellows so. I'll write
straight to my sister to hold my course.⁶ Prepare for dinner.

(*Exeunt.*)

---

1  *All … fit*  Everything is acceptable to me, so long as I can shape it to my
purposes.
2  *Steward*  Oswald is identified only as "Steward" during this scene in F.
3  *If you … services*  If you fall short of serving him as well as you have.
4  *The fault of it*  The blame for it.
5  *If he … that are one*  If things are not to his taste, let him go to my sister; I know
that she and I are of one mind about this.
6  *straight … to hold my course*  I will write immediately to my sister, and advise her to
do the same thing as I am doing.

# ACT 1, Scene 4[1]

(*Enter Kent.*)

KENT. If, but as well, I other accents borrow,[2]
That can my speech defuse, my good intent
May carry through itself to that full issue
For which I razed my likeness.[3] Now, banished Kent,
If thou canst serve where thou dost stand condemned,                5
So may it come, thy master whom thou lov'st,
Shall find thee full of labours.

(*Horns within.[4] Enter Lear and Attendants.*)

LEAR. Let me not stay a jot[5] for dinner; go get it ready. (*To Kent.*)
How now, what art thou?
KENT. A man, Sir.                                                   10
LEAR. What dost thou profess?[6] What would'st thou with us?
KENT. I do profess to be no less than I seem; to serve him truly
that will put me in trust; to love him that is honest; to converse
with him that is wise and says little; to fear judgement; to fight
when I cannot choose; and to eat no fish.[7]                        15
LEAR. What art thou?
KENT. A very honest hearted fellow, and as poor as the King.

---

1  *Scene 4*  F indicates a definite scene break here, unlike Q.
2  *other accents borrow*  I am able to disguise my way of speaking by putting on other
   accents.
3  *razed my likeness*  Concealed my appearance.
4  *within*  I.e., offstage.
5  *not stay a jot*  Not wait a moment.
6  *What ... profess*  What do you do for a living? (Kent's response puns on the word
   "profess" as also meaning "claim.")
7  *eat no fish*  The humor of this self-deflating claim has proved effective in performance regardless of whether its sense is understood; but the fact remains that it has
   yet to be satisfactorily explained. The most frequently cited explanation is that in
   abjuring fish, Kent is claiming to be a Protestant. Another suggestion is that fish-
   eating might have been regarded as a less manly taste, so Kent is claiming not to be a
   weakling. Perhaps the line should be read in the context of the regional dialect Kent
   has just adopted to disguise himself, for a certain dialect (Cornish, for example)
   could imply that he is a former fisher—a profession in which, proverbially, people
   grow sick of eating fish. The line might also be a bawdy joke (often the case with
   "fish" in Shakespeare).

LEAR.  If thou be'st as poor for a subject, as he's for a King, thou art poor enough. What would'st thou?

20 KENT.  Service.

LEAR.  Who would'st thou serve?

KENT.  You.

LEAR.  Dost thou know me fellow?

KENT.  No Sir, but you have that in your countenance which I
25 would fain call Master.[1]

LEAR.  What's that?

KENT.  Authority.

LEAR.  What services canst thou do?

KENT.  I can keep honest counsel; ride; run; mar a curious tale
30 in telling it and deliver a plain message bluntly. That which ordinary men are fit for, I am qualified in; and the best of me is diligence.

LEAR.  How old art thou?

KENT.  Not so young, Sir, to love a woman for singing, nor
35 so old to dote on her for anything. I have years on my back forty-eight.

LEAR.  Follow me, thou shalt serve me, if I like thee no worse after dinner. I will not part from thee yet. Dinner, ho, dinner! Where's my knave, my Fool?[2] Go you and call my fool
40 hither. (*To Oswald who is passing through.*) You, you sirrah! Where's my daughter?

OSWALD.  So please you …[3]

(*Exit.*)

LEAR.  What says the fellow there? Call the clot-poll[4] back! (*A Knight pursues Oswald.*) Where's my Fool? Ho! I think the world's
45 asleep! (*Knight re-enters.*) How now? Where's that mongrel?

KNIGHT.  He says, my Lord, your daughter is not well.

---

1  *that in your countenance … call Master*  Something in your appearance that leads me to want to call you Master.

2  *Fool*  For the sake of clarity, the word has been capitalized wherever it refers directly to the character so named.

3  *So please you …*  The incomplete sentence may indicate inaudibility, either due to mumbling or because Oswald walks out of the room while speaking.

4  *clot-poll*  Block head (literally, lump-of-dirt-head).

LEAR. Why came not the slave back to me when I called him?

KNIGHT. Sir, he answered me in the roundest manner, he would not.

LEAR. He would not? 50

KNIGHT. My Lord, I know not what the matter is; but to my judgement your Highness is not entertained with that ceremonious affection as you were wont. There's a great abatement of kindness appears as well in the general dependants, as in the Duke himself also, and your daughter. 55

LEAR. Ha? Sayst thou so?

KNIGHT. I beseech you pardon me, my Lord, if I be mistaken; for my duty cannot be silent, when I think your Highness wronged.

LEAR. Thou but rememb'rest me of mine own conception.[1] I 60 have perceived a most faint neglect of late, which I have rather blamed as mine own jealous curiosity,[2] than as a very pretence and purpose of unkindness. I will look further into't. But where's my Fool? I have not seen him this two days.

KNIGHT. Since my young Lady's going into France, Sir, the Fool 65 hath much pined away.

LEAR. No more of that; I have noted it well. Go you and tell my daughter I would speak with her. Go you call hither my Fool.

(*Exit Servant; Enter [Oswald]*.)

Oh you, Sir, you; come you hither, Sir. Who am I, Sir?

OSWALD. My Lady's father. 70

LEAR. "My Lady's father"? My Lord's knave, you whoreson dog, you slave, you cur.

OSWALD. I am none of these my Lord; I beseech your pardon.[3]

LEAR. Do you bandy[4] looks with me, you rascal? (*Strikes him.*)

OSWALD. I'll not be strucken, my Lord. 75

KENT. (*Tripping him.*) Nor tripped neither, you base football player.

---

1 *Thou ... conception* You have reminded me of a notion I'd had earlier.
2 *as mine own jealous curiosity* As the result of my being excessively on the lookout for signs of ill-will in others.
3 *beseech ... pardon* I.e., for contradicting Lear, not for past behavior.
4 *bandy* Insolently exchange, toss back and forth.

LEAR. I thank thee, fellow. Thou serv'st me, and I'll love thee.

KENT. Come sir, arise; away. I'll teach you differences! Away,
away! If you will measure your lubber's length[1] again, tarry; but
away, go to; have you wisdom, so.[2]

(*Exit Oswald.*)

LEAR. (*To Kent.*) Now my friendly knave, I thank thee. (*Giving
him money.*) There's earnest of thy service.[3]

(*Enter Fool.*)

FOOL. Let me hire him too; here's my coxcomb.[4]

LEAR. How now my pretty knave, how dost thou?

FOOL. Sirrah, you were best take my coxcomb.

LEAR. Why, my boy?

FOOL. Why? For taking one's part that's out of favour.[5] (*To
Kent.*) Nay, and thou canst not smile as the wind sits,[6] thou'lt
catch cold shortly. There, take my coxcomb. Why, this fellow
has banished two on's[7] daughters, and did the third a blessing
against his will; if thou follow him, thou must needs wear my
coxcomb. (*To Lear.*) How now, Nuncle?[8] Would I had two
coxcombs and two daughters.

LEAR. Why, my boy?

FOOL. If I gave them all my living, I'd keep my coxcombs
myself.[9] There's mine; beg another of thy daughters.

LEAR. Take heed Sirrah; the whip.[10]

---

1 *lubber's length* Lubber is a sailor's term for a clumsy person; his length is measured
when he is spread out on the floor.

2 *have you wisdom, so* Many editors propose adding a question mark after "wisdom."
Others suggest that it is an imperative: "have wisdom enough to do as I say."

3 *earnest of thy service* A token of thanks for serving me.

4 *coxcomb* Traditional cap of a fool, resembling the crest (comb) of a rooster
(cock).

5 *For taking ... favour* I.e., Kent should be awarded with the cap of a fool for siding
with someone (Lear) who is currently in disgrace with the host.

6 *and ... sits* If you are not perfectly happy to have the wind blow as hard and cold
as it likes.

7 *on's* Of his.

8 *Nuncle* The Fool's pet name for Lear derives from "mine uncle."

9 *If I ... myself* If I gave them everything by which I made my living, then I would
be a fool indeed.

10 *the whip* I.e., you'll be whipped if you aren't careful.

FOOL. Truth's a dog must to kennel; he must be whipped out, when the Lady Brach[1] may stand by'th' fire and stink. 100

LEAR. A pestilent gall[2] to me.

FOOL. Sirrah, I'll teach thee a speech.

LEAR. Do.

FOOL. Mark it, Nuncle:

Have more than thou showest, 105
Speak less than thou knowest,
Lend less than thou owest,
Ride more than thou goest,
Learn more than thou trowest,°                          *believe*
Set less than thou throwest;[3]                              110
Leave thy drink and thy whore,
And keep in a door,°                                      *indoors*
And thou shalt have more,
Than two tens to a score.[4]

KENT. This is nothing, Fool.                                 115

FOOL. Then 'tis like the breath of an unfeed lawyer;[5] you gave me nothing for't. (*To Lear.*) Can you make no use of nothing, Nuncle?

LEAR. Why, no boy; nothing can be made out of nothing.

FOOL. (*To Kent.*) Prithee, tell him, so much the rent of his land 120 comes to. He will not believe a fool.

LEAR. A bitter fool.

FOOL. Dost thou know the difference my boy, between a bitter fool, and a sweet one?

LEAR. No lad, teach me.                                      125

FOOL. Nuncle, give me an egg, and I'll give thee two crowns.

LEAR. What two crowns shall they be?

FOOL. Why, after I have cut the egg i'th' middle and eat[6] up the meat, the two crowns of the egg: when thou clovest[7] thy crowns

---

1  *Lady Brach*  Tongue-in-cheek title; a brach is a female hound.
2  *pestilent gall*  I.e., the Fool is a bitter source of affliction.
3  *Set ... throwest*  Stake less than you may win in a game.
4  *two tens ... score*  More than you started with (twenty shillings made an old English pound).
5  *like the breath of an unfeed lawyer*  I.e., worth nothing because unpaid.
6  *eat*  Have eaten.
7  *clovest*  Cut.

130 i'th' middle, and gav'st away both parts, thou bor'st thine ass on thy back o'er the dirt. Thou had'st little wit in thy bald crown, when thou gav'st thy golden one away. If I speak like myself[1] in this, let him be whipped that first finds it so.[2] (*Sings.*)

135 Fools had ne'er less grace in a year,
For wisemen are grown foppish,
And know not how their wits to wear,
Their manners are so apish.

LEAR.   When were you wont to be so full of songs, sirrah?

FOOL.   I have used it Nuncle, e'er since thou mad'st thy daughters
140 thy mothers; for when thou gav'st them the rod, and put'st thine own breeches, (*Sings.*)

Then they for sudden joy did weep,
And I for sorrow sung,
That such a King should play bo-peep,
145 And go the fool among.

Prithee, Nuncle, keep a schoolmaster that can teach thy Fool to lie; I would fain learn to lie.

LEAR.   And[3] you lie, Sirrah, we'll have you whipped.

FOOL.   I marvel what kin thou and thy daughters are: they'll
150 have me whipped for speaking true; thou'lt have me whipped for lying; and sometimes I am whipped for holding my peace. I had rather be any kind o' thing than a fool. And yet I would not be thee Nuncle: thou hast pared thy wit o' both sides, and left nothing i'th'middle. Here comes one o'the parings.

(*Enter Gonerill.*)

155 LEAR.   How now daughter? What makes that frontlet[4] on? You are too much of late i'th' frown.

FOOL.   Thou wast a pretty fellow when thou hadst no need to care for her frowning; now thou art an O without a figure.[5] I am better than thou art now: I am a fool; thou art nothing. (*To*

---

1  *speak like myself*  Speak seriously.
2  *let him ... so*  I.e., because to suggest that what the Fool says is not nonsense, but sense, would be impudent.
3  *And*  If.
4  *frontlet*  I.e., frown (literally, an ornamental band).
5  *an O without a figure*  A zero without a numeral before it.

*Gonerill.*) Yes, forsooth, I will hold my tongue, so your face bids     160
me, though you say nothing.
    Mum, mum,
      He that keep nor° crust, nor crumb,[1]                    *neither*
      Weary of all, shall want some.
[*Indicating Lear.*] That's a shelled peascod.[2]                                165
GONERILL.   Not only, Sir, this, your all-licenced[3] fool,
    But other of your insolent retinue
    Do hourly carp and quarrel, breaking forth
    In rank, and (not to be endured) riots, Sir.
    I had thought by making this well known unto you,                     170
    To have found a safe° redress; but now grow fearful,          *certain*
    By what yourself too late° have spoke and done,          *recently*
    That you protect this course, and put it on
    By your allowance; which, if you should, the fault
    Would not 'scape censure, nor the redresses sleep,[4]                 175
    Which in the tender of a wholesome weal,[5]
    Might in their working do you that offence,
    Which else were shame, that then necessity
    Will call discreet proceeding.[6]
FOOL.   (*To Lear.*) For you know, Nuncle:                          180
      The hedge-sparrow fed the cuckoo so long,
      That it had its head bit off by its young.[7]
    So, out went the candle, and we were left darkling.[8]
LEAR.   (*To Gonerill.*) Are you our daughter?

---

1   *crumb*  The soft inside of the bread.
2   *shelled peascod*  Empty peapod.
3   *all-licenced*  Indulged in all liberties.
4   *nor ... sleep*  Nor would your attempts to make amends pause until they had been
    fulfilled.
5   *in the tender of ... weal*  Out of concern to bring about healthy state of affairs.
6   *Might ... proceeding*  The redresses might, in the doing, cause you a sense of embar-
    rassment and humiliation, were it not that they were necessary and therefore the
    discreet thing to do.
7   *hedge-sparrow fed the cuckoo*  Cuckoos lay their eggs in the nests of other birds,
    including the smaller hedge-sparrow. The "host" bird then feeds the young cuckoo
    until it has grown so large that it endangers the host, and is allegedly able to devour
    it.
8   *So ... darkling*  Thus, the life upon which we (the Fool imagines himself to be one
    of the sparrow's chicks) depended was snuffed out, and we were left facing death.

185    GONERILL.   I would you would make use of your good wisdom
        Whereof I know you are fraught,° and put away     *supplied*
        These dispositions, which of late transport you
        From what you rightly are.
    FOOL.   May not an ass know when the cart draws the horse?
190       (*Sings.*) Whoop, Jug, I love thee.[1]
    LEAR.   Does any here know me? This is not Lear.
        Does Lear walk thus? Speak thus? Where are his eyes?
        Either his notion° weakens, or's discernings     *thinking*
        Are lethargied. Ha! Waking? 'Tis not so?
195    Who is it that can tell me who I am?
    FOOL.   Lear's shadow.
    LEAR.   Your name,[2] fair gentlewoman?
    GONERILL.   This admiration Sir, is much o'th'savour[3]
        Of other your new pranks. I do beseech you
200    To understand my purposes aright;
        As you are old, and reverend, should be wise.[4]
        Here do you keep a hundred knights and squires:
        Men so disordered, so debauched and bold,
        That this our court, infected with their manners,
205    Shows like a riotous inn; epicurism° and lust     *hedonism*
        Makes it more like a tavern, or a brothel,
        Than a graced palace. The shame itself doth speak°     *calls out*
        For instant remedy. Be then desired—
        By her that else will take the thing she begs—
210    A little to disquantity your train,[5]
        And the remainders that shall still depend,[6]

---

1  *Whoop ... thee*  Apparently the refrain of a lost comic song, which may be sung in response to some threatening gesture from Gonerill. Jug is an affectionate variation on Joan, a common name for a girl, used as Australians now use "Sheila."

2  *Who is it that can tell me ... Your name*  Additional text appears here in the Quarto version, with Lear answering his own question: "Who is it that can tell me who I am? Lear's shadow? I would learn that; for by the marks of sovereignty, knowledge, and reason, I should be false persuaded I had daughters.
    FOOL.  Which they will make an obedient father.
    LEAR.  Your name, fair gentlewoman?"

3  *This admiration ... much o'th'savour*  This show of bewilderment has much the same taste to it.

4  *As ... wise*  Given your age and status, you should show an appropriate wisdom.

5  *disquantity your train*  Reduce the number of your followers.

6  *still depend*  Continue to stay with you.

To be such men as may besort° your age,       *be suitable to*
Which know themselves, and you.

LEAR.                     Darkness and devils!
Saddle my horses; call my train together.     215
(*To Gonerill.*) Degenerate bastard, I'll not trouble thee;
Yet have I left a daughter.

GONERILL.   You strike my people, and your disordered rabble
make servants of their betters.

(*Enter [Duke of] Albany.*)

LEAR.   (*To Albany.*) Woe, that too late repents.[1]     220
Is it your will? Speak , Sir! (*To followers.*)—Prepare my horses.—
(*Spoken at large.*) Ingratitude! Thou marble-hearted fiend,
More hideous when thou show'st thee in a child,
Than the sea-monster.

ALBANY.            Pray, Sir, be patient.     225

LEAR.   (*To Gonerill.*) Detested kite,[2] thou liest!
My train are men of choice, and rarest parts,[3]
That all particulars of duty know,
And in the most exact regard, support
The worships of their name.[4] O most small fault,     230
How ugly did'st thou in Cordelia show!
Which like an engine,[5] wrenched my frame of nature[6]
From the fixed place,[7] drew from my heart all love,
And added to the gall.[8] O Lear, Lear, Lear!
Beat at this gate[9] that let thy folly in,     235
And thy dear judgement out. (*To followers.*)—Go, go, my
   people.

---

1  *Woe ... repents*  Woe to the person (i.e., Albany) who comes too late to make amends.

2  *kite*  Bird of prey associated with cowardice and treachery.

3  *of choice, and rarest parts*  Having highly valuable virtues.

4  *support ... name*  Show themselves worthy of their title (Knight).

5  *engine*  War machine (such as a battering ram or a crane used in a siege).

6  *frame of nature*  Natural disposition.

7  *fixed place*  Natural location.

8  *added to the gall*  Increased the amount of bile (thus making him, according to the medical concepts of the day, uncharacteristically bitter and angry).

9  *this gate*  I.e., his skull.

ALBANY.    My Lord, I am guiltless, as I am ignorant
    Of what hath moved you.
LEAR.                          It may be so, my Lord.
240    (*Lyrically.*) Hear Nature, hear dear Goddess, hear:
    Suspend thy purpose, if thou did'st intend
    To make this creature fruitful;
    Into her womb convey sterility;
    Dry up in her the organs of increase,°                          *womb*
245    And from her derogate° body, never spring                    *debased*
    A babe to honour her. If she must teem,°                        *bear life*
    Create her child of spleen,[1] that it may live
    And be a thwart disnatured° torment to her.                     *unnatural*
    Let it stamp wrinkles in her brow of youth,
250    With cadent° tears fret channels in her cheeks,              *dropping*
    Turn all her mother's pains and benefits
    To laughter, and contempt: that she may feel,
    How sharper than a serpent's tooth it is,
    To have a thankless child!—Away, away!

    (*Exit [Lear with Kent, Fool, and Others].*)


255    ALBANY.    Now Gods that we adore, whereof comes this?
    GONERILL.    Never afflict your self to know more of it:
    But let his disposition have that scope
    As dotage gives it.

    (*[Re-]enter Lear [with Fool].*)


    LEAR.    What! fifty of my followers at a clap?
260    Within a fortnight?[2]
    ALBANY.                        What's the matter, Sir?
    LEAR.    I'll tell thee. Life and death, I am ashamed
    That thou hast power to shake my manhood thus,
    That these hot tears, which break from me perforce

---

1    *of spleen*   Entirely malicious.
2    *What! fifty … fortnight*   In F's revision, Lear leaves briefly, and discovers that half of
    his followers have already been dismissed while he has been arguing with Gonerill.

Should make thee worth them.[1]                                    265
Blasts and fogs upon thee:
Th'untented° woundings of a father's curse            *unbandaged, raw*
Pierce every sense about thee. Old fond eyes:
Beweep this cause again, I'll pluck ye out,
And cast you with the waters that you loose                        270
To temper clay.[2] Ha? Let it be so.
I have another daughter,
Who I am sure is kind and comfortable:
When she shall hear this of thee, with her nails
She'll flay thy wolfish visage. Thou shalt find                    275
That I'll resume the shape which thou dost think
I have cast off for ever.

(*Exit [Lear].*)

GONERILL.                    Do you mark that?
ALBANY.   I cannot be so partial, Gonerill,
  To the great love I bear you.                                    280
GONERILL.   Pray you, content. (*Calls.*)—What, Oswald, ho?
  (*To Fool.*)
  You, Sir, more knave than fool: after your master.
FOOL.   Nuncle Lear, Nuncle Lear! Tarry, take the Fool with thee!
  A fox, when one has caught her,
  And such a daughter,                                             285
  Should sure to the slaughter
  If my cap would buy a halter.
  So the Fool follows after.

(*Exit.*)

GONERILL.   This man hath had good counsel: a hundred
  Knights?
  'Tis politic, and safe to let him keep                          290

---

1   *That these hot tears ... worth them*   That my involuntary tears should choose to be
    prompted by so unworthy a cause as you are.
2   *Old fond eyes ... clay*   Eyes, if you should ever betray me by weeping again, I will
    pluck you out and, along with the tears you shed, consign you to an early grave.

At point a hundred Knights! Yes, that on every dream,
Each buzz, each fancy, each complaint, dislike,
He may enguard his dotage[1] with their powers,
And hold our lives in mercy!—Oswald, I say!

295 ALBANY.    Well, you may fear too far.

GONERILL.    Safer than trust too far;
Let me still take away the harms I fear,
Not fear still to be taken.[2] I know his heart,
What he hath uttered, I have writ my sister;
300 If she sustain him, and his hundred Knights
When I have showed th'unfitness—

(*Enter [Oswald].*)

How now, Oswald?[3]
What, have you writ that letter to my sister?

OSWALD.    Aye, Madam.

305 GONERILL.    Take you some company, and away to horse,
Inform her full of my particular fear,
And thereto add such reasons of your own,
As may compact it more.[4] Get you gone,
And hasten your return. (*Exit Oswald.*)
310             (*To Albany.*) No, no, my Lord,
This milky gentleness, and course of yours,
Though I condemn not, yet, under pardon,
You are much more at task[5] for want of wisdom,
Than praised for harmful mildness.

315 ALBANY.    How far your eyes may pierce I cannot tell;
Striving to better, oft we mar what's well.

GONERILL.    Nay then—

ALBANY.    Well, well, th' event.[6]

(*Exeunt.*)

---

1   *enguard his dotage*   Protect his senile whims.
2   *Let me ... taken*   Let me remove anything I fear rather than fear to be removed myself.
3   *This man ... How now, Oswald?*   The equivalent speech in the Quarto version is one line only: "GONORILL.   What Oswald, ho!"
4   *As may compact it more*   As may give the argument more force.
5   *at task*   To be blamed, taken to task.
6   *Well ... event*   Well, we shall see what happens in the event.

(*Enter Lear, Kent, Gentleman, and Fool.*)

LEAR.  Go you before to Gloucester with these letters; acquaint
my daughter no further with anything you know than comes
from her demand out of the letter.[1] If your diligence be not
speedy, I shall be there afore you.

KENT.  I will not sleep, my Lord, till I have delivered your letter.          5

(*Exit.*)

FOOL.  If a man's brains were in's heels, were't not in danger of
kibes?[2]

LEAR.  Aye, boy.

FOOL.  Then I prithee, be merry; thy wit shall not go slipshod.[3]

LEAR.  Ha, ha, ha!          10

FOOL.  Shalt see thy other daughter will use thee kindly; for
though she's as like this as a crabbe's like an apple,[4] yet I can tell
what I can tell.

LEAR.  What canst tell boy?

FOOL.  She will taste as like this, as a crabbe does to a crab.[5]          15
Thou canst tell why one's nose stands i'th'middle on's face?

LEAR.  No.

FOOL.  Why, to keep one's eyes of either side's nose, that what a
man cannot smell out, he may spy into.

LEAR.  I did her wrong—          20

FOOL.  Canst tell how an oyster makes his shell?

LEAR.  No.

FOOL.  Nor I neither; but I can tell why a snail has a house.

LEAR.  Why?

FOOL.  Why to put's head in, not to give it away to his daughters,          25
and leave his horns without a case.

---

1   *than ... letter*  Than her reading of the letter leads her to ask.
2   *kibes*  Chilblains (inflammation of the feet).
3   *thy wit ... slipshod*  You won't have to worry about protecting your brains with
slippers, for walking to Regan's shows you have no brains in your feet.
4   *as a crabbe's ... apple*  As similar as a crab-apple is (in appearance) to a regular
apple.
5   *She will taste ... crab*  She will be that much more sour and unpleasant than Gonerill as a crab-apple is than a crab.

LEAR.  I will forget my nature. So kind a father? —Be my horses
     ready?
FOOL.  Thy asses[1] are gone about 'em. The reason why the seven
30   stars are no mo' than seven, is a pretty reason.
LEAR.  Because they are not eight.
FOOL.  Yes indeed; thou would'st make a good fool.
LEAR.  To take't again perforce[2]—monster ingratitude!
FOOL.  If thou wert my fool, Nuncle, I'd have thee beaten for
35   being old before thy time.
LEAR.  How's that?
FOOL.  Thou shouldst not have been old, till thou had'st been
     wise.
LEAR.  O let me not be mad, not mad, sweet heaven!
40   Keep me in temper, I would not be mad.

     (*Enter a Gentleman.*)

     How now? Are the horses ready?
GENTLEMAN.  Ready, my Lord.
LEAR.  Come, boy.
FOOL.  She that's a maid now, and laughs at my departure,
45   Shall not be a maid long, unless things be cut shorter.[3]

     (*Exeunt.*)


                    ACT 2, SCENE 1

     (*Enter Bastard, and Curan, severally.*)

EDMUND.  Save thee, Curan.
CURAN.  And you, Sir. I have been with your father, and given
     him notice that the Duke of Cornwall, and Regan, his Duchess,
     will be here with him this night.
5    EDMUND.  How comes that?

---

1   *asses* I.e., Lear's servants.
2   *to take't ... perforce* I.e., to re-take the kingdom forcibly.
3   *She that's ... shorter* A crude sexual gibe: she who finds this situation comic will
    have the seriousness of things thrust upon her, unless the fool loses his virility.
    (Note that in Shakespeare's time "departure" was pronounced so as to rhyme with
    "shorter.")

CURAN.   Nay, I know not. You have heard of the news abroad?—
I mean the whispered ones, for they are yet but ear-kissing
arguments.[1]

EDMUND.   Not I; pray you, what are they?

CURAN.   Have you heard of no likely wars toward, 'twixt the   10
Dukes of Cornwall and Albany?

EDMUND.   Not a word.

CURAN.   You may do then in time. Fare you well, Sir.

(*Exit.*)

EDMUND.   The Duke be here tonight? The better best;[2]
This weaves itself perforce into my business.   15
My father hath set guard to take my brother,
And I have one thing of a queasy question[3]
Which I must act. Briefness and Fortune work.

(*Enter Edgar [from above].*)

Brother, a word. Descend, brother, I say!
My father watches. O Sir, fly this place;   20
Intelligence is given where you are hid.
You have now the good advantage of the night.
Have you not spoken 'gainst the Duke of Cornwall?
He's coming hither; now, i'th'night, i'th'haste,
And Regan with him. Have you nothing said   25
Upon his party 'gainst the Duke of Albany?
Advise yourself.[4]

EDGAR.                I am sure on't, not a word.

EDMUND.   I hear my father coming. Pardon me:
In cunning,[5] I must draw my sword upon you.   30
Draw, seem to defend yourself,
Now quit you well.—
Yield! Come before my Father! Light! Hoa, here!
—Fly brother—Torches, Torches!—So farewell.

(*Exit Edgar.*)

---

1   *ear-kissing arguments*   Whispered rumors.
2   *The better best*   Better and better.
3   *of a queasy question*   Of a precarious sort.
4   *Advise yourself*   Think carefully.
5   *In cunning*   In order to maintain the deception.

35 Some blood drawn on me would beget opinion
Of my more fierce endeavour. (*Cuts himself.*) I have seen drunkards
Do more than this in sport.—Father, Father!
Stop, stop! No help?

(*Enter Gloucester, and Servants with torches.*)

GLOUCESTER. Now Edmund, where's the villain?
40 EDMUND. Here stood he in the dark, his sharp sword out,
Mumbling of wicked charms, conjuring the moon
To stand auspicious mistress.[1]
GLOUCESTER. But where is he?
EDMUND. Look sir, I bleed.
45 GLOUCESTER. Where is the villain, Edmund?
EDMUND. Fled this way, Sir, when by no means he could—
GLOUCESTER. (*To Servants.*) Pursue him, ho; go after!—By no means, what?
EDMUND. Persuade me to the murder of your Lordship.
But that I told him the revenging gods,
50 'Gainst parricides did all the thunder bend,
Spoke with how manifold and strong a bond
The child was bound to'th'father. Sir, in fine,[2]
Seeing how loathly opposite[3] I stood
To his unnatural purpose, in fell[4] motion
55 With his preparèd[5] sword, he charges home[6]
My unprovided body, latched[7] mine arm;
And when he saw my best alarumed spirits[8]
Bold in the quarrels right, roused to th' encounter—
Or whether gasted[9] by the noise I made—
60 Full suddenly he fled.
GLOUCESTER.         Let him fly far:

---

1  *Mumbling … mistress*  Invoking black magic.
2  *in fine*  In short.
3  *loathly opposite*  Horrified and opposed.
4  *fell*  Lethal.
5  *preparèd*  Ready at hand.
6  *charges home*  Swings directly at.
7  *latched*  Nicked, cut.
8  *best alarumed spirits*  Best energies aroused by the prospect of battle.
9  *gasted*  Frightened by.

Not in this land shall he remain uncaught;
And found, dispatch. The noble Duke, my master,
My worthy arch and patron comes tonight,
By his authority I will proclaim it:                                            65
That he which finds him shall deserve our thanks,
Bringing the murderous coward to the stake;
He that conceals him, death.
EDMUND.     When I dissuaded him from his intent,
And found him pight[1] to do it, with cursed speech[2]                          70
I threatened to discover him. He replied:
"Thou unpossessing bastard: dost thou think,
If I would stand against thee, would the reposal[3]
Of any trust, virtue, or worth in thee
Make thy words faithed?[4] No, what should I deny,                              75
(As this I would, though thou didst produce
My very character)[5] I'd turn it all
To thy suggestion, plot, and damnèd practise.[6]
And thou must make a dullard of the world,[7]
If they not thought the profits of my death                                    80
Were very pregnant and potential spirits[8]
To make thee seek it."


(*Tucket*[9] *within.*)


GLOUCESTER.     O strange and fastened[10] villain! Would he deny his
letter, said he?—Hark, the Duke's trumpets.
I know not wherefore he comes.                                                  85
All ports I'll bar; the villain shall not scape.

---

1   *pight*   Pitched, fixed.
2   *cursed speech*   Speech full of angry curses.
3   *reposal*   Investment.
4   *If I ... faithed?*   If I were to contradict you, do you think that any amount of virtue
    in you is going to be sufficient for anyone to believe your word against mine?
5   *very character*   Actual handwriting.
6   *I'd ... practise*   I'd make out that it was you that thought of it, planned it, and did
    it.
7   *thou must ... world*   You must think the world stupid.
8   *very pregnant ... spirits*   Full and powerful motives.
9   *Tucket*   Flourish of trumpets.
10  *strange and fastened*   Unnatural and obstinate.

The Duke must grant me that. Besides, his picture
I will send far and near, that all the kingdom
May have due note of him. And of my land—
90    Loyal and natural boy!—I'll work the means
To make thee capable.

(*Enter Cornwall, Regan, and Attendants.*)

CORNWALL.    How now, my noble friend, since I came hither—
Which I can call but now—I have heard strangeness.
REGAN.    If it be true, all vengeance comes too short
95    Which can pursue th' offender. How dost my Lord?
GLOUCESTER.    O Madam, my old heart is cracked, it's cracked.
REGAN.    What, did my father's godson seek your life?
He whom my father named, your Edgar?
GLOUCESTER.    O Lady, Lady, shame would have it hid.
100    REGAN.    Was he not companion with the riotous knights
That tended upon my father?
GLOUCESTER.    I know not Madam. 'Tis too bad, too bad.
EDMUND.    Yes, Madam; he was of that consort.
REGAN.    No marvel then; though he were ill affected,[1]
105    'Tis they have put him on the old man's death,
To have th' expense[2] and waste of his revenues.
I have this present evening from my sister
Been well informed of them,[3] and with such cautions,
That if they come to sojourn at my house,
110    I'll not be there.
CORNWALL.              Nor I, I assure thee Regan.
Edmund, I hear that you have shown your father
A child-like[4] office.
EDMUND.              It was my duty, Sir.
115    GLOUCESTER.    He did bewray his practise,[5] and received
This hurt you see, striving to apprehend him.

---

1    *ill affected*    Disposed to wickedness.
2    *expense*    Spending.
3    *them*    I.e., Lear's knights.
4    *child-like*    Appropriately filial.
5    *bewray his practise*    Expose Edgar's plot.

CORNWALL.    Is he pursued?

GLOUCESTER.    Aye, my good Lord.

CORNWALL.    If he be taken, he shall never more
Be feared of doing harm. Make your own purpose                          120
How in my strength you please.[1] For you, Edmund,
Whose virtue and obedience doth this instant
So much commend itself, you shall be ours.[2]
Natures of such deep trust, we shall much need;
You, we first seize on.                                                 125

EDMUND.                        I shall serve you Sir,
Truly, however else.

GLOUCESTER.    For him I thank your Grace.

CORNWALL.    You know not why we came to visit you?

REGAN.    —Thus out of season, threading dark-eyed night?[3]          130
Occasions, noble Gloucester, of some prize:
Wherein we must have use of your advice.
Our father he hath writ, so hath our sister,
Of differences,[4] which I best thought it fit
To answer from our home;[5] the several messengers                     135
From hence attend dispatch.[6] Our good old friend,
Lay comforts to your bosom,[7] and bestow
Your needful counsel to our businesses,
Which craves the instant use.[8]

GLOUCESTER.                        I serve you Madam.                   140
Your Graces are right welcome.

(*Exeunt. Flourish.*)

---

1   *Make your ... please*   Do what you need to do, making as much use of my forces as
    you require.
2   *ours*   The "royal we" is being used.
3   *threading ... night*   Finding our way through the darkness with difficulty (the refer-
    ent is threading the eye of a needle).
4   *differences*   Disagreements between them.
5   *answer from our home*   Reply to not from our own home but from elsewhere (Regan
    and Cornwall have left their home empty so they will not be obliged to host Lear
    and his retinue when they arrive).
6   *attend dispatch*   Await our instructions.
7   *Lay ... bosom*   Console yourself.
8   *Which ... use*   Which is needed immediately.

(*Enter Kent, and [Oswald], severally.*)

OSWALD.   Good dawning to thee, friend. Art of this house?[1]
KENT.   Aye.
OSWALD.   Where may we set our horses?
KENT.   I'th' mire.
5   OSWALD.   Prithee, if thou lov'st me, tell me.
KENT.   I love thee not.
OSWALD.   Why then I care not for thee.
KENT.   If I had thee in Lipsbury pinfold,[2] I would make thee care for me.
10   OSWALD.   Why dost thou use me thus? I know thee not.
KENT.   Fellow I know thee.
OSWALD.   What dost thou know me for?
KENT.   A knave, a rascal, an eater of broken meats;[3] a base, proud, shallow, beggarly, three-suited,[4] hundred-pound,[5] filthy
15   worsted-stocking[6] knave; a lily-livered, action-taking,[7] whoreson, glass-gazing,[8] super-serviceable,[9] finical[10] rogue; one-trunk-inheriting[11] slave; one that would'st be a bawd in way of good service, and art nothing but the composition of a knave, beggar, coward, pander, and the son and heir of a mongrel bitch—one
20   whom I will beat into clamorous whining, if thou deniest the least syllable of thy addition.[12]

---

1   *Art of this house?*   Do you live here?
2   *Lipsbury pinfold*   A pinfold is a place in which stray animals are kept. Lipsbury appears to be a made up place name, though the word might be slang for "space between the lips," so that the sentence would mean: "If I had you between my teeth, I'd make you care."
3   *broken meats*   Left-overs.
4   *three-suited*   Serving men would be given three suits in a year.
5   *hundred-pound*   The price for which one could buy a knighthood at this time, implying that Oswald has purchased his position, and is not a born gentleman.
6   *worsted-stocking*   Cheap substitute for silk stockings.
7   *action-taking*   Inclined to resort to the law rather than to fight.
8   *glass-gazing*   Inclined to admire oneself in mirrors.
9   *super-serviceable*   Sycophantic.
10   *finical*   Overly fastidious.
11   *one-trunk-inheriting*   Owning only a trunkful of property.
12   *addition*   Titles just bestowed.

OSWALD.   Why, what a monstrous fellow art thou, thus to rail on one, that is neither known of thee, nor knows thee?

KENT.   What a brazen-faced varlet art thou, to deny thou knowest me? Is it two days since I tripped up thy heels, and beat thee before the King? Draw, you rogue; for though it be night, yet the moon shines; I'll make a sop o' th' moonshine[1] of you! You whoreson cullionly barber-monger,[2] draw.   25

OSWALD.   Away, I have nothing to do with thee.

KENT.   Draw you rascal; you come with letters against the King, and take vanity-the-puppet's[3] part, against the royalty of her father! Draw, you rogue; or I'll so carbonado[4] your shanks—! Draw, you rascal; come your ways!   30

OSWALD.   Help, ho, murder, help!

KENT.   Strike, you slave! Stand, rogue; stand, you neat[5] slave, strike!   35

OSWALD.Help, hoa! Murder, murder!


(*Enter Bastard, Cornwall, Regan, Gloucester, Servants.*)


EDMUND.   How now, what's the matter? Part.

KENT.   With you[6] goodman boy,[7] if you please; come, I'll flesh[8] ye! Come on young master.   40

GLOUCESTER.   Weapons? Arms? What's the matter here?

CORNWALL.   Keep peace upon your lives.[9] He dies that strikes again. What is the matter?

REGAN.   The messengers from our sister, and the King.

CORNWALL.   What is your difference, speak?   45

OSWALD.   I am scarce in breath, my Lord.

---

1   *sop o' th' moonshine*   Sponge to soak up the moonshine (because of the holes he will leave in Oswald's body).

2   *cullionly barbermonger*   Wretched, effeminate patron of barbershops. Barbers doubled as surgeons who could medicate you for venereal disease.

3   *vanity-the-puppet*   I.e., the part of Gonerill, here identified with a stock vain and selfish character seen in morality plays.

4   *carbonado*   Cut cross-wise (as meat before grilling).

5   *neat*   Unadulterated or foppish.

6   *With you*   Let's have you.

7   *goodman boy*   Peasant boy (contemptuously).

8   *flesh*   Let you smell blood (a term from hunting, when the hounds are allowed to smell a piece of meat).

9   *upon your lives*   I.e., or suffer the punishment of execution.

KENT. No marvel, you have so bestirred your valour, you
cowardly rascal, nature disclaims in thee.[1] A tailor made thee.
CORNWALL. Thou art a strange fellow: a tailor make a man?
50 KENT. A tailor, Sir. A stone-cutter, or a painter, could not have
made him so ill, though they had been but two years o'th'trade.
CORNWALL. Speak yet, how grew your quarrel?
OSWALD. This ancient ruffian, Sir, whose life I have spared at
suit of his gray-beard—
55 KENT. Thou whoreson zed![2] Thou unnecessary letter! My Lord,
if you will give me leave, I will tread this unbolted[3] villain into
mortar, and daub the wall of a jakes[4] with him. Spare my gray-
beard, you wagtail?
CORNWALL. Peace, Sirrah!
60 You beastly knave, know you no reverence?
KENT. Yes, Sir, but anger hath a privilege.
CORNWALL. Why art thou angry?
KENT. That such a slave as this should wear a sword, Who wears
no honesty! Such smiling rogues as these—
65 Like rats oft bite the holy cords atwain,[5]
Which are too intrinced[6] unloose—smooth every passion
That in the natures of their lords rebel,[7]
Being oil to fire, snow to the colder moods,
Revenge, affirm, and turn their halcyon beaks[8]
70 With every gall,[9] and vary of their Masters,
Knowing naught (like dogs) but following.

---

1 *you have … in thee*  You have so overtaxed your courage that nature wants nothing
to do with you.
2 *zed*  I.e., the last letter of the alphabet (US: zee), often left out of dictionaries at the
time; superfluous non-entity.
3 *unbolted*  Unsifted, unrefined, a pure villain.
4 *jakes*  Outdoor toilet.
5 *holy cords atwain*  Sacred bond in two.
6 *intrinced*  Entangled.
7 *smooth … rebel*  Humor every foolish whimsical notion their masters have.
8 *halcyon beaks*  Those of the kingfisher, which was proverbially regarded as changeable; according to superstition, the kingfisher would serve as a weathervane when
hung by its neck.
9 *gall*  Difficult moment.

(*To Oswald.*) A plague upon your epileptic[1] visage!
Smile you my speeches, as I were a fool?
Goose, if I had you upon Sarum Plain,
I'd drive ye cackling home to Camelot.[2]                         75
CORNWALL.   What art thou mad, old fellow?
GLOUCESTER.   How fell you out, say that?
KENT.   No contraries hold more antipathy
Than I, and such a knave.
CORNWALL.   Why dost thou call him knave?                         80
What is his fault?
KENT.   His countenance likes me not.
CORNWALL.   No more perchance does mine; not his, nor hers.
KENT.   Sir, 'tis my occupation to be plain,
I have seen better faces in my time,                              85
Than stands on any shoulder that I see
Before me, at this instant.
CORNWALL.                          This is some fellow,
Who having been praised for bluntness, doth affect
A saucy roughness,[3] and constrains the garb                    90
Quite from his nature.[4] He cannot flatter, he!
An honest mind and plain; he must speak truth.
And they will take it so. If not, he's plain.
These kind of knaves I know, which in this plainness
Harbour more craft, and more corrupter ends,                     95
Than twenty silly-ducking observants,[5]
That stretch their duties nicely.[6]
KENT.   Sir, in good faith, in sincere verity,
Under th'allowance of your great aspect,

---

1  *epileptic*  Contorted (presumably Oswald is moving through various expressions of
   incredulity, indignation, and forced laughter).
2  *Goose ... Camelot*  Goose, presumably because of Oswald's cackling; *Sarum
   Plain*  Salisbury Plain, the site of Stonehenge, which was associated with King Arthur because it was said to have been built by Merlin;  *Camelot*  Legendary home
   of King Arthur. Kent's threat appears to allude to some Arthurian legend which is
   now lost; the general idea is that he would thrash Oswald from one place to the next,
   thus knocking the foolishness out of him.
3  *saucy roughness*  Cheeky rudeness.
4  *constrains the garb ... his nature*  Keeps any cloak of civility away from him.
5  *silly-ducking observants*  Foolishly bowing attendants.
6  *stretch ... nicely*  Bend over backwards to be precise in their work.

100 Whose influence, like the wreath of radiant fire
     On flickering Phoebus' front—[1]
     CORNWALL.   What mean'st by this?
     KENT.   To go out of my dialect, which you discommend so
        much. I know, Sir—I am no flatterer—he that beguiled you in
105     a plain accent, was a plain knave; which, for my part, I will not
        be, though I should win your displeasure to entreat me to't.[2]
     CORNWALL.   What was th'offence you gave him?
     OSWALD.   I never gave him any.
        It pleased the King, his master, very late
110     To strike at me upon his misconstruction,[3]
        When he (*Indicating Kent.*), compact,[4] and flattering his
           displeasure[5]
        Tripped me behind; being down,[6] insulted, railed,
        And put upon him such a deal of man,
        That worthied him,[7] got praises of the King,
115     For him attempting who was self-subdued,[8]
        And in the fleshment° of this dread exploit,[9]          *excitement*
        Drew on me here again.
     KENT.                        None of these rogues and cowards
        But Ajax is their fool.[10]
120 CORNWALL.                 Fetch forth the stocks.
        You stubborn ancient knave; you reverend braggart,[11]

---

1  *Sir ... front*  Kent assumes an absurdly flattering attitude to mock Cornwall's pref-
   erence for servitude, identifying Cornwall with a planetary influence and with the
   sun itself.
2  *I know ... me to't*  I know, and will say so bluntly, that whoever it was that deceived
   you by putting on plain speech was simply a knave; that's something I won't be, even
   if you were made cross by trying to persuade me to take on that attitude.
3  *upon his misconstruction*  Because of his (Lear's) misunderstanding.
4  *compact*  In league (with the King).
5  *flattering his displeasure*  Playing to Lear's bad mood.
6  *being down*  I.e., me being down.
7  *put upon ... worthied him*  Acted like such a hero that he was regarded as being of
   great worth in the eyes of others.
8  *For him ... self-subdued*  For overcoming someone who had put up no struggle.
9  *dread exploit*  Heroic deed (ironic).
10 *None ... fool*  This sort of person inevitably plays upon and prevails with the Ajax
   type (the boastful idiot described in Homer's *Iliad*, implicitly compared here to
   Cornwall).
11 *ancient ... braggart*  The thrust of Cornwall's name-calling lies in what he regards
   as the inappropriateness of Kent's insubordination to his advanced age.

We'll teach you!
KENT.                    Sir, I am too old to learn:
Call not your stocks for me; I serve the King,
On whose employment I was sent to you.                    125
You shall do small respects, show too bold malice
Against the grace and person of my master,
Stocking his messenger.
CORNWALL.                    Fetch forth the stocks.
As I have life and honour, there shall he sit till noon.                    130
REGAN.    Till noon? Till night, my Lord; and all night too.
KENT.    Why Madam, if I were your father's dog,
You should not use me so.
REGAN.                    Sir, being his Knave, I will.
CORNWALL.    This is a fellow of the self-same colour                    135
Our sister speaks of.[1] Come, bring away the stocks.

(*Stocks brought out.*)

GLOUCESTER.    Let me beseech your Grace not to do so.
The King his master, needs must take it ill
That he so slightly valued in his messenger,
Should have him thus restrained.[2]                    140
CORNWALL.                    I'll answer that.
REGAN.    My sister may receive it much more worse,
To have her gentleman abused, assaulted.

(*Kent is put in the stocks.*)

CORNWALL.    (*To Gloucester.*) Come my Lord, away.

(*Exit [Cornwall and Regan].*)

---

1    *This is ... speaks of*    This is the same sort of person that Gonerill complained of (i.e.,
Lear's followers).
2    *Let me beseech ... thus restrained*    The equivalent speech in the Quarto version is
several lines longer: "GLOUCESTER. Let me beseech your Grace not to do so. / His
fault is much, and the good King his master / Will check him for't. Your purposed
low correction / Is such as basest and damnest wretches for pilf'rings / And most
common trespasses are punished with. / The King must take it ill, that he's so slightly
valued / In his messenger; should have him thus restrained."

145 GLOUCESTER. I am sorry for thee friend. 'Tis the Duke's
    pleasure,
    Whose disposition, all the world well knows,
    Will not be rubbed¹ nor stopped. I'll entreat for thee.
    KENT. Pray, do not, Sir. I have watched² and travelled hard;
    Some time I shall sleep out, the rest I'll whistle.
150 A good man's fortune may grow out at heels.³
    Give you good morrow.
    GLOUCESTER. The Duke's to blame in this.
    'Twill be ill taken.

    (*Exit.*)

    KENT. Good King, that must approve the common
       saw:°                                      *saying, proverb*
155 Thou out of heaven's benediction com'st
    To the warm sun.⁴
    Approach thou beacon to this under globe,⁵
    That by thy comfortable beams I may
    Peruse this letter. Nothing almost sees miracles
160 But misery.⁶ I know 'tis from Cordelia,
    Who hath most fortunately been informed
    Of my obscured course;⁷ and shall find time
    From this enormous state, seeking to give
    Losses their remedies.⁸ All weary and o'er-watched.⁹
165 Take vantage, heavy eyes, not to behold

---

1 *rubbed* Diverted (a term used in lawn bowling).
2 *watched* Stayed awake.
3 *A ... heels* Even a good man has bad luck sometimes (as one's shoes must wear out).
4 *Thou ... sun* One has to leave good things and come to unpleasant things (the heat of the sun being regarded as an uncomfortable affliction).
5 *Approach ... globe* Rise, sun, and shine on the earth.
6 *Nothing ... misery* Only those who are miserable can see the possibility of miracles happening.
7 *obscured course* Disguised journey.
8 *shall find ... remedies* Shall take the time from the (French) affairs of state to come and remedy the problems here.
9 *o'er-watched* Awake too long.

This shameful lodging.[1] Fortune, goodnight;
Smile once more, turn thy wheel.[2]

(*Sleeps.*)
(*Enter Edgar.*)[3]

EDGAR.   I heard myself proclaimed,[4]
And by the happy° hollow of a tree,                                    *lucky*
Escaped the hunt. No port is free; no place                            170
That guard, and most unusual vigilance,
Does not attend my taking.[5] Whiles I may 'scape
I will preserve myself: and am bethought°                              *have decided*
To take the basest, and most poorest shape
That ever penury, in contempt of man,                                  175
Brought near to beast.[6] My face I'll grime with filth,
Blanket[7] my loins; elf all my hairs in knots,[8]
And with presented° nakedness out-face°                                *exposed / defy*
The winds, and persecutions of the sky.
The country gives me proof° and precedent                              *example*   180
Of Bedlam beggars who, with roaring voices,
Strike in their numbed and mortified arms
Pins, wooden-pricks, nails, sprigs of rosemary.
And with this horrible object,° from low farms,                        *spectacle*
Poor pelting° villages, sheep-cotes, and mills—                        *paltry*    185
Sometimes with lunatic bans,° sometime with                            *curses*
    prayers—

---

1   *Take … lodging*   Take advantage of the opportunity presented by sleep not to have
    to look at these disgraceful circumstances in which I have been left.

2   *Fortune … wheel*   Fortune was depicted as a goddess with a large wheel which
    represented the cyclical turns of a person's luck or misfortune.

3   *Enter Edgar*   Though many editions mark a new scene (Act 2, Scene 3) at this
    point, in the Folio there is no scene break; Kent, in stocks, is unable to leave the
    stage, so technically the scene is continuous. However, we are to understand that
    Edgar is at some distance from the place where Kent has been stocked.

4   *proclaimed*   I.e., publicly proclaimed an outlaw.

5   *attend my taking*   Wait to arrest me.

6   *That ever … beast*   That poverty, in stripping away the veneer of civilization, has
    been able to use to demonstrate how close a human still is to an animal.

7   *blanket*   Cover only with a blanket.

8   *elf … knots*   As mischievous elves were reputed to do, tangle the hair into matted
    lumps.

Enforce their charity. "Poor Turlygod, poor Tom!"[1]
That's something yet. Edgar I nothing am.

                                                        (*Exit.*)

(*Enter Lear, Fool, and Gentleman.*)[2]

LEAR.   'Tis strange that they should so depart from home,
190     And not send back my messengers.[3]
GENTLEMAN.                             As I learned,
        The night before, there was no purpose in them
        Of this remove.[4]
KENT.                   Hail to thee, noble master.
195  LEAR.   Ha? Mak'st thou this shame thy pastime?[5]
KENT.                                       No, my Lord.
FOOL.   Ha, ha! He wears cruel garters![6] Horses are tied by the
        heads; dogs and bears by th'neck; monkeys by th'loins; and
        men by th'legs. When a man's over-lusty[7] at legs, then he wears
200     wooden nether-stocks.[8]
LEAR.   What's he that hath so much thy place mistook[9]
        To set thee here?
KENT.               It is both he and she,
        Your son and daughter.
205  LEAR.                   No.
KENT.                     Yes.
LEAR.                              No I say.
KENT.   I say yea.

---

1   *Poor ... Tom*   Edgar is trying out the voice for his new character. The origin of the
    name Turlygod is unknown, and continues to be debated.
2   *Enter ... Gentleman*   Many editions mark a new scene (Act 2, Scene 4) as starting
    here, but in the Folio text there is no scene break. (As noted above, Kent remains
    onstage.)
3   *'Tis ... messengers*   I.e., Regan and Cornwall have left their own house to come to
    Gloucester's without sending Lear's messenger (Kent) back to tell him where they are
    so as to save him the journey.
4   *there was ... remove*   They did not declare any intention of making this move.
5   *Mak'st ... pastime*   Is this shameful thing your idea of a game?
6   *cruel garters*   Pun on the cruelty of the stocks and on crewel (slack woolen yarn,
    worsted) stockings.
7   *over-lusty*   Irrepressibly active (either just physically or sexually).
8   *nether-stocks*   Pun on nether (lower) stockings (as opposed to upper stocks, or
    breeches).
9   *thy place mistook*   Misunderstood your rank (as the King's servant).

LEAR.                    By Jupiter, I swear no.

KENT.   By Juno,[1] I swear aye.                                             210

LEAR.                             They durst not do't:
They could not, would not do't! 'Tis worse than murder,
To do upon respect such violent outrage!
Resolve me with all modest haste, which way
Thou might'st deserve, or they impose this usage,[2]               215
Coming from us.[3]

KENT.                    My Lord, when at their home
I did commend your Highness' letters to them.
Ere I was risen from the place, that showed
My duty kneeling, came there a reeking post,                       220
Stewed in his haste,[4] half breathless, panting forth
From Gonerill, his mistress, salutations;
Delivered letters spite of intermission,°          *without pausing*
Which presently they read. On those contents[5]
They summoned up their many, straight took horse,[6]              225
Commanded me to follow, and attend
The leisure of their answer;[7] gave me cold looks.
And meeting here the other messenger,
Whose welcome I perceived had poisoned mine,
Being the very fellow which of late                               230
Displayed so saucily[8] against your Highness,
Having more man than wit[9] about me, drew.
He raised° the house, with loud and coward cries.       *aroused*
Your son and daughter found this trespass worth
The shame which here it suffers.                                  235

---

1   *Jupiter/Juno*   Chief Roman god, and his consort.

2   *which way ... usage*   What you have done to deserve, or what their reasons are for
    imposing.

3   *Coming from us*   I.e., given that you are my servant.

4   *reeking ... haste*   Perspiring messenger (Oswald), steaming in the sweat which his
    haste had produced.

5   *On those contents*   On the basis of what they had read.

6   *straight took horse*   Assembled their many followers and immediately mounted their
    horses.

7   *attend ... answer*   Wait until they were ready to reply.

8   *Displayed so saucily*   Showed off so insolently.

9   *more man than wit*   More manliness than sense.

FOOL.    Winter's not gone yet, if the wild geese fly that way.[1]
    Fathers that wear rags,
        do make their children blind,[2]
    But fathers that bear bags,[3]

240         shall see their children kind.
    Fortune, that arrant whore,
        ne'er turns the key[4] to th'poor.
    But for all this thou shalt have as many dolours[5] for thy
    daughters, as thou canst tell° in a year.[6]        *count*

245 LEAR.    Oh how this mother[7] swells up toward my heart!
    *Hysterica passio*:[8] down thou climbing sorrow;
    Thy element's below.[9] Where is this daughter?
KENT.    With the Earl, Sir, here within.
LEAR.    Follow me not, stay here.


    (*Exit.*)


250 GENTLEMAN.    Made you no more offence, but what you speak
    of?
KENT.    None. How chance the King comes with so small a
    number?
FOOL.    And[10] thou hadst been set i'th' stocks for that question,
255     thoud'st well deserved it.
KENT.    Why, Fool?

---

1  *Winter's ... way*  If these acts are the signs we are to judge by (like geese flying south), more trouble is yet to come.
2  *blind*  I.e., to the needs of their fathers.
3  *bags*  I.e., of money.
4  *turns the key*  Opens the door.
5  *dolours*  Sorrows (with a pun on dollars).
6  *Winter's not gone yet ... in a year*  This speech does not appear in the Quarto version; Lear's line "Oh how this mother ..." follows directly after Kent's speech.
7  *mother*  Hysteria; the word is derived from the Greek *hysteria* (womb), which was thought to be mobile within the body and a physical source for feelings of hysteria, especially in women.
8  *Hysterica passio*  Medical term in the early seventeenth century for a feeling of rising panic and suffocation.
9  *thy element's below*  Your proper place is in the viscera (not climbing the throat and threatening to take hold of the mind).
10  *And*  If.

FOOL. We'll set thee to school to an ant,[1] to teach thee there's
no labouring i'th' winter. All that follow their noses, are led by
their eyes, but blind men; and there's not a nose among twenty,
but can smell him that's stinking.[2] Let go thy hold when a great          260
wheel runs down a hill, lest it break thy neck with following;
but the great one that goes upward, let him draw thee after.[3]
When a wise man gives thee better counsel, give me mine again.
I would ha' none but knaves use it, since a Fool gives it.

  That Sir which serves and seeks for gain,          265
   And follows but for form[4]
  Will pack, when it begins to rain,
   And leave thee in the storm.
  But I will tarry, the Fool will stay,
   And let the wise man fly.          270
  The knave turns fool that runs away,
   The Fool no knave perdy.[5]

KENT. Where learned you this, Fool?
FOOL.         Not i'th' stocks, fool.

(*Enter Lear and Gloucester.*)

LEAR. Deny to speak with me? They are sick! They are weary!          275
They have travelled all the night? Mere fetches,[6]
The images of revolt and flying off.°              *desertion*
Fetch me a better answer.
GLOUCESTER.     My dear Lord,
You know the fiery quality of the Duke,          280
How unremovable and fixed he is
In his own course.

---

1 *set thee ... ant* Have an ant be your tutor. The allusion is to the ant and the grass-
 hopper fable, wherein the ant labors through the summer and then has food in the
 winter. So Lear has failed to make prudent provision for his old age (his "winter").
2 *All that ... stinking* Anyone who has eyes to see knows that Lear is in trouble, and
 even a blind man would know the smell of a corpse.
3 *Let go ... after* Cynical summary of the opportunistic policy of most of Lear's followers: to latch onto winners and to abandon losers.
4 *for form* Out of convention (rather than loyalty).
5 *perdy* By God (from the French, *par Dieu*). The disloyal servant will be recognized
 as lacking in wisdom, but the fool, at least, will remain loyal in the eyes of God.
6 *fetches* Deceptions, excuses (literally, a nautical term describing tacking away from
 the direct course).

LEAR.                      Vengeance, plague, death, confusion!
         "Fiery?" What quality? Why Gloucester, Gloucester!
285     I'd speak with the Duke of Cornwall and his wife.
GLOUCESTER.   Well, my good Lord, I have informed them so.
LEAR.   Informed them? Dost thou understand me, man?[1]
GLOUCESTER.   Aye, my good Lord.
LEAR.   The King would speak with Cornwall! The dear father
290     Would with his daughter speak; commands, tends service.[2]
         Are they informed of this? My breath and blood!
         Fiery? The fiery Duke! Tell the hot Duke that—
         No, but not yet; maybe he is *not* well.
         Infirmity doth still neglect all office,
295     Whereto our health is bound.[3] We are not ourselves,
         When nature, being oppressed, commands the mind
         To suffer with the body. I'll forbear,
         And am fallen out with my more headier° will,              *headstrong*
         To take the indisposed and sickly fit
300     For the sound man.[4] (*Noticing Kent again.*)
                             Death on my state![5] Wherefore°             *why*
         Should he sit here? This act persuades me,
         That this remotion° of the Duke and her                    *removal*
         Is practise° only. Give me my servant forth!              *stratagem*
305     Go tell the Duke and's wife I'd speak with them
         Now, presently! Bid them come forth and hear me,
         Or at their chamber door I'll beat the drum,
         Till it cry sleep to death![6]
GLOUCESTER.   I would have all well betwixt you.

         (*Exit.*)

310     LEAR.   Oh me, my heart! My rising heart! But down.

---

1   *Well my good Lord ... understand me, man?*   These two short speeches do not appear
    in the Quarto version.
2   *tends service*   Waits to be served.
3   *Infirmity ... bound*   When we are sick, we neglect responsibilities that we would
    never think of neglecting when we are in health.
4   *To take ... man*   To assume that someone disabled by sickness has the same abilities
    as someone healthy.
5   *Death on my state*   May my royal power end (an oath similar to "I'll be damned").
6   *cry sleep to death*   I.e., Like a pack of hounds in pursuit of Sleep, intent on killing
    it.

FOOL.    Cry to it, Nuncle, as the cockney did to the eels,[1] when
she put 'em i'th'paste[2] alive. She knapped[3] 'em o'th'coxcombs[4]
with a stick, and cried: "Down wantons,[5] down!" 'Twas her
brother that, in pure kindness to his horse, buttered his hay.[6]

(*Enter Cornwall, Regan, Gloucester, Servants.*)

LEAR.    Good morrow to you both.                                        315
CORNWALL.    Hail to your Grace.

(*Kent here set at liberty.*)

REGAN.    I am glad to see your Highness.
LEAR.    Regan, I think you are. I know what reason
   I have to think so. If thou should'st not be glad,
   I would divorce me from thy mother's tomb—                           320
   Sepulch'ring an adulteress.[7] (*To Kent.*) O, are you free?
   Some other time for that.—Belovèd Regan,
   Thy sister's naught!° Oh Regan, she hath tied                *wicked*
   Sharp-toothed unkindness, like a vulture, here![8]
   I can scarce speak to thee. Thou'lt not believe                      325
   With how depraved a quality° —Oh, Regan!              *nature*
REGAN.    I pray you, Sir, take patience. I have hope
   You less know how to value her desert,
   Than she to scant her duty.
LEAR.                                Say? How is that?                   330
REGAN.    I cannot think my sister in the least
   Would fail her obligation. If, Sir, perchance
   She have restrained the riots of your followers,
   'Tis on such ground, and to such wholesome end,

---

1   *as the cockney ... eels*   This may be a reference to a story now lost. In the early
    seventeenth century "cockney" could mean "Londoner," "child," or "poor woman."
2   *paste*   Pastry.
3   *knapped*   Rapped.
4   *coxcombs*   Heads.
5   *wantons*   Naughty, playful things. The gist of the story is that the cockney woman,
    too squeamish to kill the eels before baking them, then fruitlessly attempts to scold
    them for their natural reaction, like Lear, who, having foolishly given his two selfish
    daughters power, now attempts to scold them into being kind to him.
6   *'Twas ... hay*   I.e., the foolish gesture was unappreciated, and aroused only
    ingratitude.
7   *adulteress*   I.e., because Regan could not be Lear's own child.
8   *here*   I.e., his chest.

335     As clears her from all blame.¹

LEAR.   My curses on her!

REGAN.                O, Sir, you are old.
    Nature in you stands on the very verge
    Of his confine.² You should be ruled and led
340     By some discretion that discerns your state
    Better than you yourself.³ Therefore, I pray you,
    That to our sister you do make return.
    Say you have wronged her.

LEAR.              Ask her forgiveness?
345     Do you but mark how this becomes the house:⁴
    (*Kneeling.*) "Dear daughter, I confess that I am old;
    Age is unnecessary: on my knees I beg,
    That you'll vouchsafe me raiment,° bed, and food."     *clothing*

REGAN.   Good Sir, no more: these are unsightly tricks:
350     Return you to my sister.

LEAR.         (*Rises.*) Never, Regan.
    She hath abated° me of half my train;         *cut off*
    Looked black upon me, struck me with her tongue
    Most serpent-like upon the very heart.
355     All the stored vengeances of heaven fall
    On her ingrateful top!° Strike her young bones,     *head*
    You taking airs, with lameness.⁵

CORNWALL.           Fie sir, fie.

LEAR.   You nimble lightnings, dart your blinding flames
360     Into her scornful eyes! Infect her beauty,
    You fen-sucked fogs,⁶ drawn by the powerful sun,
    To fall, and blister.

REGAN.         O the blest Gods!
    So will you wish on me, when the rash mood is on.

---

1  *Say? How is that? ... from all blame*  These six lines do not appear in the Quarto version.

2  *Nature ... confine*  I.e., you cannot live much longer.

3  *some ... yourself*  Some discreet mind that understands your condition better than you do.

4  *Do you ... the house*  Just think how becoming that would be to my royal state.

5  *Strike ... lameness*  "Young bones" was a colloquial expression for "unborn child"; Lear is calling for her progeny to be struck with disease (causing lameness) by the infected air.

6  *fen-sucked fogs*  Fogs that have risen from noxious swamps.

LEAR.   No, Regan, thou shalt never have my curse.                   365
  Thy tender-hearted nature shall not give
  Thee o'er to harshness. Her eyes are fierce, but thine
  Do comfort, and not burn. 'Tis not in thee
  To grudge my pleasures, to cut off my train,
  To bandy hasty words, to scant my sizes,[1]                        370
  And in conclusion, to oppose the bolt[2]
  Against my coming in. Thou better know'st
  The offices of nature,[3] bond of childhood,
  Effects° of courtesy, dues of gratitude.                *demonstrations*
  Thy half o'th' kingdom hast thou not forgot,                       375
  Wherein I thee endowed.
REGAN.                        Good Sir, to'th'purpose.[4]

(*Tucket within.*)

LEAR.   Who put my man i'th' stocks?

(*Enter [Oswald.]*)

CORNWALL.   What trumpet's that?
REGAN.   I know't, my sister's. This approves[5] her letter,         380
  That she would soon be here. (*To Oswald.*) Is your Lady come?
LEAR.   (*Of Oswald.*) This is a slave, whose easy borrowed[6] pride
  Dwells in the sickly grace[7] of her he follows.
  (*To Oswald.*) Out varlet, from my sight!
CORNWALL.                        What means your Grace?              385

(*Enter Gonerill.*)

LEAR.   Who stocked my servant? Regan, I have good hope
  Thou did'st not know on't.[8]—Who comes here? O, heavens,
  If you do love old men; if your sweet sway

---

1  *scant my sizes*  Reduce my allowances.
2  *oppose the bolt*  Bolt the door.
3  *offices of nature*  Natural obligations.
4  *to'th'purpose*  Come to the point.
5  *approves*  Confirms the content of.
6  *easy borrowed*  Facile and not earned.
7  *sickly grace*  Feeble favor.
8  *Who stocked ... did'st not know on't*  In the Quarto version almost identical lines are
   given to Gonorill rather than to Lear: "GONORILL. Who struck my servant? Regan I
   have good hope / Thou didst not know on't. LEAR. Who comes here?"

Allow¹ obedience; if you yourselves are old,
390    Make it your cause; send down, and take my part.
       (*To Gonerill.*) Art not ashamed to look upon this beard?
       O Regan, will you take her by the hand?
GONERILL.    Why not by th'hand, Sir? How have I offended?
       All's not offence that indiscretion finds,
395    And dotage terms so.²
LEAR.                          O sides, you are too tough!
       Will you yet hold?—How came my man i'th'stocks?
CORNWALL.    I set him there, Sir, but his own disorders³
       Deserved much less advancement.⁴
400    LEAR.                              You? Did you?
REGAN.    I pray you father, being weak, seem so.⁵
       If, till the expiration of your month,
       You will return and sojourn with my sister,
       Dismissing half your train, come then to me.
405    I am now from home, and out of that provision
       Which shall be needful for your entertainment.⁶
LEAR.    Return to her? And fifty men dismissed?
       No, rather I abjure all roofs, and choose
       To wage against the enmity o'th'air,
410    To be a comrade with the wolf and owl—
       Necessity's sharp pinch!⁷ Return with her?
       Why, the hot-bloodied France, that dowerless took
       Our youngest born: I could as well be brought
       To knee his⁸ throne, and squire-like⁹ pension beg,
415    To keep base life afoot!¹⁰ Return with her?
       Persuade me rather to be slave and sumpter°           laborer
       To this detested groom. (*Indicates Oswald.*)
GONERILL.                          At your choice, Sir.

---

1   *If you ... Allow*   If your authority approve of.
2   *All's ... terms so*   Not everything is offensive which the foolish and the senile call so.
3   *disorders*   Misbehaviors.
4   *Deserved much less advancement*   Deserved even worse.
5   *being weak, seem so*   I.e., don't pretend to a strength you no longer possess.
6   *needful ... entertainment*   Necessary to host you.
7   *Necessity's ... pinch*   The pain of not having enough.
8   *knee his*   Go on my knees before.
9   *squire-like*   As if I were his servant.
10  *To ... afoot*   Just to keep my miserable life going.

LEAR.  I prithee, daughter do not make me mad.
I will not trouble thee, my child. Farewell.                                    420
We'll no more meet, no more see one another.
But yet thou art my flesh, my blood, my daughter—
Or rather a disease that's in my flesh,
Which I must needs call mine. Thou art a bile,
A plague sore, or embossèd carbuncle°                    *swollen boil*    425
In my corrupted blood. But I'll not chide thee.
Let shame come when it will, I do not call it.
I do not bid the thunder-bearer shoot,
Nor tell tales of thee to high-judging Jove.[1]
Mend when thou canst, be better at thy leisure.                                430
I can be patient, I can stay with Regan,
I and my hundred knights.
REGAN.                           Not altogether so.
I looked not for you yet, nor am provided
For your fit welcome. Give ear, Sir, to my sister;                             435
For those that mingle reason with your passion,[2]
Must be content to think you old, and so—
But she knows what she does.
LEAR.                           Is this well spoken?
REGAN.  I dare avouch it, Sir. What, fifty followers?                          440
Is it not well? What should you need of more?
Yea, or so many? Sith that both charge and danger[3]
Speak 'gainst so great a number? How, in one house,
Should many people under two commands
Hold amity?[4] 'Tis hard, almost impossible.                                    445
GONERILL.  Why might not you, my Lord, receive attendance
From those that she calls servants, or from mine?
REGAN.  Why not, my Lord? If, then, they chanced to slack ye,[5]
We could control them. If you will come to me—

---

1  *high-judging Jove*  Jupiter/Zeus, the chief god of the Greek and Roman pantheon,
   who judges from on high.
2  *mingle ... passion*  I.e., take your emotional outbursts with a grain of salt.
3  *Sith ... danger*  Since both the expense and the risks involved.
4  *Hold amity*  Remain friendly.
5  *slack ye*  Show you poor service.

| 450 | For now I spy a danger[1]—I entreat you |
| | To bring but five and twenty. To no more |
| | Will I give place or notice.[2] |

LEAR.    I gave you all—

REGAN.                                    And in good time you gave it.

455 LEAR.    —Made you my guardians, my depositaries,°          *trustees*
But kept a reservation[3] to be followed
With such a number. What, must I come to you
With five and twenty? Regan, said you so?

REGAN.    And speak't again my Lord: no more with me.

460 LEAR.    Those wicked creatures yet do look well favoured
When others are more wicked.[4] Not being the worst
Stands in some rank of praise. (*To Gonerill.*) I'll go with thee,
Thy fifty yet doth double five and twenty,
And thou art twice her love.

465 GONERILL.                              Hear me my Lord;
What need you five and twenty? Ten? Or five?
To follow in a house, where twice so many
Have a command to tend you?

REGAN.                                    What need one?

470 LEAR.    O, reason not the need! Our basest beggars
Are in the poorest thing superfluous.[5]
Allow not nature more than nature needs,
Man's life is cheap as beast's. Thou art a lady;
If only to go warm were gorgeous,
475 Why nature needs not what thou gorgeous wear'st,
Which scarcely keeps thee warm.[6] But for true need—
You heavens, give me that patience, patience I need!
You see me here, you gods, a poor old man,
As full of grief as age, wretchèd in both.

---

1   *For now ... danger*   For I now see that there is a risk (in what I had previously agreed to).
2   *place or notice*   Lodging or acknowledgment.
3   *kept a reservation*   Specified a condition.
4   *Those ... wicked*   Even the wicked start to look good when others are worse.
5   *Our ... superfluous*   Even the poorest person possesses some small thing that is beyond absolute necessity.
6   *If only ... warm*   If being warm were your only concern, if that's what you thought gorgeous, then you would have no need of those gorgeous things you wear, which can hardly be said to keep you warm.

If it be you that stirs these daughters' hearts            480
Against their father, fool me not so much[1]
To bear it tamely; touch me with noble anger,
And let not women's weapons, water drops,
Stain my man's cheeks. No, you unnatural hags,
I will have such revenges on you both,            485
That all the world shall—I will do such things—
What they are yet, I know not, but they shall be
The terrors of the earth! You think I'll weep.
No, I'll not weep! I have full cause of weeping,

(*Storm and tempest [is heard].*)[2]

But this heart shall break into a hundred thousand            490
    flaws°            *pieces*
Or ere[3] I'll weep! O, Fool, I shall go mad.

(*Exeunt [Lear, Gentleman, Kent and Fool].*)

CORNWALL.    Let us withdraw; 'twill be a storm.
REGAN.    This house is little, the old man and's people,
  Cannot be well bestowed.°            *lodged*
GONERILL.    'Tis his own blame hath put himself from rest,            495
And must needs taste his folly.[4]
REGAN.    For his particular,[5] I'll receive him gladly,
  But not one follower.
GONERILL.           So am I purposed.
  Where is my Lord of Gloucester?            500

(*Enter Gloucester.*)

CORNWALL.    Followed the old man forth; he is returned.
GLOUCESTER.    The King is in high rage.
CORNWALL.           Whether is he going?

---

1  *fool … much*  Don't make me such a fool.
2  *Storm and tempest*  The two words now tend to be regarded as synonymous, but in the early seventeenth century "tempest" signified a more violent storm, including thunder and lightning; a "storm" might involve merely wind and rain, without any electrical activity.
3  *Or ere*  Before.
4  *'Tis … folly*  It's his own fault that he's so upset, and now he's going to have to suffer the consequences.
5  *For his particular*  As far as he himself is concerned.

GLOUCESTER. He calls to horse, but will I know not whither.

505 CORNWALL. 'Tis best to give him way; he leads himself.[1]

GONERILL. My Lord, entreat him by no means to stay.

GLOUCESTER. Alack, the night comes on, and the high winds
Do sorely ruffle.° For many miles about        *threaten, agitate*
There's scarce a bush.

510 REGAN.                              O Sir, to willful men,
The injuries that they themselves procure,
Must be their schoolmasters. Shut up your doors,
He is attended with a desperate train,
And what they may incense him to, being apt

515 To have his ear abused,[2] wisdom bids fear.

CORNWALL. Shut up your doors, my Lord, 'tis a wild night.
My Regan counsels well; come out o'th'storm.

(*Exeunt.*)

## ACT 3, SCENE 1

(*Storm still.*[3] *Enter Kent, and a Gentleman, severally.*)

KENT. Who's there besides foul weather?

GENTLEMAN. One minded like the weather: most unquietly.

KENT. I know you. Where's the King?

GENTLEMAN. Contending with the fretful elements;

5 Bids the wind blow the earth into the sea,
Or swell the curlèd waters 'bove the main,°        *land*
That things might change, or cease.[4]

KENT.                              But who is with him?[5]

GENTLEMAN. None but the Fool, who labours to outjest

10 His heart-struck injuries.[6]

---

1   *leads himself*   He'll have his own will.

2   *being apt ... abused*   Being susceptible to the knights' perverse advice.

3   *Storm still*   Here the stage direction may simply be a note to the reader that the
storm continues, but in subsequent appearances, it may be a surviving backstage
direction to those who were providing the noise of the storm.

4   *change, or cease*   Exchange places or end altogether (returning to chaos by reversing
the process described in Genesis 1.1–10).

5   *But who is with him?*   An additional eight lines appear immediately before this line
in the Quarto version.

6   *heart-struck injuries*   Sufferings which have struck him to the heart.

KENT.                    Sir, I do know you,
And dare, upon the warrant of my note
Commend a dear thing to you. There is division—
Although as yet the face of it is covered
With mutual cunning—'twixt Albany, and Cornwall,                    15
Who have—as who have not, that their great stars
Throned and set high¹—servants, who seem no less,²
Which are to France the spies and speculations³
Intelligent of our state. What hath been seen,
Either in snuffs and packings⁴ of the Dukes,                    20
Or the hard rein⁵ which both of them hath borne
Against the old kind King—or something deeper,
Whereof, perchance, these are but furnishings—⁶
GENTLEMAN.   I will talk further with you.⁷
KENT.                              No, do not.⁸                    25
For confirmation that I am much more
Than my out-wall,⁹ open this purse, and take
What it contains. If you shall see Cordelia—
As fear not but you shall—show her this ring,
And she will tell you who that fellow is                    30

---

1   *as who ... set high*   As who doesn't, who has been brought by their lucky stars into
    a state of great power.
2   *who seem no less*   Who look like ordinary servants.
3   *speculations*   What the modern military calls "intelligence advisors": those who,
    even in the absence of direct information, are able to offer informed speculation
    about the enemy.
4   *snuffs and packings*   Huffing (exchanging angry words) and plotting.
5   *hard rein*   Cruel treatment (a metaphor from horse-riding).
6   *Who have ... furnishings*   The equivalent passage in the Quarto version is longer
    and substantially different. In the Quarto version the French are said to have already
    landed: "With mutual cunning—'twixt Albany and Cornwall. / But true it is, from
    France there comes a power / Into this scattered kingdom, who already wise in our
    negligence, / Have secret feet in some of our best ports, / And are at point to show
    their open banner. / Now, to you: if on my credit you dare build so far / To make
    your speed to Dover, you shall find / Some that will thank you, making just report
    / Of how unnatural and bemadding sorrow / The King hath cause to 'plain. / I am
    a gentleman of blood and breeding, / And from some knowledge and assurance, /
    Offer this office to you."
7   *I will talk further with you*   Let's discuss this later.
8   *No, do not*   I.e., do not brush me off and assume you can talk to me later.
9   *out-wall*   Outward appearance.

That yet you do not know.[1] Fie on this storm!
I will go seek the King.

GENTLEMAN.                    Give me your hand,
Have you no more to say?

35    KENT.    Few words, but to effect more than all yet:[2]
That when[3] we have found the King. In which your pain[4]
That way, I'll this. He that first lights on° him,                    *sees*
Holla the other.

(*Exeunt.*)

## ACT 3, SCENE 2

(*Storm still. Enter Lear, and Fool.*)

LEAR.    Blow, winds, and crack your cheeks! Rage, blow!
You cataracts and hurricanoes, spout
Till you have drenched our steeples; drown the cocks![5]
You sulph'rous and thought-executing fires,[6]
5    Vaunt-couriers[7] of oak-cleaving thunder-bolts,
Singe my white head. And thou, all-shaking thunder,
Strike flat the thick rotundity o'th' world!
Crack Nature's moulds, all germens[8] spill at once
That makes ingrateful man.

10    FOOL.    O Nuncle, court holy-water in a dry house, is better than
this rain-water out o' door.[9] Good Nuncle, in, ask thy daughters'
blessing. Here's a night pities neither wisemen nor fools.

LEAR.    Rumble thy belly full; spit fire, spout rain!
Nor rain, wind, thunder, fire are my daughters;
15    I tax° not you, you elements, with unkindness.                    *accuse*

---

1    *who that fellow … know*    I.e., who I am.
2    *to effect … yet*    More important in consequence than anything I have said thus far.
3    *That when*    That I will tell you when.
4    *In which your pain*    Towards the accomplishment of which, please take the trouble
to go.
5    *cocks*    I.e., those on weather vanes.
6    *thought-executing fires*    Mind-numbing lightning.
7    *Vaunt-couriers*    Advance guard.
8    *Nature's moulds*    Forms Nature uses to make human beings; *germens*    Seeds, life.
9    *court holy water*    Phrase used to describe flattery (because the blessings offered in
court are so often empty of sincerity). The Fool suggests Lear might be better off
being insincere.

I never gave you kingdom, called you children;
You owe me no subscription.° Then let fall              *allegiance*
Your horrible pleasure!° Here I stand, your slave:                *will*
A poor, infirm, weak, and despised old man.
But yet I call you servile ministers,°                    *agents*    20
That will with two pernicious daughters join
Your high-engendered battles 'gainst a head
So old, and white as this! O, ho! 'Tis foul!
FOOL.    He that has a house to put's head in, has a good
    head-piece.[1]
        The codpiece[2] that will house[3]                    25
          before the head has any,
        The head, and he shall louse:[4]
          so beggars marry many.[5]
        The man who makes his toe,
          what he his heart should make,[6]           30
        Shall of a corn cry woe,
          and turn his sleep to wake.
For there was never yet fair woman, but she made mouths in a
    glass.[7]

(*Enter Kent.*)

LEAR.    No, I will be the pattern of all patience;[8]          35
    I will say nothing.
KENT.    Who's there?
FOOL.    Marry here's grace and a codpiece—that's a wiseman, and
    a fool.
KENT.    Alas, Sir, are you here? Things that love night,          40
    Love not such nights as these. The wrathful skies

---

1   *head-piece*  Pun on "helmet" and "brain."
2   *codpiece*  Often ostentatious covering for male genitals, sometimes, as here, stand-
    ing for the penis itself.
3   *house*  Find a home (i.e., a vagina, etc.).
4   *louse*  Get a case of lice.
5   *so ... many*  In this way, the poor have many partners (the lice).
6   *The man ... make*  The man who mistakenly sets a higher premium on lesser con-
    cerns rather than focusing on what is most essential to him.
7   *For there ... glass*  I.e., vanity is a thing to which we are all prone.
8   *No ... patience*  Lear has resolved to bear his sufferings stoically rather than
    complain.

Gallow° the very wanderers of the dark                              *terrify*
And make them keep their caves. Since I was man,
Such sheets of fire, such bursts of horrid thunder,
45    Such groans of roaring wind and rain, I never
Remember to have heard. Man's nature cannot carry
Th'affliction, nor the fear.
LEAR.                          Let the great goddess
That keep this dreadful pudder° o'er our heads,                    *racket*
50    Find out their enemies now. Tremble, thou wretch,
That hast within thee undivulgèd crimes
Unwhipped of¹ justice. Hide thee, thou bloody hand;
Thou perjured, and thou, simular° of virtue                    *counterfeit*
That art incestuous. Caitiff,° to pieces shake,                *low wretch*
55    That under covert, and convenient seeming²
Has practised on³ man's life. Close pent-up guilts,
Rive° your concealing continents,° and cry          *split / containers*
These dreadful summoners' grace.⁴ I am a man
More sinned against, than sinning.
60  KENT.                                 Alack, bare-headed?
Gracious my Lord, hard by here is a hovel,
Some friendship will it lend you 'gainst the tempest.
Repose you there, while I to this hard⁵ house—
More harder than the stones whereof 'tis raised,
65    Which even but now, demanding after you,⁶
Denied me to come in—return, and force
Their scanted courtesy.

      (*Exit.*)

LEAR.                          My wits begin to turn.
Come on, my boy. How dost my boy? Art cold?
70    I am cold myself. Where is this straw, my fellow?
The art of our necessities is strange,

---

1   *Unwhipped of* Unpunished by.
2   *convenient seeming* Opportunistic deception.
3   *practised on* Plotted against.
4   *cry … grace* Call for mercy from the awful agents who summon you before heaven's court.
5   *hard* I.e., hard-hearted.
6   *demanding after you* Seeking to know if you were there.

And can make vile things precious. Come, your hovel;
Poor Fool and knave, I have one part in my heart
That's sorry yet for thee.

FOOL.   (*Sings.*) He that has and a little tiny wit,                       75
    With heigh-ho, the wind and the rain,
    Must make content with his fortunes fit,
    Though the rain it raineth every day.[1]

LEAR.   True, boy. Come, bring us to this hovel.

(*Exit.*)

FOOL.   This is a brave night[2] to cool a courtesan.[3]                    80
I'll speak a prophecy ere I go:
When priests are more in word than matter;
When brewers mar their malt with water;
When nobles are their tailors' tutors,
No heretics burned, but wenches' suitors;[4]                                85
When every case in law is right;
No squire in debt, nor no poor knight;
When slanders do not live in tongues;
Nor cut-purses come not to throngs;
When usurers tell their gold i'th'field,                                    90
And bawds and whores do churches build,
Then shall the realm of Albion come to great confusion.
Then comes the time, who lives to see't,
That going shall be used with feet.[5]
This prophecy Merlin shall make, for I live before his time.               95

(*Exit.*)

---

1  *He that ... day*  This song is derived from the song that Feste sings at the end of
   *Twelfth Night.* The lyrics are slightly different in Q and in F, but the meaning is
   substantially the same: for the person who has little reason, it is necessary to find
   contentment in whatever fortune brings, because misfortunes will come steadily.
2  *brave night*  Pun on "brave knight."
3  *cool a courtesan*  Bring a quick end to lascivious enthusiasm.
4  *When ... suitors*  When priests are hypocrites, brewers water their beer, noblemen
   know more about clothes than tailors do, and the only people punished by "burning" are young men with syphilis.
5  *going ... feet*  People will walk on their feet (obviously an absurd truism).

(*Enter Gloucester, and Edmund.*)

GLOUCESTER. Alack, alack, Edmund, I like not this unnatural
dealing. When I desired their leave[1] that I might pity[2] him,
they took from me the use of mine own house, charged me, on
pain of perpetual displeasure, neither to speak of him, entreat
5    for him, or any way sustain[3] him.
EDMUND. Most savage and unnatural.
GLOUCESTER. Go to; say you nothing. There is division between
the Dukes, and a worse matter than that: I have received a letter
this night—'Tis dangerous to be spoken; I have locked the
10    letter in my closet. These injuries the King now bears, will be
revenged home;[4] there is part of a power already footed.[5] We
must incline to the King. I will look[6] him, and privily relieve[7]
him. Go you and maintain talk with the Duke, that my charity
be not of him perceived. If he ask for me, I am ill, and gone to
15    bed. If I die for it—as no less is threatened me—the King my
old master must be relieved. There is strange things toward,[8]
Edmund; pray you, be careful.

(*Exit.*)

EDMUND. This courtesy forbid thee,[9] shall the Duke
Instantly know, and of that letter too.
20    This seems a fair deserving,[10] and must draw[11] me
That which my father loses: no less than all.
The younger rises when the old doth fall.

(*Exit.*)

---

1    *leave*    Permission.
2    *pity*    Show pity towards.
3    *sustain*    Help.
4    *home*    To the utmost.
5    *footed*    Landed, or possibly only mobilized.
6    *look*    Seek.
7    *privily relieve*    Secretly assist.
8    *toward*    Coming.
9    *forbid thee*    Which you have already been forbidden to exercise.
10    *fair deserving*    Act likely to earn me favor.
11    *draw*    Win.

## ACT 3, Scene 4

*(Enter Lear, Kent, and Fool. Storm still.)*

KENT.    Here is the place,[1] my Lord. Good my Lord, enter;
The tyranny of the open night's too rough
For nature to endure.
LEAR.                    Let me alone.
KENT.    Good my Lord, enter here.                                    5
LEAR.                              Wilt break my heart?
KENT.    I had rather break mine own. Good my Lord, enter.
LEAR.    Thou think'st 'tis much that this contentious storm
Invades us to the skin; so 'tis to thee.
But where the greater malady is fixed,[2]                            10
The lesser is scarce felt. Thou'dst shun a bear,
But if thy flight lay toward the roaring sea,
Thou'dst meet the bear i'th' mouth. When the mind's free[3]
The body's delicate. The tempest in my mind,
Doth from my senses take all feeling else,                           15
Save what beats there: filial ingratitude.
Is it not as this mouth should tear this hand
For lifting food to't? But I will punish home—
No, I will weep no more! In such a night,
To shut me out? Pour on, I will endure!                             20
In such a night as this?[4] O, Regan, Gonerill,
Your old kind father, whose frank heart gave all—
O, that way madness lies! Let me shun that;
No more of that.
KENT.                    Good my Lord, enter here.                   25
LEAR.    Prithee, go in thyself; seek thine own ease.
This tempest will not give me leave to ponder

---

1   *the place*  The hovel spoken of in 3.2.
2   *fixed*  Lodged in the mind.
3   *free*  I.e., from care.
4   *But I will punish ... such a night as this*  The Quarto version is at this point slightly
    shorter: "For lifting food to't? But I will punish sure— / No! I will weep no more, in
    such a night as this! / O, Regan, Gonerill, your old kind father / Whose frank heart
    gave you all— / O, that way madness lies! Let me shun that; / No more of that."

On things would hurt me more— But I'll go in.
[*To Fool.*] In, boy, go first.
30   [*Begins to soliloquize.*]—You houseless poverty—
[*To others.*] Nay get thee in; I'll pray, and then I'll sleep.[1]

(*Exit [Fool].*)

—Poor naked wretches, wheresoe'er you are
That bide the pelting of this pitiless storm,
How shall your house-less heads, and unfed sides,
35   Your looped and windowed[2] raggedness defend you
From seasons such as these? O I have ta'en
Too little care of this. Take physic, pomp;[3]
Expose thyself to feel what wretches feel,
That thou mayst shake the superflux° to them,         *excess*
40   And show the heavens more just.

(*Enter Edgar [disguised], and Fool.*)

EDGAR.   Fathom and half,[4] fathom and half! Poor Tom!
FOOL.   Come not in here, Nuncle; here's a spirit! Help me, help
me!
KENT.   Give my thy hand. Who's there?
45   FOOL.   A spirit, a spirit! He says his name's Poor Tom.
KENT.   What art thou that dost grumble there i'th' straw? Come
forth.
EDGAR.   Away, the foul fiend follows me. (*Sings.*) "Through the
sharp hawthorn blow the winds—"[5] Humh, go to thy bed and
50   warm thee.
LEAR.   Did'st thou give all to thy daughters? And art thou come
to this?

---

1   *In, boy ... then I'll sleep*   These lines do not appear in the Quarto version.
2   *looped and windowed*   Loosely wrapped and full of holes.
3   *Take physic, pomp*   Take this medicine, great ones.
4   *Fathom and half*   Sailor's cry of the depth of water in a channel (presumably a comment on the rain).
5   *Through ... winds*   Probably a line from a melancholy old song, though the source
is unknown.

EDGAR.  Who gives anything to Poor Tom?—whom the foul
fiend hath led through fire and through flame,[1] through sword,
and whirlpool, o'er bog, and quagmire; that hath laid knives    55
under his pillow, and halters[2] in his pew, set ratsbane[3] by his
porridge, made him proud of heart, to ride on a bay trotting-
horse over four-inched[4] bridges, to course[5] his own shadow for
a traitor? Bless thy five wits,[6] Tom's a cold. (*Humming*.) O, do
de, do de, do de! Bless thee from whirlwinds, star-blasting,[7] and    60
taking! Do poor Tom some charity, whom the foul fiend vexes.
There could I have him now! And there! And there again! And
there!

(*Storm still.*)

LEAR.  Has his daughters brought him to this pass?
Could'st thou save nothing? Would'st thou give 'em all?    65
FOOL.  Nay, he reserved a blanket, else we had been all shamed.[8]
LEAR.  Now all the plagues that, in the pendulous° air,    *hanging*
Hang fated o'er men's faults, light on thy daughters!
KENT.  He hath no daughters, Sir.
LEAR.  Death, traitor! Nothing could have subdued nature    70
To such a lowness but his unkind daughters.
Is it the fashion, that discarded fathers,
Should have thus little mercy on their flesh?
Judicious punishment:[9] 'twas this flesh begot
Those pelican daughters.[10]    75

---

1  *fire and through flame*  The redundancy suggests there may have been a compositor's
error. The Quarto version has "ford" for "fire."
2  *halters*  Nooses.
3  *ratsbane*  Poison (along with the knives and halters, emblematic means by which
the Devil was said to tempt a person to suicide).
4  *four-inched*  Four inches wide (thus risking his life).
5  *course*  Hunt down.
6  *Bless ... wits*  Not to be confused with the five senses, the five wits were said to be
common wit, imagination, fantasy, estimation, and memory. To have them disordered or disproportionate (i.e., unblessed) would effectively mean madness.
7  *star-blasting*  Unwholesome effects of malignant stars.
8  *shamed*  Embarrassed (by his nakedness).
9  *Judicious punishment*  (On second thought) a just punishment.
10  *pelican daughters*  According to legend, the young of the pelican would feed by
sucking blood directly from the breast of the parents.

EDGAR. (*Sings.*) "Pillicock sat on Pillicock Hill: alow, alow, loo, loo."[1]

FOOL. This cold night will turn us all to fools and madmen.

EDGAR. Take heed o'th'foul fiend! Obey thy parents; keep thy
80 word's justice;[2] swear not; commit not[3] with man's sworn
spouse; set not thy sweet heart on proud array. Tom's a cold.

LEAR. What hast thou been?

EDGAR. A servingman? Proud in heart and mind; that curled
my hair, wore gloves in my cap;[4] served the lust of my mistress'
85 heart, and did the act of darkness with her; swore as many oaths
as I spake words, and broke them in the sweet face of heaven.
One that slept in the contriving of lust, and waked to do it. Wine
loved I dearly, dice dearly; and in woman, out-paramoured the
Turk.[5] False of heart, light of ear,[6] bloody of hand; hog in sloth,
90 fox in stealth, wolf in greediness, dog in madness, lion in prey.
Let not the creaking of shoes, nor the rustling of silks, betray
thy poor heart to woman. Keep thy foot out of brothels, thy
hand out of plackets,[7] thy pen from lenders' books,[8] and defy
the foul fiend! (*Sings.*) "Still through the hawthorn blows the
95 cold wind" says: (*Sings.*)

> Suum, mun, nonny,
> Dolphin[9] my boy;
> Boy, sessa:[10] let him trot by.[11]

(*Storm still.*)

---

1 *Pillicock ... loo* This song has survived in the somewhat altered form of a nursery
rhyme known from the nineteenth century: "Pillicock, pillicock, sat on a hill / If
he's not gone, he sits there still." The name is probably related to "pillock," slang for
penis, also applied to a young boy and a fool.

2 *keep thy word's justice* Don't break your promises.

3 *commit not* I.e., adultery.

4 *gloves ... cap* A dandy's pledge to his mistress.

5 *out-paramoured the Turk* Had more lovers than a Turkish Sultan has concubines.

6 *light of ear* Ready to believe slander.

7 *plackets* Openings in the front of women's skirts.

8 *thy pen from lenders' books* Do not sign your name to moneylenders.

9 *Dolphin* The usual English version of the French *dauphin*, prince, here, apparently
the name of a horse.

10 *sessa* Possibly "sa, sa!" an exhortation to a horse (like giddyup), possibly a corruption of the French "cessez."

11 In the Quarto version these three lines read as follows: "Hey no nonny, / Dolphin
my boy, my boy! / Cease, let him trot by."

LEAR.   Thou wert better in a grave, than to answer with thy
uncovered body, this extremity of the skies. Is man no more    100
than this? Consider him well. Thou ow'st the worm no silk;
the beast, no hide; the sheep, no wool; the cat, no perfume.[1]
Ha? Here's three on's[2] are sophisticated; thou art the thing itself.
Unaccommodated man is no more but such a poor, bare, forked
animal as thou art. (*Begins to remove his clothing.*) Off, off you    105
lendings![3] Come, unbutton here.

(*Enter Gloucester with a torch.*)

FOOL.   Prithee, Nuncle, be contented; 'tis a naughty night to
swim in. Now a little fire in a wild field were like an old lecher's
heart: a small spark, all the rest on's[4] body, cold. Look, here
comes a walking fire.    110
EDGAR.   This is the foul Flibbertigibbet![5] He begins at curfew,
and walks at first cock. He gives the web and the pin;[6] squints
the eye, and makes the harelip; mildews the white wheat, and
hurts the poor creature of earth.
        S'withold footed thrice the old,[7]    115
        He met the night mare, and her nine-fold;
        Bid her alight, and her troth plight,
        And aroint thee, witch, aroint thee![8]
KENT.   How fares your Grace?
LEAR.   What's he?    120

---

1   *cat, no perfume*   Civet perfumes are made from the anal glands of the civet cat (a
    creature found in Asia and Africa, related to the common cat, but more similar to
    the mongoose).
2   *on's*   Of us.
3   *lendings*   Borrowed clothes.
4   *on's*   Of his.
5   *Flibbertigibbet*   Name of a devil, according to Elizabethan demonology.
6   *web and the pin*   Cataracts of the eye.
7   *S'withold ... old*   Saint Withold, a Saxon saint, was said to have walked three times
    across Britain, banishing demons, as is remembered in this rhyme.
8   *night mare ... thee*   The word "nightmare" originally denoted a monster from folk-
    lore known as the night mare (with "mare" deriving not from the word for female
    horse but from the Old Norse word for incubus, a demon that preyed on one during
    sleep). Here it appears that the night mare is imagined as a female demon mounted
    on a horse; Saint Withold forces her to dismount, together with her nine children,
    and swear allegiance to heaven, so that the witch is commanded to depart (aroint).

KENT. Who's there? What is't you seek?

GLOUCESTER. What are you there? Your names?

EDGAR. Poor Tom, that eats the swimming frog, the toad, the
tadpole, the wall-newt and the water;[1] that, in the fury of his
125　heart, when the foul fiend rages, eats cow-dung for sallets;[2]
swallows the old rat and the ditch-dog;[3] drinks the green
mantle[4] of the standing pool; who is whipped from tithing to
tithing,[5] and stocked,[6] punished, and imprisoned; who hath
three suits to his back, six shirts to his body—
130　　　Horse to ride, and weapon to wear:
But mice, and rats, and such small deer,[7]
Have been Tom's food for seven long year:
Beware my follower![8] Peace, Smulkin![9] Peace, thou fiend!

GLOUCESTER. (*To Lear.*) What, hath your Grace no better
135　company?

EDGAR. The Prince of Darkness[10] is a gentleman. Modo he's
called, and Mahu.[11]

GLOUCESTER. (*To Lear.*) Our flesh and blood, my Lord, is grown
so vile, that it doth hate what gets it.[12]

140　EDGAR. Poor Tom's a cold.

GLOUCESTER. (*To Lear.*)
Go in with me; my duty cannot suffer°　　　　　　　　*allow me*
T'obey in all your daughters' hard commands:
Though their injunction be to bar my doors,
And let this tyrannous night take hold upon you,

---

1　*wall-newt*　Small lizard and the water newt.

2　*sallets*　Salads.

3　*ditch-dog*　Dead dog left in a ditch.

4　*green mantle*　Pond scum.

5　*tithing*　Rural district defined by ten families.

6　*stocked*　Put in stocks (as Kent had been).

7　*small deer*　Small game.

8　*follower*　Familiar, enslaved spirit.

9　*Smulkin*　Devil from Elizabethan demonology.

10　*Prince of Darkness*　The Devil (Edgar is directly contradicting Gloucester's suggestion that Lear is keeping poor company).

11　*Modo ... Mahu*　Devils from Elizabethan demonology, here spoken of by Edgar as
if they were titled nobles.

12　*Our flesh ... gets it*　We have grown so debased as human beings that children hate
their parents who begot them (Gloucester is consoling Lear with his shared misfortune, his betrayal—as he thinks—by Edgar).

Yet have I ventured to come seek you out,                                   145
And bring you where both fire and food is ready.
LEAR.    First, let me talk with this philosopher.
(*To Edgar.*) What is the cause of thunder?
KENT.    Good my Lord take his offer; go into th' house.
LEAR.    I'll talk a word with this same learnèd Theban.°          *Greek*   150
(*To Edgar.*) What is your study?
EDGAR.    How to prevent the fiend, and to kill vermin.
LEAR.    Let me ask you one word in private.
KENT.    Importune him once more to go, my Lord.
His wits begin t'unsettle.                                                   155
GLOUCESTER.                    Canst thou blame him?
His daughters seek his death. Ah, that good Kent;
He said it would be thus. Poor banished man.
Thou sayest the King grows mad; I'll tell thee, friend
I am almost mad myself. I had a son,                                        160
Now outlawed from my blood:[1] he sought my life
But lately, very late.° I loved him, friend—                   *recently*
No father his son dearer. True to tell thee,
The grief hath crazed my wits.

(*Storm still.*)

                            What a night's this?                           165
I do beseech your grace.
LEAR.                        O, cry you mercy,[2] Sir.
Noble philosopher, your company.
EDGAR.    Tom's a cold.
GLOUCESTER.    In fellow there, into th' hovel; keep thee warm.           170
LEAR.    Come, let's in all.
KENT.                        This way, my Lord.
LEAR.                                            With him;
I will keep still with my philosopher.
KENT.    Good my Lord, soothe him; let him take the fellow.               175
GLOUCESTER.    Take him you on.°                           *with you*

---

1    *outlawed ... blood*  Disowned.
2    *cry you mercy*  I beg your pardon. (In the Quarto version this line is addressed to
      Edgar, not to Gloucester.)

KENT. Sirrah, come on. Go along with us.

LEAR. Come, good Athenian.[1]

GLOUCESTER. No words, no words, hush.

180 EDGAR. Child Rowland[2] to the dark tower came,
His word was still: "Fie, fo, and fum,
I smell the blood of a British man."[3]

(*Exeunt.*)

## ACT 3 , SCENE 5

(*Enter Cornwall and Edmund.*)

CORNWALL. I will have my revenge, ere I depart his house.

EDMUND. How, my Lord, I may be censured, that nature thus
gives way to loyalty,[4] something fears me to think of.

CORNWALL. I now perceive, it was not altogether your brother's

5 evil disposition made him seek his death, but a provoking merit
set a-work by a reprovable badness in himself.[5]

EDMUND. How malicious is my fortune, that I must repent to
be just? This is the letter which he spoke of, which approves him
an intelligent party[6] to the advantages[7] of France. O, heavens!

10 That this treason were not; or not I the detector.

CORNWALL. Go with me to the Duchess.

EDMUND. If the matter of this paper be certain, you have mighty
business in hand.

---

1 *Athenian* I.e., because a Greek philosopher.

2 *Child Rowland* Hero of the French medieval epic, *Chanson de Roland* ("Child"
being the term used to denote a candidate for knighthood), and later stories and
ballads.

3 *Fie … man* The giant's lines from such tales as "Jack-and-the-Beanstalk," and "Jack
the Giant-Killer." The juxtaposition of the two stories is incongruous, and helps
indicate Edgar's "madness."

4 *that nature … loyalty* That I have allowed my natural affections to be superseded
by my loyalty to you.

5 *it was … himself* It was not Edgar's wickedness that made him plot to kill Gloucester, but his good qualities, which were activated by the badness in Gloucester.

6 *intelligent party* Spy.

7 *to the advantages* In the service.

CORNWALL.    True or false, it hath made thee Earl of Gloucester. Seek out where thy father is, that he may be ready for our apprehension.    15

EDMUND.    (*Aside.*) If I find him comforting the King, it will stuff his suspicion more fully.[1] I will persevere in my course of loyalty, though the conflict be sore between that and my blood.[2]

CORNWALL.    I will lay trust upon thee; and thou shalt find a dear father in my love.    20

(*Exeunt.*)

---

1    *stuff his suspicion more fully*    Make him more of a suspect.
2    *though ... blood*    Though it is a great hardship to maintain my loyalty to you when it conflicts with my natural affection for my father.

*(Enter Kent and Gloucester.)*

GLOUCESTER. Here[1] is better than the open air; take it thankfully.
I will piece out the comfort with what addition I can. I will not
be long from you.

KENT. All the power of his wits have given way to his impatience.
5 The gods reward your kindness.

*(Exit Gloucester.)*
*(Enter Lear, Edgar and Fool.)*

EDGAR. Fraterretto[2] calls me, and tells me Nero[3] is an angler in
the lake of darkness. Pray, innocent; and beware the foul fiend!

FOOL. Prithee, Nuncle, tell me whether a madman be a gentleman or a yeoman.

10 LEAR. A King, a King.

FOOL. No, he's a yeoman that has a gentleman to his[4] son; for
he's a mad yeoman that sees his son a gentleman before him.

LEAR. To have a thousand with red burning spits
Come hissing in upon 'em![5]

---

1 *Here* Apparently one of the outlying buildings on Gloucester's estate—likely imag-
ined as a barn or stable.

2 *Fraterretto* Shakespeare borrows names for his demons from accounts of exorcisms
in Samuel Harsnett's *A Declaration of Egregious Popish Impostures* (1603).

3 *Nero* Villainous Roman emperor. The gist seems to be that Edgar is aware that the
tyrants are looking for victims.

4 *to his* For a.

5 *To have … 'em* Lear is evidently fantasizing about a legion of devils punishing his
daughters in the afterlife.

*(Enter Gloucester, Lear, Kent, Fool, and [Edgar, still disguised as] Tom.)*

GLOUCESTER.   Here is better than the open air; take it thankfully. I will piece out the comfort with what addition I can. I will not be long from you.

KENT.   All the power of his wits have given way to impatience. The gods deserve your kindness.                                                                5

*(Exit Gloucester.)*

EDGAR.   Frateretto calls me, and tells me Nero is an angler in the lake of darkness. Pray, innocent, beware the foul fiend.

FOOL.   Prithee, Nuncle, tell me whether a madman be a gentleman or a yeoman.

LEAR.   A King, a King, to have a thousand with red burning spits      10 come hissing in upon them.

EDGAR.   The foul fiend bites my back.

FOOL.   He's mad, that trusts in the tameness of a wolf, a horse's health, a boy's love, or a whore's oath.

LEAR.   It shall be done; I will arraign them straight.                            15
   *(To Edgar.)* Come sit, thou here, most learned justice.
   *(To Fool.)* Thou, sapient[1] sir, sit here. *(To his imaginary daughters.)*—No, you she-foxes—!

EDGAR.   *(To the imaginary daughters.)* Look where he stands and glares. Want'st thou eyes?[2] At trial,[3] madam! "Come o'er the      20 broom, Bessy, to me."[4]

FOOL.   *(Sings.)* Her boat hath a leak,
   And she must not speak,
   Why she dares not come over to thee.[5]

---

1   *sapient*   Wise.

2   *Want'st thou eyes?*   Are you blind?

3   *At trial*   Take your place in the defence stand.

4   *Come ... to me*   Edgar quotes a line altered from an old song, "Come over the bourn (stream), Bessy, to me," here presumably adjusted to suit their location, in which we may imagine straw (broom) on the floor.

5   *Her boat ... thee*   The Fool joins in by parodying the song in reply.

EDGAR.  The foul fiend haunts poor Tom in the voice of a        25
    nightingale. Hoppedance[1] cries in Tom's belly for two white
    herring. Croak[2] not, black angel, I have no food for thee.
KENT.  (*To Lear.*) How do you sir? Stand you not so amazed.
    Will you lie down and rest upon the cushions?
LEAR.  I'll see their trial first. Bring in their evidence.        30
    (*To Edgar.*) Thou robèd man of justice, take thy place.
    (*To Fool.*) And thou, his yokefellow[3] of equity,
    Bench by his side. (*To Kent.*) You are o'th' commission,
    Sit you, too.
EDGAR.  Let us deal justly.        35
    (*Sings.*) Sleepest or wakest, thou jolly shepherd?
        Thy sheep be in the corn,
      And for[4] one blast of thy minikin[5] mouth,
        Thy sheep shall take no harm.[6]
    Purr[7] the cat is gray.        40
LEAR.  (*Indicating a stool.*) Arraign her first. 'Tis Gonorill. I here
    take my oath before this honourable assembly, she kicked the
    poor king her father.
FOOL.  Come hither, mistress. Is your name Gonorill?
LEAR.  She cannot deny it.        45
FOOL.  Cry you mercy, I took you for a join stool.[8]
LEAR.  And here's another whose warped looks proclaim

---

1  *Hoppedance*  Another name of a demon taken from Harsnett.
2  *Croak*  Sound of a demon, and of the growling of a stomach.
3  *yokefellow*  Partner.
4  *for*  In exchange for you making.
5  *minikin*  Shrill.
6  *Sleepest ... harm*  Variation on the nursery rhyme: "Little Boy Blue, come blow
   your horn / The sheep's in the meadow, the cow's in the corn. / But where is the boy
   who looks after the sheep? / He's under a haystack, fast asleep."
7  *Purr*  A pun: the name of a devil drawn from Elizabethan demonology, and also the
   sound a cat makes.
8  *join stool*  Stool made of jointed pieces of wood. "I took you for a join stool" was a
   common jocular way of claiming not to have noticed someone.

15    EDGAR.            Bless thy five wits.

KENT.   O, pity! Sir, where is the patience now
That you so oft have boasted to retain?

EDGAR.   (*Aside.*) My tears begin to take his part so much,
They mar my counterfeiting.[1]

20    LEAR.                  The little dogs, and all—
Trey, Blanch, and Sweetheart—see, they bark at me.

EDGAR. Tom will throw his head[2] at them.—Avaunt you curs!

      Be thy mouth or black or white,
      Tooth that poisons if it bite:

25       Mastiff, grey-hound, mongrel, grim,
      Hound or spaniel, brach° or him,°           *bitch / male*
      Or bobtail tight, or trundle tail,[3]
      Tom will make him weep and wail,
      For with throwing thus my head;

30       Dogs leapt the hatch, and all are fled.

Do, de, de, de! Sesa![4] Come, march to wakes and fairs and
market towns. Poor Tom, thy horn[5] is dry.

LEAR.   Then let them anatomize[6] Regan; see what breeds about
her heart. Is there any cause in nature that makes these hard-

35    hearts? (*To Edgar.*) You sir, I entertain for one of my hundred;
only I do not like the fashion of your garments. You will say
they are Persian;[7] but let them be changed.

(*Enter Gloucester.*)

---

1  *mar my counterfeiting*  Make it difficult to keep up the deception.

2  *throw his head*  Meet their aggression with his own (throwing his head forward as
an aggressive dog does).

3  *bobtail ... tail*  Short-tailed or long-tailed.

4  *Do, de, de, de! Sesa!*  Presumably the sound is an imitation of a trumpet used to
announce a public attraction with a following shout to the horses as they set off on
their imaginary tour.

5  *horn*  Hollowed out horns were often hung about the necks of Bedlam beggars and
used as cheap vessels for water.

6  *anatomize*  Dissect.

7  *Persian*  Persians were known for their elaborate and exotic finery (ironic).

What store her heart is made on.[1] Stop her there!
Arms, arms, sword, fire, corruption in the place!
False justicer,[2] why hast thou let her 'scape?                50
EDGAR.   Bless thy five wits.
KENT.   O, pity! Sir, where is the patience now
That you so oft have boasted to retain.
EDGAR.   (*Aside*.) My tears begin to take his part so much,
They'll mar my counterfeiting.                                  55
LEAR.   The little dogs and all—Trey, Blanch, and Sweetheart—
see, they bark at me.
EDGAR.   Tom will throw his head at them.—Avaunt, you curs!
    Be thy mouth or black or white,
    Tooth that poisons if it bite,                             60
    Mastiff, greyhound, mongrel grim
    Hound or spaniel, brach or him,
    Bobtail tyke, or trundle-tail,
    Tom will make them weep and wail,
    For with throwing thus my head,                            65
    Dogs leap the hatch and all are fled!
Loudla doodla![3] Come march to wakes and fairs, and market
towns! Poor Tom, thy horn is dry.
LEAR.   Then let them anatomize Regan; see what breeds about
her heart. Is there any cause in nature that makes this hardness?   70
(*To Edgar*.) You sir, I entertain you for one of my hundred. Only
I do not like the fashion of your garments. You'll say they are
Persian attire; but let them be changed.

---

1   *whose ... made on*   Whose wicked expression shows the material her heart is made
    out of.
2   *justicer*   Judge.
3   *Loudla doodla*   Presumably an imitation of a trumpet used to announce a public
    attraction.

KENT.   (*To Lear.*) Now good my Lord, lie here and rest awhile.
LEAR.   Make no noise, make no noise, draw the curtains:[1] so, so.
40      We'll go to supper i'th' morning.
FOOL.   And I'll go to bed at noon.


GLOUCESTER.   Come hither, friend. Where is the King my master?
KENT.   Here Sir, but trouble him not. His wits are gone.
GLOUCESTER.   Good friend, I prithee take him in thy arms;
45      I have o'er-heard a plot of death upon him.
        There is a litter[2] ready; lay him in't,
        And drive toward Dover, friend, where thou shalt meet
        Both welcome, and protection. Take up thy master,
        If thou should'st dally half an hour, his life
50      With thine, and all that[3] offer to defend him,
        Stand in assurèd loss. Take up, take up,
        And follow me, that will to some provision°          *supplies*
        Give thee quick conduct.




                        Come, come away.


(*Exeunt.*)

---

1   *curtains*   Presumably imaginary.
2   *litter*   Mobile couch enclosed with curtains.
3   *and all that*   And the lives of all those who.

KENT.   Now good my Lord, lie here awhile.

LEAR.   Make no noise, make no noise. Draw the curtains. So, so,   75
so. We'll go to supper i'th morning. So, so, so.

(*Enter Gloucester.*)

GLOUCESTER.   Come hither, friend. Where is the King my master?

KENT.   Here sir, but trouble him not. His wits are gone.

GLOUCESTER.   Good friend, I prithee, take him in thy arms.
I have o'erheard a plot of death upon him.   80
There is a litter ready; lay him in't.
And drive towards Dover, friend, where thou shalt meet
Both welcome and protection. Take up thy master.
If thou should'st dally half an hour, his life
With thine, and all that offer to defend him,   85
Stand in assurèd loss. Take up the King
And follow me, that will to some provision
Give thee quick conduct.

KENT.                              Oppressèd nature sleeps.
This rest might yet have balmed° thy broken sinews,[1]   *healed*   90
Which, if convenience will not allow, stand in hard cure.[2]
(*To Fool.*) Come, help to bear thy master. Thou must not stay
behind.

GLOUCESTER.   Come, come away.

(*Exit [Lear, Kent, Gloucester, and the Fool].*)

EDGAR.   When we our betters see bearing our woes,
We scarcely think our miseries our foes.[3]   95
Who alone suffers, suffers most i'th' mind,
Leaving free things and happy shows behind.[4]

---

1   *broken sinews*   Figuratively, shattered nerves.

2   *stand ... cure*   Will be hard to cure.

3   *When ... foes*   It is so upsetting to see our superiors suffer that we begin to forget
our own misfortunes.

4   *free*   Carefree;   *happy shows*   Displays of happiness;   *Who ... behind*   The worst
thing about suffering alone is the mental anguish at having left behind ordinary
happiness (that others still enjoy).

But then the mind much sufferance doth o'erskip
When grief hath mates; and bearing fellowship,
How light and portable my pain seems now,                           100
When that which makes me bend, makes the King bow.[1]
He childed as I fathered.[2] Tom, away:
Mark the high noises[3] and thyself bewray°                  *reveal*
When false opinion, whose wrong thoughts°      *misconceptions*
  defile thee,
In thy just proof repeals and reconciles thee.[4]                   105
What will hap more tonight, safe 'scape the King.[5]
Lurk, lurk.

(*Exit.*)

## ACT 3, SCENE 7

(*Enter Cornwall, Regan, Gonerill, Bastard, and Servants.*)

CORNWALL. (*To Gonerill.*) Post speedily to my Lord your husband; show him this letter. The army of France is landed. (*To
Servants.*) Seek out the traitor Gloucester.

(*Exeunt some servants.*)

REGAN.   Hang him instantly.
GONERILL.   Pluck out his eyes.                                       5

---

1   *But ... bow*   But suffering is much lessened when misery has company, and now
    that I'm no longer alone, I find my own suffering much easier to bear, by seeing how
    much more deeply affected the King is by his own troubles.
2   *He childed ... fathered*   I.e., he had children who now seek his death, as I have a
    father who now seeks mine.
3   *Mark the high noises*   Keep your eye on the brewing problems amongst those in
    power (i.e., Gonorill and Regan and their husbands).
4   *In thy ... thee*   In proving your true innocence, ends your sentence of banishment
    and reconciles you to your father.
5   *What ... King*   Whatever else happens, may the King escape safely.

CORNWALL. Leave him to my displeasure. Edmund, keep you our sister company: the revenges we are bound to take upon your traitorous Father, are not fit for your beholding. Advise the Duke where you are going—to a most festinate[1] preparation.

10 We are bound to the like. Our posts shall be swift and intelligent betwixt us. (*To Gonerill.*) Farewell, dear sister. (*To Bastard.*) Farewell, my Lord of Gloucester.

(*Enter [Oswald, the] Steward.*)

How now? Where's the King?
OSWALD. My Lord of Gloucester hath conveyed him hence.
15 Some five or six and thirty of his knights,
Hot questrists° after him, met him at gate,                    seekers
Who, with some other of the Lord's dependents,[2]
Are gone with him toward Dover, where they boast
To have well armed friends.
20 CORNWALL. Get horses for your Mistress.

(*Exit Oswald.*)

GONERILL. Farewell sweet Lord, and Sister.

(*Exit [Gonerill and Edmund].*)

CORNWALL. Edmund, farewell. (*To Servants.*) Go seek the traitor Gloucester.
Pinion him like a thief; bring him before us.

(*Exit Servants.*)

Though well we may not pass upon his life
25 Without the form of justice, yet our power
Shall do a court'sy to our wrath, which men
May blame, but not control.

---

1  *festinate*  Hasty.
2  *Lord's dependents*  Gloucester's attendants.

*(Enter Gloucester [brought in by] Servants.)*

Who's there? The traitor?
REGAN.   Ingrateful fox, 'tis he.
CORNWALL.   (*To Servants.*) Bind fast his corky[1] arms.                30
GLOUCESTER.   What means your Graces?
  Good my friends, consider: you are my guests!
  Do me no foul play, friends.
CORNWALL.   (*To Servants.*) Bind him, I say.
REGAN.   Hard, hard! O, filthy traitor.                                   35
GLOUCESTER.   Unmerciful lady, as you are,[2] I'm none.
CORNWALL.   (*To Servants.*) To this chair bind him.
  Villain, thou shalt find—

*(Regan plucks Gloucester's beard.)*

GLOUCESTER.   By the kind gods, 'tis most ignobly done
  To pluck me by the beard.                                               40
REGAN.   So white, and such a traitor?
GLOUCESTER.                              Naughty[3] lady,
  These hairs which thou dost ravish from my chin
  Will quicken[4] and accuse thee. I am your host.
  With robbers' hands my hospitable favours                              45
  You should not ruffle thus. What will you do?
CORNWALL.   Come, Sir: what letters had you late from France?
REGAN.   Be simple answered,[5] for we know the truth.
CORNWALL.   And what confederacy have you with the traitors
  Late footed[6] in the kingdom?                                         50
REGAN.                              To whose hands
  You have sent the lunatic King? Speak.
GLOUCESTER.   I have a letter guessingly set down[7]

---

1   *corky*   Dry (because old).
2   *as you are*   I.e., a traitor.
3   *Naughty*   Evil (the word "naughty" did not have then the playful connotation it has
    now).
4   *quicken*   Come to life.
5   *Be simple answered*   Answer straightforwardly.
6   *Late footed*   Who have recently gained a foothold.
7   *guessingly set down*   Written speculatively.

Which came from one that's of a neutral heart,
55 And not from one opposed.
CORNWALL.                     Cunning.
REGAN.                                          And false.
CORNWALL.   Where hast thou sent the King?
GLOUCESTER.                                        To Dover.
60 REGAN.   Wherefore to Dover? Wast thou not charged,[1] at
peril—[2]
CORNWALL.   Wherefore to Dover? Let him answer that.
GLOUCESTER.   I am tied to'th'stake, and I must stand the
course.[3]
REGAN.   Wherefore to Dover?
GLOUCESTER.   Because I would not see thy cruel nails
65 Pluck out his poor old eyes, nor thy fierce sister,
In his anointed[4] flesh, stick boarish fangs!
The sea, with such a storm as his bare head,
In hell-black night endured, would have buoyed up
And quenched the stellèd° fires.                          *starry*
70 Yet poor old heart, he holp° the heavens to rain.[5]   *helped*
If wolves had at thy gate howled that stern time,
Thou should'st have said "Good porter, turn the key."
All cruels else subscribe;[6] but I shall see
The wingèd[7] vengeance overtake such children.
75 CORNWALL.   See't shalt thou never. (*To Servants.*) Fellows, hold
the chair.
(*To Gloucester.*) Upon these eyes of thine, I'll set my foot.
GLOUCESTER.   He that will think to live, till he be old,
Give me some help!

---

1  *charged*   Ordered.
2  *at peril*   On peril (of losing your life).
3  *stand the course*   Endure the assaults to come.
4  *anointed*   Consecrated. Kings and Queens of England were anointed with holy oil
   at their coronations as a sign that they were sanctified by God as lawful rulers.
5  *he holp the heavens to rain*   The Quarto version here reads, "he helped the heavens
   to rage."
6  *All cruels else subscribe*   All other cruelties tolerate. (Gloucester addresses the
   heavens.)
7  *wingèd*   I.e., that of Furies, whose assigned role included the punishing of ill-be-
   haved children, as well as those who damaged familial bonds.

*(Cornwall forces out one of Gloucester's eyes.)*

           —O, cruel! O, ye gods!

REGAN.    One side will mock another: Th' other too.    80
CORNWALL.    *(To Gloucester.)* If you see vengeance—
SERVANT.              Hold your hand, my Lord:
  I have served you ever since I was a child;
  But better service have I never done you,
  Than now to bid you hold.    85
REGAN.                 How now, you dog?
SERVANT.    If you did wear a beard upon your chin,
  I'd shake it on this quarrel.[1] *(To Cornwall.)* What do you
    mean?
CORNWALL.    My villain?
SERVANT.    Nay then, come on, and take the chance of anger.    90

*(They begin to fight; Cornwall is wounded.)*

REGAN.    *(To another Servant.)* Give me thy sword. A peasant
  stand up thus?

*(Kills him.)*

SERVANT.    Oh, I am slain! *(To Gloucester.)* My Lord, you have
  one eye left
  To see some mischief on him. Oh.

*(He dies.)*

CORNWALL.    Lest it see more, prevent it. Out, vile jelly.
  *(He forces out Gloucester's other eye.)* Where is thy luster now?    95
GLOUCESTER.    All dark and comfortless? Where's my son
  Edmund?
  Edmund, enkindle all the sparks of nature
  To quit this horrid act.
REGAN.                Out, treacherous villain!

---

1  *If you ... quarrel*  If you were a man, I'd challenge you to a duel.

100　Thou call'st on him that hates thee. It was he
　　That made the overture of thy treasons to us,
　　Who is too good to pity thee.
　　GLOUCESTER.　O, my follies! Then Edgar was abused,
　　Kind Gods, forgive me that, and prosper him.
105　REGAN.　(*To Servants.*) Go thrust him out at gates, and let him smell
　　His way to Dover.

(*Exit [Servants] with Gloucester.*)

　　How is't my Lord? How look you?
　　CORNWALL.　I have received a hurt. Follow me, Lady.
　　Turn out that eyeless villain. Throw this slave
110　Upon the dunghill. Regan, I bleed apace,
　　Untimely comes this hurt. Give me your arm.[1]

(*Exeunt.*)

ACT 4, SCENE 1

(*Enter Edgar.*)

　　EDGAR.　Yet better thus, and known to be condemned,
　　Than still condemned and flattered.[2] To be worst,
　　The lowest and most dejected thing of Fortune,
　　Stands still in esperance, lives not in fear.[3]

---

1　*Give me your arm*　Following this line in the Quarto version, the scene concludes with an exchange between two servants, who have remained on the stage: "Untimely comes this hurt. Give me your arm. / (*Exit [Cornwall and Regan].*) / 2ND SERVANT. I'll never care what wickedness I do, / If this man come to good. 3RD SERVANT. If she live long, / And in the end meet the old course of death, / Women will all turn monsters. 2ND SERVANT. Let's follow the old Earl, and get the bedlam / To lead him where he would. His roguish madness / Allows itself to anything. 3RD SERVANT. Go thou; I'll fetch some flax and whites of eggs / To apply to his bleeding face. Now heaven help him. / (*Exeunt.*)"

2　*better ... flattered*　Better to be a despised madman and beggar and know it than to be secretly despised yet openly flattered.

3　*Stands ... fear*　Still exists within the realm of hope (*esperance*: French for hope) yet with no more fear of things becoming worse.

The lamentable change is from the best;                              5
The worst returns to laughter.[1] Welcome then,
Thou unsubstantial air that I embrace;
The wretch that thou hast blown unto the worst,
Owes nothing to thy blasts.[2]

(*Enter Gloucester and an Old Man.*)

                           But who comes here?                       10
My father, poorly[3] led? World, world, O world![4]
But that thy strange mutations make us hate thee,
Life would not yield to age.[5]

OLD MAN.   O, my good Lord, I have been your tenant,
And your father's tenant, these fourscore years.                     15

GLOUCESTER.   Away, get thee away. Good friend, be gone.
Thy comforts can do me no good at all,
Thee, they may hurt.

OLD MAN.                You cannot see your way.

GLOUCESTER.   I have no way, and therefore want no eyes;             20
I stumbled when I saw. Full oft, 'tis seen,
Our means secure us, and our mere defects
Prove our commodities.[6] Oh, dear son Edgar—
The food[7] of thy abusèd father's wrath:
Might I but live to see thee in my touch,                            25
I'd say I had eyes again.

OLD MAN.                How now? who's there?

EDGAR.   (*Aside.*) O gods! Who is't can say I am at the worst?
I am worse than e'er I was.

---

1   *The lamentable ... laughter*   The change to be lamented is descending from good
    fortune to bad; once one is at bottom, one can look forward to laughing again.
2   *The wretch ... blasts*   Because it has caused nothing but harm to him, Edgar owes
    the air no debt of gratitude.
3   *poorly*   By a poor person.
4   *Welcome then ... O world!*   In the Quarto version Gloucester and the Old Man do
    not enter until after Edgar's speech, which is at this point somewhat different and
    shorter: "The worst returns to laughter. / Who's here? / My father, parti-eyed? World,
    world, O world!"
5   *But that ... age*   Were it not that the grotesque changes of the world make us hate
    it, we would not succumb to death in our old age.
6   *Our means ... commodities*   Our livelihood gives us a false sense of security, whereas
    our simple defects turn out to be to our advantage.
7   *food*   I.e., the object on which Gloucester's wrath nourished itself.

30  OLD MAN.                        'Tis poor mad Tom.

EDGAR  (*Aside.*) And worse I may be yet; the worst is not,
    So long as we can say: "This is the worst."

OLD MAN.   Fellow, where goest?

GLOUCESTER.  Is it a beggar-man?

35  OLD MAN.   Madman, and beggar too.

GLOUCESTER.  He has some reason, else he could not beg.
    I'th'last night's storm I such a fellow saw;
    Which made me think a man a worm. My son
    Came then into my mind, and yet my mind

40   Was then scarce friends with him. I have heard more since.
    As flies to wanton boys, are we to th'gods,
    They kill us for their sport.

EDGAR.                         (*Aside.*) How should this be?[1]
    Bad is the trade[2] that must play fool to sorrow,

45   Ang'ring itself and others. (*To Old Man.*) Bless thee, master.

GLOUCESTER.  Is that the naked fellow?

OLD MAN.                            Aye, my Lord.

GLOUCESTER.  Get thee away. If for my sake
    Thou wilt o'er-take us hence a mile or twain

50   I'th'way toward Dover,[3] do it for ancient° love;     *long-surviving*
    And bring some covering for this naked soul,
    Which I'll entreat to lead me.

OLD MAN.                        Alack sir, he is mad.

GLOUCESTER.  'Tis the time's plague,[4] when madmen lead the
       blind.

55   Do as I bid thee; or rather, do thy pleasure;
    Above the rest, be gone.[5]

OLD MAN.   I'll bring him the best 'parel° that I have,     *apparel*
    Come on't what will.


    (*Exit.*)

---

1  *How should this be*  How is this to be done? (I.e., playing the part of Poor Tom
   under these circumstances.)
2  *trade*  Line of work (i.e., pretending to be Poor Tom).
3  *o'er-take … Dover*  Catch up with us a mile or two along the road towards Dover.
4  *time's plague*  Misfortune characteristic of the age.
5  *Above … gone*  Whatever else [you do], be gone.

GLOUCESTER.          Sirrah, naked fellow—

EDGAR.   Poor Tom's a cold. (*Aside.*) I cannot daub it further.[1]          60

GLOUCESTER.   Come hither fellow.

EDGAR.   (*Aside.*) And yet I must. (*Aloud.*) Bless thy sweet eyes, they bleed.

GLOUCESTER.   Know'st thou the way to Dover?

EDGAR.   Both stile and gate; horse-way and foot-path. Poor Tom          65
hath been scared out of his good wits. Bless thee, good man's son, from the foul fiend.[2]

GLOUCESTER.   Here take this purse, thou whom the heavens' plagues
Have humbled to all strokes.[3] That I am wretchèd
Makes thee the happier. Heavens, deal so still:[4]          70
Let the superfluous[5] and lust-dieted man
That slaves your ordinance,[6] that will not see
Because he does not feel, feel your power quickly;
So distribution should undo excess,
And each man have enough. Dost thou know Dover?          75

EDGAR.   Aye, master.

GLOUCESTER.   There is a cliff, whose high and bending° head          *overhanging*
Looks fearfully in the confinèd deep:
Bring me but to the very brim of it,
And I'll repair the misery thou dost bear          80
With something rich about me. From that place,
I shall no leading need.

EDGAR.          Give me thy arm.
Poor Tom shall lead thee.


(*Exeunt.*)

---

1  *daub it further*   Paint (i.e., dissemble, put on the assumed identity) any longer.

2  *from the foul fiend*   This speech of Edgar's is extended in the Quarto version as follows: "Bless the good man from the foul fiend! Five fiends have been in poor Tom at once: of lust, as Obidicut; Hobbididence, prince of dumbness; Mahu, of stealing; Modo, of murder; Flibbertigibbet of mobbing and mowing, who since possesses chambermaids and waiting women. So, bless thee master."

3  *humbled ... strokes*   Reduced to suffering all humiliations.

4  *Heavens ... still*   May the heavens continue to do this.

5  *superfluous*   Possessing too much.

6  *slaves your ordinance*   Enslaves, uses to his own ends injunctions from heaven.

## ACT 4, SCENE 2
### (FOLIO EDITION)

(*Enter Gonerill and Edmund.*)

GONERILL.  Welcome my Lord. I marvel our mild husband
Not met° us on the way.                                    *did not meet*

(*Enter Oswald.*)

                          —Now, where's your master?
OSWALD.    Madam, within; but never man so changed.
5      I told him of the army that was landed;
       He smiled at it. I told him you were coming,
       His answer was "The worse." Of Gloucester's treachery,
       And of the loyal service of his son
       When I informed him, then he called me "sot,"
10     And told me I had turned the wrong side out.
       What most he should dislike, seems pleasant to him;
       What like,¹ offensive.
GONERILL.    (*To Edmund.*) Then shall you go no further.
       It is the cowish terror of his spirit
15     That dares not undertake. He'll not feel² wrongs
       Which tie him to an answer. Our wishes on the way³
       May prove effects. Back, Edmund, to my brother,
       Hasten his musters, and conduct his powers.⁴
       I must change names⁵ at home, and give the distaff⁶
20     Into my husband's hands. This trusty servant
       Shall pass between us. Ere long you are like to hear—
       If you dare venture in your own behalf—
       A mistress's command.

---

1   *What like*   What he should like.
2   *not feel*   I.e., not acknowledge that he feels.
3   *Our wishes on the way*   What we were wishing on the way here.
4   *Hasten … powers*   Get him to hurry the readying of his troops, and then lead them
    back here.
5   *change names*   I.e., master for mistress.
6   *distaff*   Staff on which wool is wound for spinning (a symbol of womanhood).

(*Enter Gonorill and Bastard.*)

GONORILL.    Welcome my Lord, I marvel our mild husband
Not met us on the way.

(*Enter [Oswald the] Steward.*)

                              Now where's your master?
OSWALD.    Madame, within; but never man so changed.
I told him of the army that was landed;                                    5
He smiled at it. I told him you were coming;
His answer was "The worse." Of Gloucester's treachery,
And of the loyal service of his son
When I informed him, then he called me "sot,"
And told me I had turned the wrong side out.                        10
What he should most despise seems pleasant to him,
What like, offensive.
GONORILL.    (*To Bastard.*) Then shall you go no further,
It is the cowish cure[1] of his spirit
That dares not undertake. He'll not feel wrongs                      15
Which tie him to an answer. Our wishes on the way
May prove effects. Back, Edmund, to my brother;
Hasten his musters, and conduct his powers.
I must change arms[2] at home, and give the distaff
Into my husband's hands. This trusty servant                          20
Shall pass between us, ere long you are like to hear—
If you dare venture in your own behalf—
A mistress's command.

---

1    *cure*    Conditioning (as leather is "cured").
2    *change arms*    I.e., pick up the sword and hand off the distaff.

(*Presenting him with a locket.*)

Wear this—spare speech;
25    Decline your head. This kiss, if it durst speak
Would stretch thy spirits up into the air.
Conceive, and fare thee well.
EDMUND.    Yours in the ranks of death.

(*Exit.*)

GONERILL.                     My most dear Gloucester.
30    Oh, the difference of man, and man,
To thee a woman's services are due.
My fool usurps my body.
OSWALD.    Madam, here comes my Lord.

(*Enter Albany [and exit Oswald].*)

GONERILL.    I have been worth the whistle.[1]
35    ALBANY.                    Oh, Gonerill,
You are not worth the dust which the rude wind
Blows in your face.

---

1   *I have ... whistle*   "So, you decided to come and look for me after all." The allusion
is to a proverb: "It is a poor dog that is not worth the whistling."

*(Presenting him with a locket.)*

                    Wear this—spare speech;
Decline your head. This kiss, if it durst speak,                    25
Would stretch thy spirits up into the air.
Conceive, and fare you well.
BASTARD.    Yours in the ranks of death.


GONORILL.                              My most dear Gloucester:

To thee, woman's services are due.                              30

*(Exit Bastard.)*

My foot usurps my body.[1]
OSWALD.    Madam, here comes my Lord.

*(Exit Oswald [and enter Albany].)*

GONORILL.    I have been worth the whistle.
ALBANY.                              O Gonorill,
You are not worth the dust which the rude wind           35
Blows in your face. I fear your disposition.
That nature which contemns its origin[2]
Cannot be bordered certain[3] in itself.
She that herself will sliver and disbranch
From her material sap,[4] perforce must wither,              40
And come to deadly use.[5]

---

1  *My foot usurps my body*  "A fool usurps my bed" in the "corrected" version of the
   Quarto edition; "My foot usurps my head" in later Quarto editions.
2  *contemns its origin*  Despises the source from which it sprung (as Gonorill has
   Lear).
3  *bordered certain*  Confidently defined.
4  *material sap*  Life-giving substance (i.e., family blood).
5  *deadly use*  To be used as one does dead branches, for burning.

Gonerill.                          Milk-livered[1] man,
  That bear'st a cheek for blows, a head for wrongs,
40  Who hast not in thy brows an eye discerning
  Thine honour from thy suffering—[2]

---

1  *Milk-livered*  Cowardly, lily-livered (the liver was regarded as the source of courage).
2  *Who hast ... thy suffering*  Who doesn't have the eyes to see the difference between doing something honorable and simply suffering.

GONORILL.                    No more, the text[1] is foolish.
ALBANY.    <u>Wisdom and goodness to the vile seem vile;</u>
   Filths savour but themselves. What have you done?
   Tigers, not daughters! What have you performed?                    45
   A father, and a gracious agèd man,
   Whose reverence even the head-lugged[2] bear would lick—

   Most barbarous, most degenerate!—have you madded.[3]
   Could my good brother[4] suffer you to do it?
   A man, a prince, by him so benefacted?[5]                    50
   If that the heavens do not their visible spirits
   Send quickly down to tame the vile offences,
   It will come: humanity must perforce
   Prey on itself, like monsters of the deep![6] **Humans acting like animals**
GONORILL.                            Milk livered man!    55
   That bearest a cheek for blows, a head for wrongs,
   Who hast not in thy brows an eye deserving thine honour!
   From thy suffering, that not know'st fools, do those villains
      pity
   Who are punished ere they have done their mischief![7]
   Where's thy drum?                    60
   France spreads his banners in our noiseless land!

---

1    *text*  Figuratively, the biblical text that is used as the basis for a sermon.
2    *head-lugged*  Pulled by the head (usually with a ring through its nose) into the bear-
     baiting pit, where, naturally, it was furious.
3    *have you madded*  You have made (this father) mad, insane.
4    *good brother*  I.e., brother-in-law—Cornwall.
5    *by him so benefacted*  From whom he had received so many benefits.
6    *If that ... deep*  If heaven does not send some clear vengeance, humanity will de-
     scend into a subhuman savagery.
7    *Milk livered ... mischief*  You gutless man, who turns the other cheek to blows, and
     who tolerates wrongs done to you; who lacks the sense befitting one of your rank;
     out of your compassion for suffering—which you don't seem to know is self-decep-
     tive—go ahead and pity those villains, who are simply receiving pre-emptive justice
     before they can commit crimes.

ALBANY.                                    See thyself, devil;
   Proper deformity seems not in the fiend
   So horrid as in woman.[1]
45  GONERILL.                          Oh, vain fool—

(*Enter a Messenger.*)

---

1  *Proper deformity ... woman*  Deformity, appropriate to the fiend, seems horrid in a
  woman.

With plumèd helm, thy slayer begins threats[1]
Whil'st thou, a moral fool, sits still and cries
"Alack, why does he so?"

ALBANY.                         See thyself, devil!                         65
Proper deformity seems not in the fiend
So horrid as in woman.

GONORILL.                   O vain fool!

ALBANY.   Thou changèd, and self-covered[2] thing, for shame
Be-monster not thy feature![3] Wer't my fitness[4]                         70
To let these hands obey my blood,°                    *impulses*
They are apt enough to dislocate and tear
Thy flesh and bones! Howe'er thou art[5] a fiend,
A woman's shape doth shield thee.

GONORILL.   Marry your manhood now—[6]                         75


(*Enter a Gentleman.*)

---

1   *With plumèd … threats*   Wearing a plumed helmet (i.e., with a display of aristo-
    cratic bellicosity), the adversary who will kill you has begun to make open threats.
    Gonorill speaks of Albany, a head of state (one of two, as far as these two know),
    as if he were a single knight challenging his opponent to chivalric combat. This is
    substantially the text as it originally appeared in the first Quarto (an "s" has been
    added to "begin"). The speculative emendation embraced by almost all editors since
    Charles Jennens introduced it in 1770—"thy state begins to threat."—seems unnec-
    essary, and tends to weaken the synecdoche (a poetic figure in which a part is taken
    for the whole).
2   *changèd and self-covered*   Transformed and self-deluded.
3   *Be-monster … feature*   Don't let your inner monster show externally.
4   *my fitness*   Appropriate for me.
5   *Howe'er thou art*   However much you may be.
6   *Marry … now*   This is the Q1 reading, the sense of which is: "try to wed your wom-
    anly disposition to your male sex, and—" (the rest of the line, which would presum-
    ably have to do with Gonorill urging Albany to get ready to fight, is cut off by the
    messenger's appearance). In Q2, "now" was changed to "mew," an alteration which
    has become widely accepted, though it is arguably the weaker of the two versions.
    In that revised reading, "Marry" becomes an exclamation and with "mew," usually
    Gonorill is assumed to imitate a cat, so that the sense of the line becomes: "Honestly,
    what is one to say about your masculinity, except that it is cat-like." Another reading
    glosses "mew" as "coop up," so that the sense of the line is: "Go ahead and hide your
    manhood away."

MESSENGER. Oh my good Lord: the Duke of Cornwall's dead,
Slain by his servant, going to[1] put out
The other eye of Gloucester.
ALBANY.                                    Gloucester's eyes?
50 MESSENGER. A servant that he bred,[2] thrilled with[3] remorse,
Opposed against the act, bending his sword
To his great master, who, threat-enraged[4]
Flew on him, and amongst them[5] felled him dead;
But not without that harmful stroke, which since
55 Hath plucked him after.[6]
ALBANY. (*To gods.*) This shows you are above,
You justices, that these our nether[7] crimes
So speedily can venge.—But O, poor Gloucester!
Lost he his other eye?
60 MESSENGER.                    Both, both, my Lord.
(*To Gonerill.*) This letter, Madam, craves a speedy answer:
'Tis from your sister.
GONERILL. (*Aside.*) One way I like this well.
But being widow, and my Gloucester with her,

65 May all the building in my fancy pluck
Upon my hateful life.[8] Another way
The news is not so tart. (*Aloud.*)—I'll read, and answer.

---

1  *going to*  While about to.
2  *he bred*  Cornwall had raised.
3  *thrilled with*  Deeply affected by.
4  *threat-enraged*  Infuriated by being threatened.
5  *amongst them*  With assistance from others.
6  *plucked him after*  Dragged him behind the servant into death.
7  *nether*  Below (committed on earth).
8  *May ... life*  (This situation) may bring all the building of dreams (of marrying Edmund) which I have been doing in my imagination crashing down onto my horrible life. (This sense requires reading "pluck" as "pluck down.")

ALBANY.　What news?

GENTLEMAN.　O my good Lord: the Duke of Cornwall's dead,
　　Slain by his servant, going to put out
　　The other eye of Gloucester.

ALBANY.　　　　　　　　　　Gloucester's eyes?　　　　　　　　80

GENTLEMAN.　A servant that he bred, thralled with remorse,
　　Opposed against the act, bending his sword
　　To his great master, who, thereat enraged,[1]
　　Flew on him, and amongst them, felled him dead;
　　But not without that harmful stroke, which since　　85
　　Hath plucked him after.

ALBANY.　(*To gods.*) This shows you are above,
　　You justices, that these our nether crimes
　　So speedily can venge. —But O, poor Gloucester!
　　Lost he his other eye?　　　　　　　　　　　　　　　90

GENTLEMAN.　　　　　Both, both my Lord.
　　(*To Gonorill.*) This letter, madam, craves a speedy answer:
　　'Tis from your sister.

GONORILL.　(*Aside.*) One way I like this well;
　　But, being widow, and my Gloucester with her,　　95
　　Another way the news is not so took.[2]
　　May all the building on my fancy pluck
　　Upon my hateful life.[3] (*Aloud.*)—I'll read and answer.

(*Exit.*)

---

1　*thereat enraged*　Infuriated by that (being opposed).

2　*One way ... took*　On the one hand, this is good news (that Cornwall is dead be-
　　cause it likely means that Albany—and therefore Gonorill—will likely take over the
　　rule of the entire kingdom), but given that Edmund is now with the newly available
　　Regan, this is not such good news. *Another ... took*　This line has been placed
　　here by the current editor; in Q the line appears, as it does in F, after "hateful
　　life." Compare F for an unamended reading.

3　*May ... hateful life*　I pray that all the planning I have been doing in my imagina-
　　tion (about marrying Edmund and becoming Queen) will pull upon (as one plucks
　　on a thread of yarn and thereby unravels a sweater) my hateful life. Again, compare
　　F for a very different reading.

ALBANY.    Where was his son, when they did take his eyes?
MESSENGER.    Come with my Lady hither.
70   ALBANY.                                         He is not here.
MESSENGER.    No my good Lord, I met him back again.[1]
ALBANY.    Knows he the wickedness?
MESSENGER.    Aye, my good Lord: 'twas he informed against
     him,[2]
     And quit the house on purpose that their punishment
75   Might have the freer course.
ALBANY.                              Gloucester, I live
     To thank thee for the love thou showedst the King,
     And to revenge thine eyes.—Come hither, friend,
     Tell me what more thou know'st.

     (*Exeunt.*)

---

1   *back again*   On his way back again.
2   *he ... him*   Edmund who informed against his father.

ALBANY.    Where was his son when they did take his eyes?
GENTLEMAN.    Come with my Lady hither.                                    100
ALBANY.                        He is not here.
GENTLEMAN.    No, my good Lord. I met him back again.
ALBANY.    Knows he the wickedness?
GENTLEMAN.    Aye, my good Lord: 'twas he informed against
   him,
   And quit the house on purpose that their punishment          105
   Might have the freer course.
ALBANY.                        Gloucester, I live
   To thank thee for the love thou showedst the King,
   And to revenge thy eyes.—Come hither, friend;
   Tell me what more thou knowest.                              110

(*Ex[eun]t.*)

## ACT 4, SCENE 3

(*Enter Kent and a Gentleman.*[1])

KENT.    Why the King of France is so suddenly gone back, know
   you no reason?
GENTLEMAN.    Something he left imperfect in the state,[2]
   Which since his coming forth is thought of, which
   Imports° to the kingdom so much fear and          *would mean*     5
      danger
   That his personal return was most required and necessary.
KENT.    Who hath he left behind him general?
GENTLEMAN.    The Marshall of France, Monsieur la Far.
KENT.    Did your letters pierce° the queen to any          *move*
   demonstration of grief?
GENTLEMAN.    Aye, sir. She took them, read them in my presence,     10
   And now and then an ample tear trilled down
   Her delicate cheek. It seemed she was a queen

---

1   *Gentleman*   This is not the same gentleman who was speaking to Albany in the last
    scene.
2   *imperfect in the state*   Unresolved in his own kingdom.

Over her passion, who[1] most rebel-like,
Sought to be King o'er her.

KENT.                                         O, then it moved her.                    15

GENTLEMAN.    Not to a rage; patience and sorrow strove
Who should express her goodliest.[2] You have seen
Sunshine and rain at once? Her smiles and tears
Were like—a better way.[3] Those happy smilets,[4]
That played on her ripe lip seemed not to know          20
What guests were in her eyes, which parted thence,
As pearls from diamonds dropped. In brief,
Sorrow would be a rarity most belovèd,
If all could so become it.[5]

KENT.                               Made she no verbal question?        25

GENTLEMAN.   Faith, once or twice she heaved the name of "father"
Pantingly forth as if it pressed her heart;
Cried "Sisters, sisters! Shame of ladies, sisters!
Kent! Father! Sisters! What, i'th'storm? I'th'night?
Let pity not be believed!" There she shook              30
The holy water from her heavenly eyes,
And clamour moistened her.[6] Then away she started[7]
To deal with grief alone.

KENT.                            It is the stars,
The stars above us govern our conditions.[8]            35
Else one self mate and make could not beget
Such different issues.[9] You spoke not with her since?

---

1   *who*  Which (the passion).
2   *patience ... goodliest*  Her patience and her solemn grief competed as to which was
    the most accurate (and most moral) expression of her character.
3   *Were like ... way*  Were similar to that—only in an improved manner.
4   *smilets*  Little smiles.
5   *Sorrow ... become it*  Sadness would be a precious commodity if it were as becom-
    ing (flattering) to others as it was to her.
6   *clamour moistened her*  She began to weep openly.
7   *started*  Moved quickly.
8   *govern our conditions*  Determine our characters.
9   *Else ... issues*  Otherwise it wouldn't be possible for the same husband and wife to
    produce such completely different daughters.

(FOLIO EDITION)

GENTLEMAN.  No.

KENT.  Was this before the King returned?

GENTLEMAN.                              No, since.                    40

KENT.  Well sir, the poor distressèd Lear's i'th'town,
  Who some time in his better tune[1] remembers
  What we are come about, and by no means
  Will yield to see his daughter.

GENTLEMAN.                    Why good sir?                    45

KENT.  A sovereign shame so elbows him.[2] His own unkindness
  That stripped her from his benediction, turned her
  To foreign casualties,[3] gave her dear rights
  To his dog-hearted daughters—these things sting
  His mind so venomously that burning shame            50
  Detains him from Cordelia.

GENTLEMAN.                    Alack, poor gentleman!

KENT.  Of Albany's and Cornwall's powers[4] you heard not?

GENTLEMAN.  'Tis so: they are afoot.

KENT.  Well sir, I'll bring you to our master, Lear,         55
  And leave you to attend him. Some dear cause,[5]
  Will in concealment wrap me up awhile.
  When I am known aright you shall not grieve
  Lending me this acquaintance.
  I pray you go along with me.                          60

  (Ex[eun]t.)

---

1  *better tune*  Saner moments (his insanity being compared to a musical instrument that has fallen out of tune).
2  *sovereign ... him*  Overpowering shame prods him.
3  *turned her to foreign casualties*  Cast her to the fortune she would find in a foreign land.
4  *powers*  Troops.
5  *dear cause*  Important reason.

## ACT 4, SCENE 4[1]

*(Enter with Drum and Colours, Cordelia, Gentlemen, and Soldiers.)*

CORDELIA.    Alack, 'tis he! Why, he was met even now,
As mad as the vexèd sea, singing aloud,
Crowned with rank fumitor,[2] and furrow weeds,[3]
With hardocks,[4] hemlock,[5] nettles, cuckoo flowers,[6]
5  Darnel,[7] and all the idle weeds that grow
In our sustaining corn. A century[8] send forth;
Search every acre in the high-grown field,
And bring him to our eye. What can man's wisdom
In the restoring his bereavèd sense?[9]
10 He that helps him, take all my outward worth.
GENTLEMAN.    There is means, Madam.
Our foster nurse of nature is repose:
The which he lacks. That to provoke in him
Are many simples operative, whose power
15 Will close the eye of anguish.[10]
CORDELIA.                                    All blest secrets,
All you unpublished virtues[11] of the earth
Spring with my tears; be aidant, and remediate

---

1  Since the Folio does not include the preceeding scene, this scene is numbered 4.3 in
   the Folio, and there are corresponding differences in scene numbering through to
   the end of Act 4.
2  *rank fumitor*  Thick climbing vine (now known as fumitory).
3  *furrow weeds*  Weeds growing in the furrows of ploughed fields.
4  *hardocks*  Prickly, burr-bearing weed more commonly known as burdock.
5  *hemlock*  Fern-like, poisonous plant with white flowers (not related to the spruce
   trees known as hemlock in North America).
6  *cuckoo flowers*  Wildflowers with white or pink petals that bloom in the spring,
   when the cuckoo bird is heard.
7  *Darnel*  Grass-like weed.
8  *century*  One hundred soldiers.
9  *What can ... sense*  The verb "do" is understood, following "wisdom."
10 *Our foster ... anguish*  The natural means of curing a disordered mind is rest; this
   is all he lacks; but we can remedy that by giving him any of several simple sedative
   medicines that will allow the suffering person to sleep.
11 *unpublished virtues*  Undiscovered medicinal properties.

In the goodman's desires.[1] Seek, seek for him,
Lest his ungoverned rage dissolve the life                                    20
That wants the means to lead it.

(*Enter Messenger.*)

MESSENGER.                                  News, Madam:
The British[2] powers are marching hitherward.
CORDELIA.     'Tis known before; our preparation stands
In expectation of them. O, dear father,                                       25
It is thy business that I go about:
Therefore great France
My mourning, and importuned tears hath pitied.
No blown° ambition doth our arms incite,                        *inflated*
But love, dear love, and our aged father's right.                             30
Soon may I hear, and see him.


(*Exeunt.*)


## ACT 4, SCENE 5


(*Enter Regan, and Steward.*)


REGAN.     But are my brother's[3] powers set forth?
OSWALD.     Aye, Madam.
REGAN.     Himself in person there?
OSWALD.     Madam, with much ado. Your sister is the better
    soldier.
REGAN.     Lord Edmund spake not with your Lord at home?          5
OSWALD.     No, Madam.
REGAN.     What might import my sister's letter to him?
OSWALD.     I know not, Lady.
REGAN.     Faith, he is posted hence on serious matter.
    It was great ignorance, Gloucester's eyes being out          10
    To let him live. Where he arrives, he moves

---

1   *aidant and … goodman's desires*   Helpful and curative in the hopes of the gentleman
    (to find an herbal cure).
2   *British*   I.e., those of Cornwall (now under the command of Edmund) and
    Albany.
3   *brother's*   I.e., brother-in-law's (Albany's).

All hearts against us.[1] Edmund, I think, is gone
In pity of his misery, to dispatch
His nighted[2] life; moreover to descry

15      The strength o'th'enemy.
OSWALD.    I must needs after him, Madam, with my letter.
REGAN.    Our troops set forth tomorrow; stay with us;
The ways are dangerous.
OSWALD.                              I may not, Madam.

20      My Lady charged my duty[3] in this business.
REGAN.    Why should she write to Edmund?
Might not you transport her purposes by word?
    belike,°                                                                          *probably*
Some things—I know not what. I'll love thee much;
Let me unseal the letter.

25    OSWALD.                              Madam, I had rather—
REGAN.    I know your Lady does not love her husband.
I am sure of that; and at her late being here,
She gave strange *oeillades*,° and most speaking looks     *stares*
To noble Edmund. I know you are of her bosom.

30    OSWALD.    I, Madam?
REGAN.    I speak in understanding. Y'are; I know't.
Therefore, I do advise you, take this note:[4]
My Lord is dead; Edmund and I have talked,
And more convenient is he for my hand

35    Than for your Lady's: you may gather more.
If you do find him, pray you give him this,[5]
And when your mistress hears thus much[6] from you,
I pray, desire her call her wisdom to her.
So, fare you well.

40    If you do chance to hear of that blind traitor,
Preferment[7] falls on him that cuts him off.[8]

---

1    *Where ... us*  Wherever Gloucester goes, the people's pity for him incites their an-
     ger against Regan and her allies.
2    *nighted*  Darkened (because blinded).
3    *charged my duty*  Commanded me to be strictly obedient.
4    *take this note*  Note what I am about to say.
5    *this*  Probably a token such as a ring.
6    *thus much*  I.e., that I have asked you to give Edmund this token.
7    *Preferment*  Promotion.
8    *cuts him off*  Kills him (before he reaches Dover).

OSWALD.  Would I could meet him Madam; I should show
What party I do follow.
REGAN.                    Fare thee well.


(*Exeunt.*)


ACT 4, SCENE 6


(*Enter Gloucester and Edgar.*)


GLOUCESTER.  When shall I come to th'top of that same hill?
EDGAR.  You do climb up it now. Look how we labour.
GLOUCESTER.  Methinks the ground is even.
EDGAR.                                    Horrible steep.
Hark, do you hear the sea?                                        5
GLOUCESTER.                  No, truly.
EDGAR.  Why, then your other senses grow imperfect
By your eyes' anguish.
GLOUCESTER.              So may it be indeed.
Methinks thy voice is altered, and thou speak'st            10
In better phrase and matter than thou did'st.
EDGAR.  Y'are much deceived; in nothing am I changed
But in my garments.
GLOUCESTER.            Methinks y'are better spoken.
EDGAR.  Come on, Sir. Here's the place. Stand still. How fearful   15
And dizzy 'tis, to cast ones eyes so low!
The crows and choughs,[1] that wing the midway air
Show scarce so gross° as beetles. Half-way down         *large*
Hangs one that gathers samphire[2]—dreadful trade!
Methinks he seems no bigger than his head.               20
The fishermen that walked upon the beach
Appear like mice; and yond tall anchoring bark°            *ship*
Diminished to her cock;[3] her cock a buoy
Almost too small for sight. The murmuring surge,

---

1  *choughs*  Crow-like birds.
2  *samphire*  Carrot-like plant that grows on cliffs near the seashore and can be eaten
   if pickled; gathering it was considered a "dreadful trade" because, notoriously, one
   risked one's life in clambering down the cliffs to get to it.
3  *cock*  Small dinghy attached to a large ship.

25 That on th' unnumbered idle pebble chafes
Cannot be heard so high. I'll look no more,
Lest my brain turn, and the deficient sight
Topple down headlong.[1]
GLOUCESTER.                    Set me where you stand.
30 EDGAR   Give me your hand. You are now within a foot
Of th' extreme verge. For all beneath the moon
Would I not leap upright.
GLOUCESTER.                         Let go my hand.
Here, friend, 's another purse; in it, a jewel
35 Well worth a poor man's taking. Fairies and gods
Prosper it[2] with thee. Go thou further off.
Bid me farewell, and let me hear thee going.
EDGAR.   (*Pretending to move much farther away.*)
Now fare ye well, good Sir.
40 GLOUCESTER.                    With all my heart.[3]
EDGAR.   (*Aside.*) Why I do trifle thus with his despair
Is done to cure it.
GLOUCESTER.   (*On his knees.*) O you mighty Gods!
This world I do renounce, and in your sights
45 Shake patiently my great affliction off:
If I could bear it longer, and not fall
To quarrel with your great opposeless wills,
My snuff, and loathèd part of nature,[4] should
Burn itself out. If Edgar live, O bless him!
50 —Now fellow, fare thee well!
EDGAR.                              Gone Sir, farewell!

(*Gloucester falls forward.*)

(*Aside.*) And yet I know not how conceit may rob
The treasury of life,[5] when life itself
Yields to the theft. Had he been where he thought,

---

1   *Lest my brain ... headlong*   Lest I am overcome by vertigo, and with my vision having failed, fall over the edge.
2   *Prosper it*   Make it multiply (a talent which fairies were said to possess).
3   *With all my heart*   I.e., and I return the same sentiments to you with all my heart.
4   *snuff ... nature*   Spirit (seen as the flickering wick of a candle) and body.
5   *I know not ... life*   I wonder to what degree imagination can bring one close to
death.

By this,[1] had thought been past.—Alive, or dead?    55
(*To Gloucester*.) Hoa, you Sir! Friend! Hear you, Sir? Speak![2]
(*Aside*.) Thus might he pass indeed; yet he revives.
What are you Sir?

GLOUCESTER.    Away, and let me die.

EDGAR.    Had'st thou been aught but gossamer, feathers, air,    60
So many fathom down precipitating
Thou'dst shivered° like an egg! But thou dost    *shattered*
   breathe,
Hast heavy substance, bleed'st not, speak'st, art sound!
Ten masts at each,[3] make not the altitude
Which thou hast perpendicularly fell,    65
Thy life's a miracle. Speak yet again.

GLOUCESTER.    But have I fall'n, or no?

EDGAR.    From the dread summit of this chalky
   bourn!°    *boundary*
Look up a height, the shrill-gorged° lark so far    *throated*
Cannot be seen, or heard. Do but look up!    70

GLOUCESTER.    Alack, I have no eyes:
Is wretchedness deprived that benefit
To end itself by death? 'Twas yet some comfort,
When misery could beguile the tyrant's rage,
And frustrate his proud will.[4]    75

EDGAR.    Give me your arm.
Up, so. How is't? Feel you your legs? You stand.

GLOUCESTER.    Too well, too well.

EDGAR.    This is above all strangeness.
Upon the crown o'th'cliff, what thing was that    80
Which parted from you?

GLOUCESTER.    A poor unfortunate beggar.

EDGAR.    As I stood here below, methought his eyes
Were two full moons; he had a thousand noses,
Horns whelked[5] and waved like the enragèd sea:    85

---

1  *this*  This point.
2  *Friend ... Speak!*  Beginning with this line, Edgar drops the Poor Tom disguise, and
   pretends to be a resident of Dover.
3  *at each*  Placed end to end.
4  *frustrate his proud will*  I.e., by committing suicide.
5  *whelked*  Shaped like the shell of a whelk (large marine snail with a pointed, spiral
   shell).

It was some fiend. Therefore, thou happy father,
Think that the clearest° gods, who make them                    *purest*
    honours
Of men's impossibilities, have preserved thee.[1]
GLOUCESTER.   I do remember now; henceforth I'll bear
90   Affliction till it do cry out itself:
"Enough, enough!" and die. That thing you speak of,
I took it for a man; often 'twould say
"The fiend, the fiend." He led me to that place.
EDGAR.   Bear free[2] and patient thoughts.

(*Enter Lear.*)

95                                            But who comes here?
The safer sense will ne'er accommodate
His master thus.[3]
LEAR.   No, they cannot touch me for crying.[4] I am the King
    himself.
100  EDGAR.   O thou side-piercing[5] sight!
LEAR.   Nature's above art, in that respect.[6]—There's your press-
    money.[7] That fellow handles his bow like a crow-keeper![8] Draw
    me a clothier's yard![9]—Look, look, a mouse! Peace, peace. This

---

1   *who ... thee*   Who become honored and revered because they accomplish that
    which it is impossible for human beings to achieve. Edgar is trying to persuade
    Gloucester that he was literally led towards his suicide attempt by a devil, and to
    remind Gloucester that his life is, religiously speaking, not his own to take.
2   *free*   I.e., free according to Christian and Stoic doctrine, i.e., free of despair.
3   *The safer ... thus*   Gloucester's newly regained senses will not be able to withstand
    the blow of encountering Lear in his present state.
4   *touch ... crying*   Censure me for weeping in public. Q's "coining" may be preferable
    for reasons mentioned below.
5   *side-piercing*   Heart-rending (with an overtone of the piercing of the side of Jesus
    by the Roman soldier—John 19.34).
6   *Nature's ... respect*   Allusion to the ongoing Renaissance debate as to the superiority
    of nature or art.
7   *press-money*   Money paid out to men who were forced, or "pressed," into service as
    sailors or soldiers.
8   *crow-keeper*   Scarecrow.
9   *clothier's yard*   Tailor's measurement of a yard of fabric, achieved by holding the
    fabric from his breastbone to his outstretched wrist. (Lear imagines himself pressing
    soldiers; one holds his bow weakly, as if he is made of straw; in drill-sergeant fashion,
    Lear demands that the bow be stretched to the utmost limit.)

piece of toasted cheese will do't.[1] There's my gauntlet; I'll prove
it on a giant.[2] Bring up the brown bills![3]—O, well flown bird!   105
I'th'clout, i'th'clout![4] Hewgh! (*To Edgar.*) Give the word![5]

EDGAR.   Sweet marjoram.[6]

LEAR.   Pass.

GLOUCESTER.   I know that voice.

LEAR.   Ha! Gonerill with a white beard? They flattered me like   110
a dog,[7] and told me I had the white hairs[8] in my beard, ere the
black ones were there. To say aye and no, to every thing that I
said—aye and no too!—was no good divinity.[9] When the rain
came to wet me once, and the wind to make me chatter; when
the thunder would not peace at my bidding, there I found 'em,   115
there I smelt 'em out.[10] Go to, they are not men o'their words;
they told me I was everything. 'Tis a lie! I am not ague-proof.[11]

GLOUCESTER.   The trick of that voice, I do well remember:
Is't not the King?

LEAR.               Aye, every inch a King.   120
When I do stare, see how the subject quakes.
I pardon that man's life. What was thy cause?
Adultery? Thou shalt not die. Die for adultery?
No, the wren goes to't, and the small gilded fly
Does lecher in my sight. Let copulation thrive!   125
For Gloucester's bastard son was kinder to his father,
Than my daughters got° 'tween the lawful sheets.[12]   *begotten*

---

1  *do't*  I.e., comprise a sufficiently large fee to entice the mouse into joining his imaginary army.

2  *prove it on a giant*  Maintain my challenge even against a giant (let alone a mouse).

3  *brown bills*  Troops carrying the weapon so named—a sort of shorter version of the pike.

4  *well flown ... clout*  Probably the "bird" is an imaginary arrow which hits its target (clout), but Lear may be remarking on the flight of an actual bird, seeking prey.

5  *word*  I.e., password.

6  *Sweet marjoram*  Herb thought to have medicinal values for mental illness.

7  *like a dog*  I.e., as a dog flatters its master.

8  *white hairs*  I.e., the sign of wisdom (more flattery).

9  *no good divinity*  Distorted theology.

10  *there I smelt 'em out*  In this I was able to detect their deceptiveness.

11  *ague-proof*  Immune to fevers.

12  *For Gloucester's ... sheets*  Lear does not yet know of Edmund's treachery.

To't! Luxury pell-mell, for I lack soldiers.[1]
Behold yond simp'ring dame, whose face between
130  Her forks presages snow;[2] that minces virtue,
And does shake the head to hear of pleasure's name.[3]
The fitchew,[4] nor the soilèd horse[5] goes to't with
A more riotous appetite. Down from the waist
They are centaurs,[6] though women all above;
135  But° to the girdle do the gods inherit;                    *only*
Beneath is all the fiends. There's hell; there's darkness;
There is the sulphurous pit: burning, scalding,
Stench, consumption! Fie, fie, fie; pah, pah!—Give me
An ounce of civet,° good apothecary;                      *perfume*
140  Sweeten my imagination. There's money for thee.
GLOUCESTER.   O let me kiss that hand.
LEAR.   Let me wipe it first. It smells of mortality.
GLOUCESTER.   O ruined piece of nature! This great world
Shall so wear out to naught.[7]—Dost thou know me?
145  LEAR.   I remember thine eyes well enough. Dost thou squint at
me? No, do thy worst blind Cupid, I'll not love. Read thou this
challenge;[8] mark but the penning of it.
GLOUCESTER.   Were all thy letters suns, I could not see.
EDGAR.   I would not take this from report; it is, and my heart
150  breaks at it.
LEAR.   Read.
GLOUCESTER.   What! With the case[9] of eyes?

---

1 *Luxury ... soldiers*   Let people indulge their lechery in any which way, because they may beget me children who will become my army.
2 *whose face ... snow*   Who, judging by the look on her face, would be frigid between her legs.
3 *does shake ... name*   Shakes her head in disapproval merely to hear the word "plea-sure" spoken.
4 *fitchew*   Polecat (a member of the weasel family, reputed to be lecherous, and its name accordingly applied to prostitutes).
5 *soilèd horse*   Horse left to run in pasture and therefore more sexually enthusiastic than a stabled horse.
6 *Down ... centaurs*   They have bestial appetites below the waist, like centaurs, who have the torsos of men and the bodies of horses.
7 *Shall so ... naught*   Shall come to nothing (in the same way that Lear has).
8 *challenge*   The paper may be imaginary.
9 *case*   Empty eye-sockets.

LEAR. Oh ho, are you there with me? No eyes in your head, nor
no money in your purse? Your eyes are in a heavy case, your
purse in a light; yet you see how this world goes.                    155
GLOUCESTER. I see it feelingly.
LEAR. What, art mad? A man may see how this world goes,
with no eyes. Look with thine ears. See how yond justice rails
upon yond simple[1] thief. Hark in thine ear: change places, and
handy-dandy, which is the justice, which is the thief? Thou hast      160
seen a farmer's dog bark at a beggar?
GLOUCESTER. Aye, Sir.
LEAR. And the creature run from the cur? There thou might'st
behold the great image of authority: a dog's obeyed in office.
Thou, rascal beadle,[2] hold thy bloody hand; why dost thou          165
lash that whore? Strip thy own back; thou hotly lusts to use
her in that kind, for which thou whip'st her. The usurer hangs
the cozener.[3] Through tattered clothes, great vices do appear;
robes and furred gowns hide all. Plate sins with gold, and the
strong lance of justice hurtless breaks; arm it in rags, a pigmy's   170
straw does pierce it.[4] None does offend; none, I say none. I'll
able 'em.[5] Take that of me, my friend, who have the power
to seal th'accuser's lips.[6] Get thee glass-eyes, and like a scurvy[7]
politician, seem to see the things thou dost not. Now, now, now,
now. Pull off my boots. Harder, harder—so.                           175
EDGAR. O matter and impertinency[8] mixed.
Reason in madness.
LEAR. If thou wilt weep my fortunes, take my eyes.
I know thee well enough; thy name is Gloucester.
Thou must be patient. We came crying hither;                         180

---

1  *simple*  Petty.
2  *beadle*  Constable.
3  *The usurer ... cozener*  The moneylender hangs the petty cheat.
4  *Plate ... pierce it*  Cover sinfulness with wealth (plate it with gold) and it acts as
   armor; but sinfulness in rags has no protection, and can be penetrated by the merest
   trifle.
5  *able 'em*  Vouch for them.
6  *Plate sins ... th'accuser's lips*  These four sentences do not appear in the Quarto
   version.
7  *scurvy*  Corrupt.
8  *matter and impertinency*  Sense and nonsense.

Thou know'st, the first time that we smell the air
We wail and cry. I will preach to thee. Mark:
GLOUCESTER.   Alack, alack the day.
LEAR.   When we are born, we cry that we are come
To this great stage of fools. This a good block.[1]
It were a delicate stratagem to shoe
A troop of horse with felt![2] I'll put't in proof,
And when I have stol'n upon these son-in-laws,
Then kill, kill, kill, kill, kill, kill!

(*Enter a Gentleman.*)

GENTLEMAN.   Oh here he is. (*To Edgar.*) Lay hand upon him, Sir.
(*To Lear.*) Your most dear daughter—
LEAR.   No rescue? What, a prisoner? I am even
The natural fool[3] of Fortune. Use me well;
You shall have ransom. Let me have surgeons;
I am cut to'th' brains.
GENTLEMAN.                  You shall have anything.
LEAR.   No seconds?[4] All myself?
Why, this would make a man a man of salt,[5]
To use his eyes for garden water-pots.
I will die bravely, like a smug bridegroom.[6]
What? I will be jovial. Come, come.
I am a king, masters, know you that?
GENTLEMAN.   You are a royal one, and we obey you.
LEAR.   Then there's life in't.[7] Come, and you get it,
You shall get it by running: Sa, sa, sa, sa![8]

(*Exit.*)

---

1   *This a good block*   The meaning is debated.
2   *shoe … felt*   I.e., so their approaching hooves could not be heard.
3   *The natural fool*   Born to be a fool ("a natural" was an expression for those born
    mentally challenged).
4   *seconds*   Assistants, as in a duel.
5   *make a man a man of salt*   Make a man cry salt tears.
6   *die bravely … smug bridegroom*   Embrace death as if it were a bride.
7   *there's life in't*   There's hope yet.
8   *Sa, sa, sa, sa*   Cry used to urge on horses when hunting.

GENTLEMAN.   A sight most pitiful in the meanest wretch,
  Past speaking of in a king. Thou hast a daughter
  Who redeems nature from the general curse
  Which twain have brought her to.[1]
EDGAR.   Hail gentle° Sir.                                              *noble*   210
GENTLEMAN.   Sir, speed you.[2] What's your will?
EDGAR.   Do you hear ought, Sir, of a battle toward.[3]
GENTLEMAN.   Most sure, and vulgar:[4]
  Every one hears that, which can distinguish sound.
EDGAR.   But, by your favour, how near's the other army?        215
GENTLEMAN.   Near, and on speedy foot: the main descry
  Stands on the hourly thought.[5]
EDGAR.                                     I thank you Sir, that's all.
GENTLEMAN.   Though that the Queen on special cause is here
  Her army is moved on.                                                  220
EDGAR.                      I thank you Sir.


(*Exit [Gentleman].*)


GLOUCESTER.   You ever gentle gods, take my breath from me,
  Let not my worser spirit[6] tempt me again
  To die before you please.
EDGAR.                            Well pray you,[7] father.[8]          225
GLOUCESTER.   Now good sir, what are you?
EDGAR.   A most poor man, made tame to Fortune's blows[9]
  Who, by the art of known and feeling sorrows,

---

1  *general curse ... her to*  Pun: the curse of family blood which Gonerill and Regan
   have brought upon her, and the state of original sin left us by Adam and Eve.
2  *speed you*  God speed you.
3  *battle toward*  Impending battle.
4  *vulgar*  Common knowledge.
5  *main descry ... thought*  Sighting of the main part of the army is expected any
   hour.
6  *worser spirit*  Bad angel, wicked side.
7  *Well pray you*  That's a good prayer.
8  *father*  Though ambiguous, used here as a manner of addressing an older man who
   is a stranger (Edgar has yet to reveal himself).
9  *tame ... blows*  As a dog or horse is made timid by a cruel master.

Am pregnant to good pity.[1] Give me your hand;
230  I'll lead you to some biding.°                           *abode*
GLOUCESTER.                     Hearty thanks;
The bounty, and the benison° of heaven                    *blessing*
To boot, and boot.[2]


(*Enter [Oswald].*)


OSWALD.                     A proclaimed prize![3] Most happy!
235  That eyeless head of thine, was first framed[4] flesh
To raise my fortunes, thou old, unhappy traitor!
Briefly thyself remember;[5] the sword is out
That must destroy thee.
GLOUCESTER.                     Now let thy friendly[6] hand
240  Put strength enough to't.


(*Edgar intervenes.*)


OSWALD.                          Wherefore, bold peasant,
Dar'st thou support a published[7] traitor? Hence,
Lest that th'infection of his fortune take
Like hold on thee. Let go his arm.
245  EDGAR.  Chill not let go, Zir, without vurther 'casion.[8]
OSWALD.   Let go, slave, or thou diest.

---

1  *by the art … pity*   Having been instructed by the sorrows I have known and deeply
   felt, I am susceptible to feeling sympathy for others.
2  *To boot, and boot*   To reward you, and again. (Boot can mean both "to reward" and
   "again" or "in addition.")
3  *proclaimed prize*   Wanted man with a price on his head.
4  *framed*   Created.
5  *Briefly … remember*   Say your prayers quickly.
6  *friendly*   Welcome (because it brings death).
7  *published*   Publicly declared.
8  *Chill … 'caison*   I will not let go, Sir, without being given further occasion to do so
   (i.e., without hearing an explanation of why I should). The line is written in a rural
   dialect more reminiscent of today's Somerset than Kent. The convention does not
   appear in Edgar's lines immediately preceding these, but, because we cannot know
   how closely the Folio and Quarto texts conform to Shakespeare's intentions, we can
   only speculate as to whether he meant Edgar to have been using the same dialect
   to deceive Gloucester since his attempted suicide, or whether Edgar actually only
   adopts the dialect here to deceive Oswald. While readers can side-step the question,
   an actor performing the role must make a definite choice.

EDGAR. Good Gentleman, go your gate, and let poor volk pass. And 'chud ha'bin zwaggerd out of my life, 'twould not ha'bin zo long as 'tis, by a vortnight.[1] Nay, come not near th'old man. Keep out che vor'ye, or I'ce try whether your costard,[2] or my ballow[3] be the harder, chill be plain with you. 250
OSWALD. Out, dunghill.
EDGAR. Chill pick your teeth,[4] Zir. Come, no matter vor your foins.[5]


(*They fight.*)


OSWALD. Slave, thou hast slain me. Villain, take my purse; 255
If ever thou wilt thrive, bury my body,
And give the letters which thou find'st about me,
To Edmund, Earl of Gloucester. Seek him out
Upon the English party.[6] Oh, untimely death! Death!


(*He dies.*)


EDGAR. I know thee well: serviceable[7] villain, 260
As duteous to the vices of thy mistress,
As badness would desire.
GLOUCESTER.                 What, is he dead?
EDGAR. Sit you down, father; rest you.—(*Aside.*)
Let's see these pockets; the letters that he speaks of 265
May be my friends.—(*To Gloucester.*) He's dead; I am only
     sorry
He had no other deathsman. (*Aside.*)—Let us see;

---

1 *And ... vortnight*   If it were possible for me to have been swaggered to death, I would have died some time ago;   *vortnight*  I.e., fortnight, two weeks.
2 *costard*  Literally, apple, but in this case, slang for head.
3 *ballow*  Cudgel.
4 *pick your teeth*  Slug you in the jaw (a figurative threat, like "kick butt").
5 *foins*  Thrusts (with a sword).
6 *Upon ... party*  Amongst the English troops (as opposed to Cordelia's French party).
7 *serviceable*  Unscrupulously ready to be employed in anyone's service.

Leave gentle wax; and manners blame us not[1]
To know our enemies' minds. We rip their hearts;
270 Their papers is more lawful.

(*Reads the letter.*)

"Let our reciprocal vows be remembered. You have many
opportunities to cut him off; if your will want not,[2] time
and place will be fruitfully offered. There is nothing done if
he return the conqueror; then am I the prisoner, and his bed,
275 my gaol—from the loathèd warmth whereof, deliver me, and
supply the place for your labour.[3]
     Your (wife, so I would[4] say) affectionate servant, Gonerill."
Oh indistinguished space[5] of woman's will!
A plot upon her virtuous husband's life;
280 And the exchange my brother! (*To Oswald's corpse.*) Here, in
     the sands
Thee I'll rake up, the post unsanctified[6]
Of murderous lechers; and in the mature time,[7]
With this ungracious paper strike the sight
Of the death-practised Duke.[8] For him, 'tis well,
285 That of thy death, and business, I can tell.

(*Exit Edgar, with the body of Oswald.*)

GLOUCESTER.   The King is mad; how stiff is my vile sense,
That I stand up, and have ingenious feeling

---

1  *Leave gentle wax and manners blame us not*   I ask your leave (permission), noble
   sealing wax (which must be broken to read the letter), let it not be considered ill-
   mannered that we open another's letter.
2  *if your will want not*   If you are not lacking in resolve.
3  *supply ... labour*   By killing him, make room for yourself to have sex.
4  *would*   Would like to.
5  *indistinguished space*   Unfathomable scope.
6  *post unsanctified*   Wicked messenger (about to be buried in unsanctified ground).
7  *in the mature time*   At the most opportune time (when the time is ripe).
8  *death-practised Duke*   Duke whose death is plotted (i.e., Albany).

Of my huge sorrows?[1] Better I were distract,°          *insane*
So should my thoughts be severed from my griefs,

(*Drum afar off. [Re-enter Edgar.]*)

And woes, by wrong imaginations,[2] lose          290
The knowledge of themselves.
EDGAR.                              Give me your hand;
Far off methinks I hear the beaten drum.
Come, father; I'll bestow you with a friend.

(*Exeunt.*)

## ACT 4, SCENE 7

(*Enter Cordelia, Kent, and Gentleman.*)

CORDELIA.    O, thou good Kent! How shall I live and work
To match thy goodness? My life will be too short,
And every measure° fail me.                    *attempt*
KENT.    To be acknowledged, Madam, is o'er-paid.
All my reports go with the modest truth,          5
Nor more, nor clipped,[3] but so.
CORDELIA.                          Be better suited.[4]
These weeds° are memories of those worser hours;     *clothes*
I prithee, put them off.
KENT.                        Pardon, dear Madam;          10
Yet to be known shortens my made° intent.     *deliberate*
My boon I make it,[5] that you know me not,
Till time, and I, think meet.°                *appropriate*

---

1   *The King ... sorrows*   "Given that the King is insane, how cunningly contrived
    my senses be that I can still bear up and have an acute awareness of my immense
    misfortunes."
2   *wrong imaginations*   Deluded imaginings.
3   *Nor more, nor clipped*   Not exaggerated, nor cut short.
4   *suited*   Clothed (Kent is still wearing the servant costume he assumed in his "Caius"
    disguise).
5   *My boon ... it*   The favor I request is.

CORDELIA.   Then be't so. (*To Gentleman.*) My good Lord, how
does the King?

GENTLEMAN.   Madam, sleeps still.

CORDELIA.                              O you kind Gods!
Cure this great breach in his abusèd nature,
Th'untuned and jarring senses, O wind up,[1]
Of this child-changed[2] father.

GENTLEMAN.                           So please your Majesty,
That we may wake the King? He hath slept long.

CORDELIA.   Be governed by your knowledge, and proceed
I'th'sway of your own will. Is he arrayed?

GENTLEMAN.   Aye, Madam; in the heaviness of sleep,
We put fresh garments on him.


(*Enter Lear in a chair carried by Servants.*)


Be by, good Madam, when we do awake him.
I doubt of his temperance.[3]

CORDELIA.                        O my dear Father! Restoration[4] hang
Thy medicine on my lips, and let this kiss
Repair those violent harms that my two sisters
Have in thy reverence[5] made.

KENT.                             Kind and dear princess!

CORDELIA.   Had you not been their father, these white flakes[6]
Did challenge[7] pity of them. Was this a face
To be opposed against the jarring winds?
Mine enemy's dog, though he had bit me,
Should have stood that night against my fire,[8]
And was't thou fain, poor father,
To hovel thee with swine and rogues forlorn,

---

1   *Th'untuned … wind up*   Tighten the untuned strings of his mind (as one might
    tune a lyre), so that they are restored to sense and harmony.
2   *child-changed*   Become child-like (or changed thanks to children).
3   *I doubt … temperance*   I'm not sure how self-controlled he will be.
4   *Restoration*   I.e., the powers of restoration to health.
5   *reverence*   Dignity, venerable state.
6   *flakes*   Wisps of hair.
7   *Did challenge*   Would have demanded.
8   *against my fire*   By my fireplace.

In short[1] and musty straw? Alack, alack!
'Tis wonder that thy life and wits at once
Had not concluded all. (*To Gentleman.*) He wakes, speak to
  him.
GENTLEMAN.   Madam do you, 'tis fittest.
CORDELIA.   How does my Royal Lord? How fares your       45
  Majesty?
LEAR.   You do me wrong to take me out o'th'grave.
  Thou art a soul in bliss; but I am bound
  Upon a wheel of fire,[2] that mine own tears
  Do scald, like molten lead.
CORDELIA.             Sir, do you know me?       50
LEAR.   You are a spirit I know. Where did you die?
CORDELIA.   (*To Gentleman.*) Still, still, far wide.[3]
GENTLEMAN.   He's scarce awake. Let him alone a while.
LEAR.   Where have I been? Where am I? Fair daylight?
  I am mightily abused.° I should e'en die with pity    *deluded*   55
  To see another thus. I know not what to say:
  I will not swear these are my hands. Let's see:
  I feel this pin prick. Would I were assured
  Of my condition.
CORDELIA.          O look upon me, Sir,       60
  And hold your hand in benediction o'er me.
  You must not kneel.
LEAR.            Pray do not mock me:
  I am a very foolish fond old man—
  Fourscore and upward;[4] not an hour more, nor less—   65
  And to deal plainly,
  I fear I am not in my perfect mind.
  Methinks I should know you, (*Of Kent.*) and know this man;
  Yet I am doubtful. For I am mainly ignorant
  What place this is; and all the skill I have       70
  Remembers not these garments; nor I know not

---

1  *short*  Broken, much used.
2  *wheel of fire*  Binding a person on a wheel and breaking his bones was a form of
   execution. There's a sort of wheel of fire in Hell in the illustrated Kalendar of Shep-
   herds (1498).
3  *wide*  I.e., wide of the mark.
4  *Fourscore and upward*  Over eighty.

Where I did lodge last night. Do not laugh at me,
For, as I am a man, I think this lady
To be my child, Cordelia.

75 CORDELIA.                    And so I am. I am.

LEAR.  Be your tears wet? Yes, faith. I pray, weep not;
If you have poison for me, I will drink it.
I know you do not love me, for your sisters
Have, as I do remember, done me wrong.

80 You have some cause, they have not.

CORDELIA.  No cause, no cause.

LEAR.  Am I in France?

KENT.  In your own kingdom, Sir.

LEAR.  Do not abuse° me.                          *deceive*

85 GENTLEMAN.  Be comforted good Madam, the great rage,
You see, is killed in him. Desire him to go in;
Trouble him no more till further settling.

CORDELIA.  Wilt please your Highness walk?

LEAR.  You must bear with me.

90 Pray you now, forget, and forgive:
I am old and foolish.[1]


(*Exeunt.*)

---

1  In the Quarto version Kent and a Gentleman remain on stage after the others exit
here, and conclude the scene as follows: "GENTLEMAN.  Holds it true, Sir, that the
Duke of Cornwall was so slain?
KENT.  Most certain, Sir.
GENTLEMAN.  Who is conductor of his people?
KENT.  As 'tis said, the bastard son of Gloucester.
GENTLEMAN.  They say Edgar, his banished son, is with the Earl of Kent in
Germany.
KENT.  Report is changeable. 'Tis time to look about. The powers of the kingdom
approach apace.
GENTLEMAN.  The arbitrament is like to be bloody. Fare you well, Sir. (*Exit.*)
KENT.  My point and period will be throughly wrought, / Or well, or ill, as this
day's battle's fought. (*Exit.*)"

(*Enter with Drum and Colours, Edmund, Regan, Gentlemen, and Soldiers.*)

EDMUND.    Know of the Duke if his last purpose hold,
Or whether since he is advised by ought
To change the course. He's full of alteration,
And self-reproving. Bring his constant pleasure.[1]

(*Exit Messenger.*)

REGAN.    Our sister's man is certainly miscarried.[2]                    5
EDMUND.    'Tis to be doubted, Madam.
REGAN.                                    Now, sweet Lord,
You know the goodness I intend upon you;
Tell me but truly—but then speak the truth—
Do you not love my sister?                                        10
EDMUND.                          In honoured love.
REGAN.    But have you never found my brother's way[3]
To the forfended° place?                                    *forbidden*
EDMUND.                          No,[4] by mine honour, Madam.
REGAN.    I never shall endure her. Dear my Lord,              15
Be not familiar with her.
EDMUND.              Fear not—
She and the Duke her husband.

(*Enter, with drum and colours, Albany, Gonerill, Soldiers.*)

---

1   *constant pleasure*  Final decision.
2   *is ... miscarried*  Has definitely come to some harm.
3   *But have ... way*  But have you never followed the path of my brother-in-law (Albany); i.e., have you never had sex with her?
4   *To the forfended place ... No*  The Quarto version here includes an additional exchange, as follows: "REGAN.    But have you never found my brother's way / To the forfended place?
    BASTARD.    That thought abuses you.
    REGAN.    I am doubtful that you have been conjunct / And bosomed with her, as far as we call her's.
    BASTARD.    No, by mine honour Madam.
    REGAN.    I never shall endure her. Dear my Lord, / Be not familiar with her.
    BASTARD. Fear me not— / She and the Duke her husband."

ALBANY.    (*To Regan.*) Our very loving sister, well be-met.[1]

20    (*To Edmund.*)[2] Sir, this I heard: the King is come to his
      daughter
    With others, whom the rigour of our state[3]
    Forced to cry out.[4]

REGAN.                Why is this reasoned?[5]

GONERILL.    Combine together 'gainst the enemy;

25    For these domestic and particular broils[6]
    Are not the question here.

ALBANY.    Let's then determine with th'ancient of war[7]
    On our proceeding.

REGAN.                Sister, you'll go with us?[8]

30  GONERILL.    No.

REGAN.    'Tis most convenient, pray go with us.

GONERILL.    Oh ho, I know the riddle,[9] I will go.


    (*Exeunt both the armies [except Albany].*)
    (*Enter Edgar [still disguised].*)


EDGAR.    If e'er your Grace had speech with man so poor,
    Hear me one word.

35  ALBANY.    (*To those departing.*) I'll overtake you.
    (*To Edgar.*) Speak.

EDGAR.    Before you fight the battle, ope this letter.
    If you have victory, let the trumpet sound
    For him that brought it:[10] Wretchèd though I seem,

---

1    *well be-met*   It is good to see you.
2    *to Edmund*   Albany addresses Edmund in F, though he ignores him in Q.
3    *rigour of our state*   Tyranny of our governance.
4    *Forced to cry out*   The Quarto version here includes several additional lines, as fol-
     lows: "Forced to cry out. Where I could not be honest / I never yet was valiant. For
     this business, / It touches us, as France invades our land, / Now bolds the King, with
     others whom I fear. / Most just and heavy causes make oppose."
5    *Why is this reasoned*   Why do you think to bring this up (now)?
6    *domestic and particular broils*   Personal quarrels.
7    *th'ancient of war*   Those with experience of war.
8    *us*   Me (rather than Edmund).
9    *riddle*   Secret (reason for asking).
10   *him that brought it*   I.e., me.

I can produce a champion, that will prove[1]                    40
What is avouchèd° there. If you miscarry,                *maintained*
Your business of° the world hath so an end,                    *in*
And machination ceases.[2] Fortune loves you.

(*He begins to leave.*)

ALBANY.    Stay till I have read the letter.
EDGAR.                                     I was forbid it.       45
    When time shall serve, let but the herald cry,
    And I'll appear again.

(*Exit.*)

ALBANY.    Why, fare thee well. I will o'er-look thy paper.

(*Enter Edmund.*)

EDMUND.    The enemy's in view; draw up your powers.

(*Hands Albany a paper.*)

    Here is the guess of their true strength and forces          50
    By diligent discovery; but your haste
    Is now urged on you.[3]
ALBANY.                          We will greet the time.

(*Exit.*)

EDMUND.    To both these sisters have I sworn my love:
    Each jealous° of the other, as the stung          *suspicious*   55
    Are of the adder. Which of them shall I take?
    Both? One? Or neither? Neither can be enjoyed

---

1  *prove*  I.e., by combat.
2  *If you … ceases*  If, on the other hand, you lose the battle, you won't be worried
   about what is happening in the world, and this plan will be called off.
3  *Here is … on you*  This is the best estimate of the size of the enemy's numbers according to careful spying; but don't read it now, you need to hurry.

If both remain alive: To take the widow,
Exasperates, makes mad her sister Gonerill.
60  And hardly¹ shall I carry out my side,²
Her husband being alive. Now then, we'll use
His countenance³ for the battle; which being done,
Let her who would be rid of him devise
His speedy taking off.° As for the mercy                    *murder*
65  Which he intends to Lear and to Cordelia:
The battle done, and they within our power,
Shall never see his pardon; for my state
Stands on me to defend, not to debate.⁴

(*Exit.*)


## ACT 5, SCENE 2

(*Alarum within. Enter, with drum and colours, Lear, Cordelia, and Soldiers, over the stage, and exeunt.*)

(*Enter Edgar and Gloucester.*)

EDGAR    Here, father, take the shadow of this tree
For your good host.⁵ Pray that the right°                   *righteous*
    may thrive;
If ever I return to you again,
I'll bring you comfort.
5  GLOUCESTER.               Grace go with you Sir.

(*Exit Edgar.*)
(*Alarum and retreat within. [Re-]enter Edgar.*)

---

1  *hardly*  With difficulty.
2  *my side*  I.e., of the bargain.
3  *use … countenance*  Use him as a figurehead (to muster the troops).
4  *my state … debate*  My circumstances make it imperative for me to defend myself, not to weigh questions of right and wrong.
5  *For … host*  As shelter.

EDGAR.   Away, old man! Give me thy hand; away!
King Lear hath lost; he and his daughter ta'en.[1]
Give me thy hand; come on.
GLOUCESTER.   No further, Sir! A man may rot even here.
EDGAR.   What in ill thoughts again? Men must endure                    10
Their going hence, even as their coming hither.
Ripeness is all. Come on.
GLOUCESTER.                    And that's true too.


(*Exeunt.*)

---

1   *ta'en*   Have been taken (prisoner).

## ACT 5, SCENE 3
## (FOLIO EDITION)

*(Enter in conquest, with drum and colours, Edmund; Lear and Cordelia, as prisoners; Soldiers, Captain.)*

EDMUND.     Some officers take them away. Good guard,[1]
　　Until their greater pleasures first be known
　　That are to censure them.[2]
CORDELIA.     *(To Lear.)*     We are not the first,
5　　Who with best meaning have incurred the worst.
　　For thee, oppressèd King, I am cast down;°　　　　　desolate
　　Myself could else out-frown false Fortune's frown.
　　Shall we not see these daughters, and these sisters?
LEAR.   No, no, no, no; come let's away to prison.
10　　We two alone will sing like birds i'th'cage.
　　When thou dost ask me blessing, I'll kneel down
　　And ask of thee forgiveness. So we'll live
　　And pray, and sing, and tell old tales, and laugh
　　At gilded butterflies; and hear (poor rogues)
15　　Talk of court news; and we'll talk with them too—
　　Who loses, and who wins; who's in, who's out—
　　And take upon's the mystery of things,[3]
　　As if we were God's spies. And we'll wear out,°　　　　outlast
　　In a walled prison, packs and sects of great ones
20　　That ebb and flow by th'moon.[4]
EDMUND.     *(To Soldiers.)*     Take them away.[5]

---

1　*Good guard*　Guard them well.
2　*Until … them*　Until the will of those who will be passing judgement upon these prisoners (i.e., Albany, Gonerill, and Regan) is known.
3　*take upon's … things*　Observe and comment upon the wonders of life and death.
4　*packs … th'moon*　The cliques and factions of the powerful that rise and fall like the (moon-influenced) tides.
5　*Take them away*　Evidently, the soldiers are reluctant to obey; they have already been given the order at the top of the scene.

## ACT 5, SCENE 3
## (QUARTO EDITION)

*(Enter Edmund [and Soldiers], with Lear and Cordelia prisoners.)*

BASTARD.    Some officers take them away. Good guard
  Untill their greater pleasures best be known
  That are to censure them.
CORDELIA.    (*To Lear.*)    We are not the first
  Who with best meaning have incurred the worst.    5
  For thee, oppressèd King, am I cast down;
  Myself could else out-frown false Fortune's frown.
  Shall we not see these daughters, and these sisters?
LEAR.    No, no; come let's away to prison.
  We two alone will sing like birds i'th'cage.    10
  When thou dost ask me blessing, I'll kneel down
  And ask of thee forgiveness. So we'll live
  And pray, and sing, and tell old tales, and laugh
  At gilded butterflies; and hear poor rogues
  Talk of court news; and we'll talk with them too—    15
  Who loses, and who wins; who's in, who's out—
  And take upon's the mystery of things
  As if we were God's spies. And we'll wear out,
  In a walled prison, packs and sects of great ones
  That ebb and flow by th'moon.    20
BASTARD.    (*To Soldiers.*)    Take them away.

LEAR.  (*To Cordelia.*) Upon such sacrifices,[1] my Cordelia,
The gods themselves throw incense.[2] Have I caught thee?
He that parts us,[3] shall bring a brand° from heaven,                  *torch*
25    And fire us hence, like foxes![4] Wipe thine eyes,
The good years[5] shall devour them, flesh and fell,°                   *skin*
Ere they shall make us weep! We'll see 'em starved first!
Come.

(*Ex[eunt Lear and Cordelia under guard].*)

EDMUND.    Come hither, Captain. Hark:
30    Take thou this note; go follow them to prison.
One step I have advanced thee;[6] if thou dost
As this instructs thee, thou dost make thy way
To noble fortunes.[7] Know thou this: that men
Are as the time is; to be tender minded
35    Does not become a sword. Thy great employment
Will not bear question; either say thou'lt do't,
Or thrive by other means.
CAPTAIN.                              I'll do't my Lord.
EDMUND.    About it, and write happy,[8] when th'hast done.
40    Mark, I say: instantly, and carry it so
As I have set it down.[9]

---

1    *such sacrifices*  I.e., as Lear and Cordelia will make in turning our backs on the
     world.
2    *throw incense*  Cast incense, an act normally performed by a priest.
3    *He that parts us*  I.e., the only person able to part us (will be divine).
4    *fire ... foxes*  The reference is to a hunting technique in which a fire is lit at one or
     more holes of a den to force the fox out another opening.
5    *good years*  Perhaps a Biblical reference to years of God's favor in which enemies are
     afflicted (Genesis 41).
6    *One step ... thee*  I have promoted you once.
7    *make ... fortunes*  You will have earned promotion to the ranks of the nobility.
8    *About it, and write happy*  Go to it immediately, and call yourself fortunate.
9    *set it down*  Written it down.

LEAR.  (*To Cordelia.*) Upon such sacrifices, my Cordelia,
The gods themselves throw incense. Have I caught thee?
He that parts us shall bring a brand from heaven,
And fire us hence like foxes! Wipe thine eyes;                        25
The good shall devour 'em, flesh and fell,
Ere they shall make us weep! We'll see 'em starve first. Come.


(*Exeunt Lear and Cordelia, under guard.*)

BASTARD.    Come hither, Captain. Hark:
Take thou this note; go follow them to prison.
One step I have advanced thee; if thou dost                           30
As this instructs thee, thou dost make thy way
To noble fortunes. Know thou this: that men
Are as the time is; to be tender minded
Does not become a sword. Thy great employment
Will not bear question; either say thou'lt do't,                     35
Or thrive by other means.
CAPTAIN.                    I'll do't, my Lord.
BASTARD.    About it, and write happy when thou hast done.
Mark, I say: instantly, and carry it so
As I have set it down.                                                40
CAPTAIN.                I cannot draw a cart,
Nor eat dried oats; if it be man's work, I'll do't.[1]

---

1  *I cannot ... do't*  I cannot do honest drudge work as an animal can; being a human
being, I will do the sort of work (i.e., evil) that human beings do.

(*Exit Captain.*)
(*Flourish. Enter Albany, Gonerill, Regan, Soldiers.*)

ALBANY.    (*To Edmund.*) Sir, you have showed today your valiant
    strain
    And Fortune led you well. You have the captives
    Who were the opposites° of this day's strife;       *opponents*
45    I do require them of you, so to use them,
    As we shall find their merits and our safety
    May equally determine.
EDMUND.              Sir, I thought it fit
    To send the old and miserable King to some retention—
50    Whose age had charms[1] in it, whose title, more,
    To pluck the common bosom on his side,[2]
    And turn our impressèd lances[3] in our eyes
    Which do command them. With him I sent the Queen—
    My reason all the same—and they are ready
55    Tomorrow, or at further space, t'appear
    Where you shall hold your session.[4]

ALBANY.               Sir, by your patience,
    I hold you but a subject of[5] this war,
    Not as a brother.

---

1   *charms*  Persuasive power.
2   *Whose age ... on his side*  I.e., if Lear is not locked away, the hearts of the common
    people might be swayed by sympathy for him (as an old man) and respect for him
    (as king) such that they would turn against the rebels (and convince the soldiers to
    do the same).
3   *impressèd lances*  Conscripted ordinary soldiers (and their lances, in the eye-piercing metaphor).
4   *session*  Trial.
5   *hold you but a subject of*  Consider you only as a subordinate in.

*(Exit.)*
*(Enter [Albany, Gonorill, Regan] and others.)*

ALBANY.    (*To Bastard.*) Sir, you have showed today your valiant
    strain;
    And Fortune led you well. You have the captives
    That were the opposites of this day's strife;                     45
    We do require then, of you, so to use them,
    As we shall find their merits and our safety
    May equally determine.
BASTARD.                        Sir, I thought it fit
    To save the old and miserable King to some retention—             50
    Whose age has charms in it, whose title, more,
    To pluck the common bosoms of his side,
    And turn our impressèd lances in our eyes
    Which do command them. With him I sent the Queen—
    My reason all the same—and they are ready                         55
    Tomorrow, or at further space, to appear
    Where you shall hold your session. At this time,
    We sweat and bleed; the friend hath lost his friend
    And the best quarrels in the heat are curst
    By those that feel their sharpness.[1]                            60
    The question of Cordelia and her father
    Requires a fitter place.
ALBANY.                        Sir, by your patience,
    I hold you but a subject of this war,
    Not as a brother.                                                 65

---

1  *At this time … sharpness*  In circumstances such as these, when suffering and passion abound, it is inadvisable to go to trial, because even a righteous argument (i.e.,
   against Lear and Cordelia) is going to be difficult to bear.

60   Regan.                That's as we list[1] to grace him.
      Methinks our pleasure might have been demanded
      Ere you had spoke so far. He led our powers,
      Bore the commission of my place and person,[2]
      The which immediacy may well stand up,
65     And call itself your brother.[3]
      Gonerill.                Not so hot.
      In his own grace he doth exalt himself,
      More than in your addition.[4]
      Regan.               In my rights,
70     By me invested,[5] he compeers° the best.         *equals*
      Albany.   That were the most, if he should husband you.
      Regan.   Jesters do oft prove prophets.
      Gonerill.                Hola, hola![6]
      That eye that told you so, looked but asquint.
75     Regan.   Lady, I am not well; else I should answer
      From a full-flowing stomach.[7] (*To Edmund.*) General:
      Take thou my soldiers, prisoners, patrimony.
      Dispose of them, of me; the walls[8] are thine.
      Witness the world, that I create thee here
80     My Lord and Master.
      Gonerill.         Mean you to enjoy him?
      Albany.   The let-alone[9] lies not in your good will.
      Edmund.   Nor in thine, Lord.

---

1   *we list*   I choose (the royal pronoun is used here and below).
2   *Bore … person*   Represented my personal, royal authority.
3   *The which … brother*   The temporary expedient of which may be made permanent, which would demand that you consider Edmund a sort of brother.
4   *In his … addition*   His own merits demand his promotion and respect more than any title you give him.
5   *In my rights … invested*   In the rights belonging to me that I have conferred on him.
6   *Hola, hola*   Expostulation roughly equivalent to "now, now" or "hang on."
7   *full-flowing stomach*   Bellyful of rage.
8   *walls*   Regan speaks figuratively, as if she were a fortress taken by Edmund after a long siege.
9   *let-alone*   Say-so, permission.

REGAN.                That's as we list to grace him.
  Methinks our pleasure should have been demanded
  Ere you had spoke so far. He led our powers,
  Bore the commission of my place and person,
  The which immediate may well stand up,                    70
  And call itself your brother.
GONORILL.                    Not so hot.
  In his own grace he doth exalt himself
  More than in your advancement.
REGAN.                            In my right,             75
  By me invested, he compeers the best.
GONORILL.   That were the most, if he should husband you.
REGAN.   Jesters do oft prove prophets.
GONORILL.                            Hola, hola!
  That eye that told you so, looked but asquint.           80
REGAN.   Lady, I am not well; else I should answer
  From a full-flowing stomach. (*To Bastard*.) General:
  Take thou my soldiers, prisoners, patrimony.

  Witness the world that I create thee here
  My lord and master.                                      85
GONORILL.              Mean you to enjoy him, then?
ALBANY.   The let-alone lies not in your good will.
BASTARD.   Nor in thine, Lord.

ALBANY.                                    Half-blooded[1] fellow, yes.

85  REGAN.   Let the drum strike, and prove my title[2] thine.

ALBANY.   Stay yet, hear reason. Edmund, I arrest thee
On capital treason; and in thy arrest,[3] (*Indicating Gonerill.*)
This gilded serpent. (*To Regan.*) For your claim, fair sister,
I bar it in the interest of[4] my wife.

90  'Tis *she* is sub-contracted to this Lord;
And I, her husband, contradict your banns.[5]
If you will marry, make your loves to me.[6]
My Lady is bespoke.

GONERILL.                          An interlude![7]

95  ALBANY.   (*To Edmund.*) Thou art armed Gloucester; let the
trumpet sound.[8]
If none appear to prove[9] upon thy person
Thy heinous, manifest, and many treasons,

(*He throws down his glove.*)

There is my pledge. I'll make it[10] on thy heart,
Ere I taste bread, thou art in nothing less
100  Than I have here proclaimed thee.

REGAN.                                    Sick, O sick!

GONERILL.   (*Aside.*) If not, I'll ne'er trust medicine.

EDMUND.   (*To Albany, throwing down his own glove.*)
There's my exchange.[11] What in the world[12] he is

---

1  *Half-blooded*   Illegitimate.
2  *my title*   I.e., the title I have given you.
3  *in thy arrest*   In connection with your arrest (i.e., as accessory to your crimes).
4  *in the interest of*   On behalf of.
5  *banns*   Formal declaration of the intent to marry.
6  *to me*   I.e., because if Gonerill can make a sub-contract, so can Albany (spoken facetiously).
7  *interlude*   Short farcical play, by now old-fashioned.
8  *let the trumpet sound*   I.e., to announce a challenge to a duel.
9  *prove*   I.e., by combat.
10  *make it*   Make it good, prove it.
11  *exchange*   Acceptance of the duel (symbolized through the exchange of gloves).
12  *What in the world*   Whoever in the world.

ALBANY.                    Half-blooded fellow, yes.

BASTARD.    Let the drum strike, and prove my title good.                    90

ALBANY.    Stay yet, hear reason. Edmund, I arrest thee
On capital treason; and in thine attaint,[1] (*Indicating Gonorill.*)
This gilded serpent. (*To Regan.*) For your claim, fair sister,
I bar it in the interest of my wife.
'Tis *she* is subcontracted to this lord,                    95
And I, her husband, contradict the banns.
If you will marry, make your love to me.
My Lady is bespoke.

(*To Bastard.*) Thou art armed, Gloucester;

If none appear to prove upon thy head                    100
Thy heinous, manifest, and many treasons,

(*He throws down his glove.*)

There is my pledge. I'll prove it on thy heart,
Ere I taste bread, thou art in nothing less
Than I have here proclaimed thee.

REGAN.                    Sick, o sick.                    105

GONORILL.    (*Aside.*) If not, I'll ne'er trust poison.

BASTARD.    (*To Albany, throwing down his own glove.*)
There's my exchange. What in the world he is

---

1   *in thine attaint*   Sharing your corruption.

105    That names me traitor, villain-like he lies.
Call by the trumpet. He that dares approach—
On him, on you; who not?—I will maintain
My truth and honour firmly.
ALBANY.                A herald, ho!

(*Enter a Herald.*)

110    Trust to thy single virtue, for thy soldiers
All levied in my name, have in my name
Took their discharge.[1]
REGAN.             My sickness grows upon me.
ALBANY.    She is not well, convey her to my tent.

(*Exit Regan with one or more soldiers.*)

115    Come hither, herald. Let the trumpet sound,
And read out this.

(*A trumpet sounds.*)


HERALD.    (*Reads.*) "If any man of quality or degree,[2] within the lists[3] of the army, will maintain upon Edmund, supposèd Earl of Gloucester, that he is a manifold traitor, let him appear by the
120    third sound of the trumpet. He is bold in his defence.

(*1st trumpet.*)

HERALD.    Again.

(*2nd trumpet.*)

HERALD.    Again.

(*3rd trumpet. Trumpet answers within.*)

---

1   *Trust ... discharge*   You're on your own, because all of your soldiers, who were recruited using my name, have been discharged by my authority.
2   *quality or degree*   Noble rank or important position.
3   *lists*   Rolls.

That names me traitor, villain-like he lies.
Call by thy trumpet. He that dares approach—                    110
On him, on you; who not?—I will maintain
My truth and honour firmly.
ALBANY.   A herald, ho!
BASTARD.                    A herald ho! A herald!

ALBANY.   Trust to thy single virtue, for thy soldiers,         115
All levied in my name, have in my name
Took their discharge.
REGAN.                    This sickness grows upon me.
ALBANY.   She is not well; convey her to my tent.

(*Exit Regan with one or more soldiers. Enter a Herald.*)

Come hither, herald. Let the trumpet sound,                     120
And read out this.
CAPTAIN.   Sound trumpet!

(*A trumpet sounds.*)

HERALD.   (*Reads.*) "If any man of quality or degree, in the host[1]
of the army, will maintain upon Edmund, supposèd Earl of
Gloucester, that he's a manifold traitor, let him appear at the   125
third sound of the trumpet. He is bold in his defence."
BASTARD.   Sound!

(*Trumpeter sounds a second time.[2]*)

Again!

(*Trumpeter sounds a third time.*)

---

1   *host*   Body.
2   *second time*   In Q, the trumpets are counted from that which preceded the herald;
in F, from after the herald's announcement.

(*Enter Edgar, armed.*[1])

ALBANY.    Ask him his purposes, why he appears
Upon this call o'th'trumpet.

125    HERALD.                              What are you?
Your name, your quality, and why you answer
This present summons?

EDGAR.                            Know my name is lost
By treason's tooth: bare-gnawn, and canker-bit.[2]

130    Yet am I noble as the adversary
I come to cope.[3]

ALBANY.              Which is that adversary?

EDGAR.    What's he that speaks for Edmund, Earl of Gloucester?

EDMUND.    Himself, what say'st thou to him?

135    EDGAR.                                        Draw thy sword,
That, if my speech offend a noble heart,
Thy arm may do thee justice. Here is mine.

(*He draws his sword.*)

Behold; it is my privilege,
The privilege of mine honours,

140    My oath, and my profession.[4] I protest—[5]
*Malgré*[6] thy strength, place, youth, and eminence,
Despite thy victor-sword,[7] and fire-new fortune,
Thy valour, and thy heart—thou art a traitor:
False to thy gods, thy brother, and thy father,

145    Conspirant 'gainst this high illustrious Prince,[8]
And from th'extremest upward of thy head,

---

1    *armed*    A helmet conceals his face.
2    *canker-bit*    Worm-eaten.
3    *cope*    Deal with; encounter in battle.
4    *profession*    Vows and role as a knight.
5    *protest*    Claim.
6    *Malgré*    Despite.
7    *victor-sword*    Victorious sword (in the battle just fought).
8    *Prince*    I.e., Albany.

*(Enter Edgar [armed] at the third sound, a trumpet before him.*[1]*)*

ALBANY.    Ask him his purposes, why he appears
  Upon this call o'th'trumpet.                                                130
HERALD.    (*To Edgar.*)   What are you?
  Your name and quality, and why you answer
  This present summons?
EDGAR.                          O know, my name is lost;
  By treason's tooth, bare-gnawn and canker-bit.                        135
  Yet, ere I move't,[2] where is the adversary
  I come to cope withal?[3]
ALBANY.                         Which is that adversary?
EDGAR.   What's he that speaks for Edmund, Earl of Gloucester?
BASTARD.    Himself, what sayest thou to him?                              140
EDGAR.                                          Draw thy sword,
  That, if my speech offend a noble heart, thy arm
  May do thee justice. Here is mine.

*(He draws his sword.)*

Behold; it is the privilege of my tongue,

  My oath, and my profession. I protest—                               145
*Malgré* thy strength, youth, place and eminence;
  Despite thy victor-sword, and fire-new fortune,
  Thy valour and thy heart—thou art a traitor:
  False to thy gods, thy brother, and thy father;
  Conspirate 'gainst this high, illustrious prince,                    150
  And from th'extremest upward of thy head,

---

1    *before him*   I.e., sound in response, just before his entrance.
2    *ere I move't*   Before I declare my case against him.
3    *cope withal*   Encounter by means of this (challenge).

To the descent and dust below thy foot,
A most toad-spotted traitor. Say thou "no":
This sword, this arm, and my best spirits are bent
150     To prove upon thy heart, whereto I speak,
Thou liest.
EDMUND.    In wisdom I should ask thy name,[1]
But since thy outside looks so fair and warlike,
And that thy tongue (some say)[2] of breeding breathes,
155     What safe and nicely I might well delay°                  *avoid*
By rule of knighthood, I disdain and spurn.
Back do I toss these treasons to thy head.
With the hell-hated[3] lie, o'er-whelm thy heart,
Which, for they yet glance by and scarcely bruise,
160     This sword of mine shall give them instant way,[4]
Where they shall rest for ever. Trumpets, speak!

(*The trumpets sound. Edgar and Edmund fight; Edgar wounds
and overcomes Edmund and holds him at his mercy.*)

ALBANY.    Save him, save him.[5]
GONERILL.    (*To Edmund.*) This is practice,[6] Gloucester.
By th'law of war, thou wast not bound to answer

---

1   *In wisdom ... name*   It would be prudent because, if his adversary were a man
of lower social rank, according to the rules of chivalry he could honorably refuse
combat.

2   *(some say)*   This provides an interesting example of the effect of a compositor's
punctuation on the sense of a line. While in most cases, the punctuation of both
Q and F has been altered to make the best sense to a contemporary reader, the
parentheses around "some say" have been left here to show the transformation of the
meaning according to the original compositor's understanding of the line. While in
Q, "some say" is to be understood as "some assay" (or hint), the object of "breathes,"
in F Edmund appears to be reporting the rumors he has heard; but there has been
no such opportunity for him to hear anything said about his masked adversary.

3   *hell-hated*   Hated as much as hell.

4   *give ... way*   Make a passage for them (to your heart).

5   *save him*   Spare him (i.e., not a cry for help, but a request that Edgar allow Edmund
to live—presumably so he can make a full confession).

6   *practice*   Trickery.

To the descent and dust beneath thy feet,
A most toad-spotted traitor. Say thou "no":
This sword, this arm—and my best spirit—is bent
To prove upon thy heart, whereto I speak,                              155
Thou liest.

BASTARD.    In wisdom I should ask thy name;
But since thy outside looks so fair and warlike,
And that thy being some say[1] of breeding breathes,

My right of knighthood, I disdain and spurn.                          160
Here do I toss those treasons to thy head.
With the hell hated lie o'er-turn thy heart,
Which, for they yet glance by and scarcely bruise,
This sword of mine shall give them instant way,
Where they shall rest for ever. Trumpets, speak!                      165

(*The trumpets sound. Edgar and Bastard fight; Edgar wounds and
overcomes Bastard and holds him at his mercy.*)

ALBANY.    Save him, save him.
GONORILL.    (*To Bastard.*) This is mere practice, Gloucester!
By the law of arms, thou art not bound to answer

---

1    *some say*  Some hint, or taste (i.e., "given that your being breathes a hint of
breeding").

165     An unknown opposite! Thou art not vanquished,
But cozened, and beguiled.
ALBANY.               Shut your mouth, dame,
Or with this paper[1] shall I stop it!—Hold, Sir.—[2]
Thou worse than any name, read thine own evil.
170     No tearing Lady, I perceive you know it.
GONERILL.    Say if I do, the laws are mine not thine,[3]
Who can arraign me for't?[4]

(*Exit.*)

ALBANY.              Most monstrous! (*To Edmund.*)
O, know'st thou this paper?
175     EDMUND.            Ask me not what I know.

ALBANY.    (*To Soldiers.*) Go after her. She's desperate; govern her.
EDMUND.    What you have charged me with, that have I done;
And more, much more; the time will bring it out.
'Tis past, and so am I.[5] But what art thou
180     That hast this fortune on me? If thou'rt noble,
I do forgive thee.
EDGAR.          Let's exchange charity:
I am no less in blood than thou art, Edmund;
If more,[6] the more th'hast wronged me.

(*Removes his helmet.*)

185     My name is Edgar, and thy father's son.

---

1  *this paper*  The letter from Gonerill to Edmund that Oswald was carrying when Edgar killed him.
2  *Hold, Sir*  Perhaps addressed to Edgar, who stands ready to kill Edmund, or perhaps to Edmund, who is trying to rise.
3  *mine not thine*  Gonerill is of royal blood; although Albany is the effective ruler, technically, he is only the consort.
4  *Who ... for't*  I.e., there is no one of higher rank to bring a sovereign to trial.
5  *so am I*  He is dying from a wound he received in the fight.
6  *If more*  In that he is legitimate.

An unknown opposite! Thou art not vanquished,
But cozened and beguiled! 170
ALBANY.                    Stop your mouth, dame,
 Or with this paper shall I stopple it![1]
 Thou, worse than anything, read thine own evil.
 Nay, no tearing, Lady; I perceive you know't.
GONORILL.   Say if I do: the laws are mine, not thine; 175
 Who shall arraign me for't?


ALBANY.                    Most monstrous!
 Know'st thou this paper?
GONORILL.                    Ask me not what I know.[2]

(*Exit Gonorill.*)

ALBANY.   (*To Soldiers.*) Go after her. She's desperate; govern her. 180
BASTARD.   What you have charged me with, that have I done;
 And more, much more; the time will bring it out.
 'Tis past, and so am I. But what art thou
 That hast this fortune on me? If thou be'st noble
 I do forgive thee. 185
EDGAR.             Let's exchange charity.
 I am no less in blood than thou art, Edmund;
 If more, the more thou hast wronged me.

(*Removes his helmet.*)

My name is Edgar, and thy father's son.

---

1  *stopple it*  Put a stopper in it (as a cork is put in a bottle).
2  *Ask ... know*  Cf. F's assignment of this line to Edmund.

The gods are just, and of our pleasant vices
Make instruments to plague us;
The dark and vicious place[1] where thee he got,°         *begot*
Cost him his eyes.
190  EDMUND.              Th'hast spoken right; 'tis true;
The wheel is come full circle;[2] I am here.
ALBANY.   (*To Edgar.*) Methought thy very gait did prophesy
A royal nobleness. I must embrace thee.
Let sorrow split my heart, if ever I
195  Did hate thee, or thy father.
EDGAR.                    Worthy Prince, I know't.
ALBANY.   Where have you hid yourself?
How have you known the miseries of your father?
EDGAR.   By nursing them, my Lord. List[3] a brief tale;
200  And when 'tis told, O that my heart would burst!
The bloody proclamation[4] to escape
That followed me so near—O, our lives' sweetness,
That we the pain of death would hourly die,
Rather then die at once![5]—taught me to shift
205  Into a mad-man's rags, t'assume a semblance
That very dogs disdained. And in this habit°         *costume*
Met I my father with his bleeding rings,
Their precious stones° new lost; became his guide,         *eyes*
Led him, begged for him, saved him from despair.
210  Never—O fault!—revealed myself unto him,
Until some half hour past, when I was armed.
Not sure, though hoping of this good success,
I asked his blessing, and from first to last

---

1  *dark and vicious place*  Place of sin (adultery).
2  *wheel ... circle*  I.e., just as Gloucester's dark sin left him with darkened sight, so has Edmund's plan to overcome Edgar resulted in Edgar's overcoming him.
3  *List*  I.e., listen to.
4  *bloody proclamation*  Announcement that he was a traitor and was wanted dead or alive.
5  *our lives' ... once*  This is a sign of how dearly we value life, that we would accept a situation so painful that it felt as if we were dying every hour rather than confronting certain death and thereby getting it over and done with.

The gods are just, and of our pleasant virtues                    190
Make instruments to scourge us;
The dark and vicious place where thee he got
Cost him his eyes.
BASTARD.          Thou hast spoken truth;
The wheel is come full circled; I am here.                        195
ALBANY.   (*To Edgar.*) Methought thy very gait did prophesy
A royal nobleness. I must embrace thee.
Let sorrow split my heart if I did ever hate
Thee or thy father.
EDGAR.           Worthy Prince, I know't.                         200
ALBANY.   Where have you hid yourself?
How have you known the miseries of your father ?
EDGAR.   By nursing them, my Lord. List a brief tale;
And when 'tis told, O that my heart would burst!
The bloody proclamation to escape                                 205
That followed me so near—O, our lives, sweetness,
That with the pain of death would hourly die,
Rather than die at once!—taught me to shift
Into a mad-man's rags, to assume a semblance
That very dogs disdained. And in this habit                       210
Met I my father with his bleeding rings,
The precious stones new lost; became his guide,
Led him, begged for him, saved him from despair.
Never—O Father!—revealed myself unto him,
Until some half hour past, when I was armed.                      215
Not sure, though hoping of this good success,
I asked his blessing, and from first to last,

Told him our pilgrimage. But his flawed heart—
215     Alack, too weak the conflict to support!—
Twixt two extremes of passion, joy and grief,
Burst smilingly.   *How Gloucester died*
EDMUND.      This speech of yours hath moved me,
And shall perchance do good. But speak you on;
220     You look as you had something more to say.
ALBANY.    If there be more, more woeful, hold it in,
For I am almost ready to dissolve,[1]
Hearing of this.

---

1   *dissolve*   I.e., into tears.

Told him my pilgrimage. But his flawed heart—
Alack, too weak the conflict to support!—
Twixt two extremes of passion, joy and grief,                    220
Burst smilingly.
BASTARD.          This speech of yours hath moved me,
And shall perchance do good. But speak you on;
You look as you had something more to say,
ALBANY.   If there be more, more woeful, hold it in,              225
For I am almost ready to dissolve,
Hearing of this.
EDGAR.            This would have seemed a period°        *ending*
To such as love not sorrow;
But another to amplify—too much                                  230
Would make much more and top extremity—[1]
Whil'st I was big in clamour,[2] came there in a man,
Who having seen me in my worst estate,°        *condition*
Shunned my abhorred society; but then, finding
Who 'twas that so endured,[3] with his strong arms             235
He fastened on my neck and bellowed out
As he'd burst heaven; threw him on my father,[4]
Told the most piteous tale of Lear and him
That ever ear received—which, in recounting,
His grief grew puissant° and the strings of life[5]   *overpowering*  240
Began to crack. Twice, then, the trumpets sounded,
And there I left him tranced.
ALBANY.                     But who was this?
EDGAR.   Kent sir, the banished Kent; who, in disguise,
Followed his enemy king and did him service                     245
Improper for a slave.[6]

---

1  *This would ... extremity*  This incident would have seemed a tragic enough ending
   for those with no taste for tragedies, but to tell (amplify) another story—if I were to
   add much more than this, it would surpass the utmost of what humans can bear.
2  *big in clamour*  Weeping loudly.
3  *so endured*  Had been forced to be Poor Tom.
4  *my father*  The body of Gloucester.
5  *strings of life*  Heart-strings.
6  *Improper ... slave*  Entailing more hardship than would be expected of a slave.

(*Enter a Gentleman.*)

GENTLEMAN.    Help, help! O help!
225  EDGAR.                              What kind of help?
ALBANY.                                        Speak, man.
EDGAR.    What means this bloody knife?
GENTLEMAN.                            'Tis hot, it smokes!
It came even from the heart of—O, she's dead!
230  ALBANY.    Who dead? Speak, man!
GENTLEMAN.    Your Lady, Sir, your Lady! And her sister
By her is poisoned; she confesses it.
EDMUND.    I was contracted to them both, all three
Now marry in an instant.
235  EDGAR.                        Here comes Kent

(*Enter Kent.*)

ALBANY.    Produce the bodies, be they alive or dead.

(*Some Soldiers go to recover the bodies.*[1])

This judgement of the heavens that makes us tremble
Touches us not with pity. (*Of Kent.*) O, is this he?

The time will not allow the compliment
240  Which very manners urges.[2]
KENT.                              I am come
To bid my King and Master aye° good night.          *forever*
Is he not here?
ALBANY.            Great thing of us forgot,
245  Speak, Edmund, where's the King? And where's Cordelia?

1  *Some … bodies*  F has the next stage direction (*Gonerill and Regan's bodies brought out*) placed at this point, though it is clear that the action of retrieving the bodies merely begins here.
2  *compliment … urges*  Formal greeting which mere manners would dictate.

(*Enter one with a bloody knife.*)

GENTLEMAN.   Help, help!

ALBANY.   What kind of help? What means that bloody knife?
GENTLEMAN.   It's hot, it smokes! It came even from the heart of
...
ALBANY.   Who, man, speak?                                              250
GENTLEMAN.   Your Lady, Sir, your Lady! And her sister
  By her is poisoned; she hath confessed it.
BASTARD.   I was contracted to them both, all three
  Now marry in an instant.

ALBANY.   Produce their bodies, be they alive or dead.                  255

(*Some Soldiers go to recover the bodies.*)

This justice of the heavens that makes us tremble,
  Touches us not with pity.
EDGAR.                    Here comes Kent, Sir.

(*Enter Kent.*)

ALBANY.   O, 'tis he! The time will not allow
  The compliment that very manners urges.                              260
KENT.   I am come
  To bid my King and master aye good night.
  Is he not here?
ALBANY.          Great thing of us forgot!
  Speak Edmund, where's the King? And where's Cordelia?               265

(*Gonerill and Regan's bodies brought out.*)

ALBANY.    Seest thou this object, Kent?[1]
KENT.    Alack, why thus?
EDMUND.                    Yet Edmund was beloved:
    The one the other poisoned for my sake,
250    And after slew herself.
ALBANY.                    Even so. Cover their faces.
EDMUND.    I pant for life; some good I mean to do
    Despite of mine own nature. Quickly send—
    Be brief in it!—to'th'castle; for my writ
255    Is on the life of Lear and on Cordelia!
    Nay, send in time.
ALBANY.    (*To Soldiers.*) Run, run, O run!
EDGAR.    (*Stopping them.*) To who my Lord? (*To Edmund.*) Who
    has the office?[2]
    Send thy token of reprieve.
260    EDMUND.                    Well thought on.
    Take my sword; give it the Captain.
EDGAR.    (*Giving the sword to the Soldiers.*) Haste thee, for thy life!

(*Exit one or more Soldiers.*)[3]

EDMUND.    (*To Albany.*) He hath commission from thy wife and
    me,
    To hang Cordelia in the prison, and
265    To lay the blame upon her own despair,
    That she fordid herself.[4]
ALBANY.                    The gods defend her!
    Bear him hence awhile.

---

1    *Seest ... Kent*    In both Q and F, this line is assigned to Albany, but for reasons of dramatic effectiveness, it is occasionally reassigned in performance to Edmund.
2    *office*    Orders (to kill Lear and Cordelia).
3    *Exit ... Soldiers*    Cf. Q and note.
4    *fordid herself*    Committed suicide.

*(The bodies of Gonorill and Regan are brought in.)*

BASTARD.    Seest thou this object, Kent?[1]

KENT.   Alack, why thus?

BASTARD.                       Yet Edmund was beloved,
The one the other poisoned for my sake,
And after slew herself.                                                   270

ALBANY.                     Even so. Cover their faces.

BASTARD.   I pant for life; some good I mean to do,
Despite of my own nature. Quickly send—
Be brief, in't!—to th'castle; for my writ,
Is on the life of Lear and on Cordelia,                      275
Nay send in time.

ALBANY.   *(To Edgar.)* Run, run, O run!

EDGAR.   To who my Lord? *(To Edmund.)* Who hath the office?
Send thy token of reprieve.

BASTARD.                     Well thought on.              280
Take my sword—the Captain; give it the Captain!

ALBANY.   *(To Edgar)* Haste thee, for thy life!


*(Exit Edgar.[2])*

BASTARD.   He hath commission from thy wife and me,

To hang Cordelia in the prison, and to lay
The blame upon her own despair,                             285
That she fordid her self.

ALBANY.                     The gods defend her!
Bear him hence a while.

---

1   *Seest ... Kent*   See note on this line in F.

2   *To Edgar ... Exit Edgar*   No stage directions are offered here in either Q or F. Most
    editors suppose that it is the Second Captain, who appears shortly thereafter, who is
    sent. But an exit here could not plausibly give him time to witness Lear's killing of
    the first Captain. Furthermore, the assignment of "Haste thee for thy life" to Albany
    in Q, together with Edgar's preceding dialogue, suggests that it is more probably
    Edgar who goes.

(*Soldiers bear Edmund off.*)
(*Enter Lear with Cordelia in his arms, [followed by a Gentleman].*)

LEAR.    Howl, howl, howl! O, you are men of stones!
270    Had I your tongues and eyes,[1] I'd use them so
That heavens' vault[2] should crack! She's gone for ever.
I know when one is dead, and when one lives;
She's dead as earth. Lend me a looking-glass.
If that her breath will mist or stain the stone,
275    Why then, she lives.
KENT.                              Is this the promised end?[3]
EDGAR.    Or image of that horror.
ALBANY.                                        Fall and cease.[4]
LEAR.    This feather stirs;[5] she lives! If it be so,
280    It is a chance which does redeem all sorrows
That ever I have felt.
KENT.                           O, my good Master—
LEAR.    Prithee, away.
EDGAR.                           'Tis noble Kent, your friend.
285    LEAR.    A plague upon you; murderers, traitors all!
I might have saved her; now she's gone for ever!—
Cordelia, Cordelia, stay a little—Ha?
What is't thou say'st?—Her voice was ever soft,
Gentle, and low: an excellent thing in woman.—
290    I killed the slave that was a-hanging thee.
GENTLEMAN.    'Tis true, my Lords, he did.

---

1  *tongues and eyes*  I.e., eyes for seeing the horror, tongues for protesting it.
2  *heavens' vault*  The sky (conceived of as an arched roof in which the stars were fixed).
3  *promised end*  Generally taken as an allusion to Judgement Day, the end of the world prophesied in the Bible (Mark 13, Revelations 16, etc.), but see the note on this line in Q.
4  *Fall and cease*  Let the heavens fall and the world cease.
5  *feather stirs*  Lear mistakenly believes a feather is stirred by Cordelia's breath.

*(Soldiers bear Bastard off.)*
*(Enter Lear with Cordelia in his arms.)*
*(Edgar follows behind with the Second Captain.)*

LEAR.    Howl, howl, howl, howl! O you are men of stones!
  Had I your tongues and eyes, I would use them so                    290
  That heavens' vault should crack! She's gone for ever.
  I know when one is dead, and when one lives;
  She's dead as earth. Lend me a looking-glass;
  If that her breath will mist or stain the stone,
  Why then, she lives.                                                  295
KENT.                     Is this the promised end?[1]
EDGAR.    Or image of that horror.
ALBANY.                     Fall and cease.
LEAR.    This feather stirs; she lives! If it be so,
  It is a chance which does redeem all sorrows                          300
  That ever I have felt.
KENT.                     Ah, my good master—
LEAR.    Prithee, away!
EDGAR.                     'Tis noble Kent, your friend.
LEAR.    A plague upon you, murderous traitors all!                          305
  I might have saved her; now she's gone for ever!—
  Cordelia, Cordelia, stay a little—Ha?
  What is't thou sayest?—Her voice was ever soft,
  Gentle and low: an excellent thing in women.—
  I killed the slave that was a-hanging thee.                           310
[2ND] CAPTAIN.    'Tis true my Lords, he did.

---

1  *promised end*  Kent may be speaking of Judgement Day, the end of the world, but there remain the possibilities that he is referring either (as some critics have argued) to the end of the chain of events begun in the first scene of the play with the abdication of Lear, or to the "top [ping of] extremity" mentioned earlier in this scene (in Q, though not in F), when Edgar had talked about the consequences of adding one sad story on top of another. In any case, Edgar certainly takes Kent's line as an apocalyptic reference.

LEAR.                                                    Did I not, fellow?
I have seen the day, with my good biting falchion[1]
I would have made him skip. I am old now,
295   And these same crosses spoil me.[2] (*To Kent.*) Who are you?
Mine eyes are not o'th'best, I'll tell you straight.
KENT.   If Fortune brag of two she loved and hated,
One of them we behold.[3]
LEAR.   This is a dull sight, are you not Kent?
300   KENT.                                          The same—
Your servant Kent. Where is your servant Caius?[4]
LEAR.   He's a good fellow, I can tell you that,
He'll strike and quickly too. He's dead and rotten.
KENT.   No my good Lord, I am the very man—
305   LEAR.   I'll see that straight.[5]
KENT.   —that from your first of difference and decay,[6]
Have followed your sad steps.
LEAR.                                    You are welcome hither.
KENT.   Nor no man else.[7] All's cheerless, dark, and deadly.
310   Your eldest daughters have fordone themselves,
And desperately° are dead.                                      *in despair*
LEAR.                              Aye, so I think.
ALBANY.   He knows not what he says; and vain is it
That we present us to him.
315   EDGAR.                              Very bootless.°                    *useless*

(*Enter a Messenger.*)

MESSENGER.   Edmund is dead, my Lord.

---

1   *biting falchion*   Sharp curved sword.
2   *these ... spoil me*   These sorts of confrontation ruin my strength.
3   *If Fortune ... behold*   Kent offers Lear a clue in a sort of riddle: i.e., "If Fortune
    brought her greatest extremes to two people, each of us beholds one of them."
4   *Caius*   This is the only mention of the name Kent took when in disguise.
5   *I'll ... straight*   I'll look into that in a moment.
6   *first ... decay*   First days of your change and decline in fortune.
7   *Nor no man else*   This line could finish off Kent's previous speech (i.e., "the very man,
    and no one else") or it could be a response to Lear's line (i.e., "No, I don't suppose I am
    welcome, nor is anyone else").

LEAR.                                     Did I not, fellow?
  I have seen the day, with my good biting falchion
  I would have made them skip. I am old now,
  And these same crosses spoil me. (*To Kent.*) Who are you?        315
  Mine eyes are not o'the best, I'll tell you straight.
KENT.    If Fortune bragged of two she loved or hated,
  One of them we behold.
LEAR.                       Are not you Kent?
KENT.    The same, your servant Kent. Where is your servant,        320
  Caius?
LEAR.    He's a good fellow, I can tell that,
  He'll strike and quickly too. He's dead and rotten.
KENT.    No my good Lord, I am the very man—
LEAR.    I'll see that straight.
KENT.    —that from your life of difference and decay,              325
  Have followed your sad steps.
LEAR.                         You're welcome hither.
KENT.    Nor no man else. All's cheerless, dark and deadly.
  Your eldest daughters have fordone themselves,
  And desperately are dead.                                         330
LEAR.                       So think I, too.
ALBANY.    He knows not what he sees; and vain it is,
  That we present us to him.
EDGAR.                       Very bootless.

  (*Enter [another] Captain.*)

[3RD] CAPTAIN.    Edmund is dead my Lord.                           335

ALBANY.                                    That's but a trifle here.
You Lords and noble friends, know our intent:
What comfort to this great decay may come,[1]
320   Shall be applied. For us, we[2] will resign,
During the life of this old majesty,
To him our absolute power. (*To Edgar and Kent.*) You to your
    rights,
With boot,[3] and such addition as your honours
Have more than merited. All friends shall
325   Taste the wages of their virtue, and all foes
The cup of their deservings.—O see, see.
LEAR.    And my poor fool[4] is hanged. No, no, no life?
Why should a dog, a horse, a rat have life,
And thou, no breath at all? Thou'lt come no more.
330   Never, never, never, never, never.
Pray you, undo this button.[5] Thank you, Sir.
Do you see this? Look on her? Look her lips,
Look there, look there—
(*He dies.*)
EDGAR.    He faints. (*To Lear.*) My Lord? My Lord?
335   KENT.    Break heart, I prithee break.
EDGAR.    Look up, my Lord.
KENT.    Vex not his ghost. O let him pass. He hates him,
That would upon the rack[6] of this tough world
Stretch him out longer.

---

1   *What comfort ... come*   Whatever may be done to help the general disaster we have
    experienced.
2   *us, we*   Albany is using "the royal we" to refer to himself.
3   *boot*   Extra measure.
4   *fool*   Likely a term of endearment, used with reference to Cordelia, but possibly
    also a reference to the Fool, absent from the play since Act 3. The line has been much
    discussed, with some critics suggesting that Lear's madness leads him to conflate the
    two.
5   *button*   Presumably the button at his own throat.
6   *rack*   Instrument of torture on which the limbs of victims were painfully
    stretched.

ALBANY.                                    That's but a trifle here.
　You Lords and noble friends, know our intent:
　What comfort to this decay may come,
　Shall be applied. For us, we will resign
　During the life of this old majesty                              340
　To him our absolute power. (*To Edgar and Kent.*)
　You to your rights with boot, and such addition
　As your honour have more than merited.
　All friends shall taste the wages of their virtue,
　And all foes the cup of their deservings—                        345
　(*Looking at Lear.*) O see, see!
LEAR.　And my poor fool is hanged. No, no life.
　Why should a dog, a horse, a rat have life,
　And thou, no breath at all? O, thou wilt come no more.
　Never, never, never. Pray you:                                   350
　Undo this button? Thank you sir. O, o, o, o.


EDGAR.　He faints. (*To Lear.*) My Lord? My Lord?
LEAR.　Break heart, I prithee break.
EDGAR.　Look up, my Lord.
KENT.　Vex not his ghost. O, let him pass. He hates him           355
　That would upon the rack of this tough world
　Stretch him out longer.

　(*Lear dies.*[1])

---

1　*Lear dies*　This is the latest the death might take place; unlike F, Q does not include
　a stage direction to mark the exact point of Lear's death.

340    Edgar.            He is gone indeed.

Kent.   The wonder is, he hath endured so long,
He but usurped his life.[1]

Albany.   (*To Soldiers.*) Bear them from hence. Our present business
Is general woe. (*To Edgar and Kent.*) Friends of my soul, you twain

345    Rule in this realm, and the gored state sustain.

Kent.   I have a journey, Sir, shortly to go;
My master calls me; I must not say no.

Edgar.[2]  The weight of this sad time we must obey,°     *submit to*
Speak what we feel, not what we ought to say.

350    The oldest hath borne° most; we that are young,     *suffered*
Shall never see so much, nor live so long.


(*Exeunt with a dead march.*)


[*End of Play.*]
—1623


---

1   *usurped his life*  Kept life longer than he was entitled to.

2   *EDGAR*  Note that this last speech is assigned to Albany in Q. By convention, the last speech in most tragedies is given to the character of highest social rank. But the references within the speech itself, to youth, and to speaking from the heart rather than according to protocol, have been cited by some critics as evidence that the speech is, indeed, intended for Edgar.

EDGAR.              O, he is gone indeed.
KENT.    The wonder is, he hath endured so long.
  He but usurped his life.                                         360
ALBANY.    (*To Soldiers.*) Bear them from hence. Our present
    business
  Is to general woe. (*To Edgar and Kent.*) Friends of my soul, you
    'twain
  Rule in this kingdom, and the gored state sustain.
KENT.    I have a journey, Sir, shortly to go;
  My master calls, and I must not say no.                    365
ALBANY.[1]    The weight of this sad time we must obey,
  Speak what we feel, not what we ought to say.
  The oldest have borne most; we that are young,
  Shall never see so much, nor live so long.

(*Exeunt, bearing the bodies.*)

[*End of Play.*]
—1608

---

1    *ALBANY*   Note that this last speech is assigned to Edgar in F.

*In Context*

# The Shakespearean Theater

## The Swan Theatre

The illustration on the next page, a "Sketch of The Swan Theatre" by Johannes De Witt, is the best visual guide we have of the physical arrangement of the interior of London's four playhouses of the late sixteenth century. The sketch, by a Dutch visitor, is accompanied by the following note (translated here from the Latin):

There are four amphitheatres in London of notable beauty, which from their diverse signs bear diverse names. In each of them a different play is daily exhibited to the populace. The two more magnificent of these are situated to the southward beyond the Thames, and from the signs suspended before them are called the Rose and Swan. The two others are outside the city towards the north on the highway which issues through the Episcopal Gate, called in the vernacular Bishopsgate. There is also a fifth, but of dissimilar structure, devoted to the baiting of beasts, where are maintained in separate cages and enclosures many bears and dogs of stupendous size, which are kept for fighting, furnishing thereby a most delightful spectacle to men. Of all the theatres, however, the largest and the most magnificent is that one of which the sign is a swan, called in the vernacular the Swan Theatre; for it accommodates in its seats three thousand persons, and is built of a mass of flint stones (of which there is a prodigious supply in Britain), and supported by wooden columns painted in such excellent imitation of marble that it is able to deceive even the most cunning. Since its form resembles that of a Roman work, I have made a sketch of it above.

"Sketch of The Swan Theatre" by Johannes De Witt.

Henry Peacham, from a manuscript in the library of the Marquess of Bath at Longleat (c. 1595). This illustration (known as "the Longleat drawing") is the only surviving image of a play of Shakespeare's in performance during his lifetime. The drawing is accompanied by forty lines of verse from the play.

The Plot of an Elizabethan Play

The plot of *The Seven Deadly Sins* (c. 1590). Originally the "plot" was a physical object listing the scenes of a play, which was hung backstage as an aid for the actors. In this detail of the plot of *The Seven Deadly Sins, Part Two* the square from which the plot hung during a performance is visible.

# *Early Editions of* King Lear

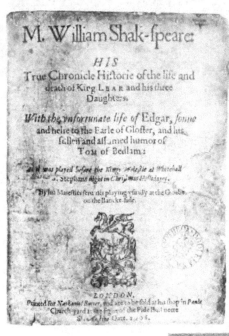

King Lear, title page, first
Quarto edition (1608).

*King Lear*, opening page,
first Quarto edition (1608).

Title page, Folio edition (1623). The page facing the title page includes a prefatory poem by Ben Jonson.

M. William Shak-ſpeare: 7

*HIS*
True Chronicle Hiſtorie of the life and
death of King L E A R and his three
Daughters.

*With the vnfortunate life of* Edgar, *ſonne*
and heire to the Earle of Gloſter, and his
ſullen and aſſumed humor of
T O M of Bedlam :

*As it was played before the Kings Maieſtie at Whitehall vpon*
*S.* Stephans *night in Chriſtmas Hollidayes.*

By his Maieſties ſeruants playing vſually at the Gloabe
on the Bancke-ſide.

*LONDON,*
Printed for *Nathaniel Butter,* and are to be ſold at his ſhop in *Pauls*
Church-yard at the ſigne of the Pide Bull neere
S⁺. *Auſtins* Gate. 1 6 0 8.

*King Lear,* title page, first Quarto edition (1608).

# Source Material

### from Geoffrey of Monmouth, *The History of the Kings of Britain*[1] (12th century)

The earliest known account of the story of Lear appears in Geoffrey of Monmouth's twelfth century work *The History of the Kings of Britain*, a book that was enormously popular and influential through the late medieval period and into the Tudor era; that account is provided here. We do not know if Shakespeare read Geoffrey's history in the Latin, or simply drew on details of the story both as recounted by Geoffrey and as they appear in later histories.

from Book 2, Sections 30-32

[30] Bladud the son of Rud Hud Hudibras succeeded him and governed the kingdom for twenty years. He built the town of Kaer Badon, which is now known as Bath, and there he made hot baths ready for the use of men. He dedicated them to the goddess Minerva and placed inextinguishable fires in her temple, fires whose flames never failed, since when they began to die down they were turned about on stone spheres. In those days Elijah prayed that no rain would fall upon the earth and it did not rain for three years and six months.[2] This Bladud, however, was a most clever man and taught necromancy throughout the island of Britain. Not content with mere illusions, he had wings made for himself in an attempt to attain the zenith of the sky. But he fell to his death atop the Temple of Apollo in the city of Trinovant, consumed by vain error.

[31] With Bladud thus consigned to his doom, his son Leir was elevated to the kingship and ruled the land for sixty years. Leir built a city on the banks of the Soar which derives its name from him in the British tongue as Kaer Leir and in the Saxon tongue

---

1    *The History of the Kings of Britain*    The translation from the Latin of Geoffrey's *Historia regum brittaniae* excerpted here is that prepared by Michael Faletra for the Broadview edition of *The History of the Kings of Britain*; Faletra's annotations have also been drawn on extensively here.

2    *Elijah ... months*    Cf. Luke 4:25; 1 Kings 17:10-16.

as Leicester. Denied any male offspring, he nonetheless had three daughters whose names were Goneril, Regan, and Cordelia. Their father loved them all greatly, but he loved his youngest daughter, Cordelia, most of all. And so, when he began to grow old he thought about how to divide his kingdom among them and he sought to find such husbands as would share the rule of the land with them. In order to determine which of his three daughters was more worthy of the greater part of the kingdom, he went and asked them one by one who loved him the best. Posed this question by her father, Goneril the eldest daughter took the gods in heaven as witness that she bore for him a greater love than she bore for the soul that was in her own body. Her father then said to her, "Since in my old age you place me above all else, I shall marry you, my most beloved daughter, to whatever young man you should choose, and I shall give you a third of the kingdom of Britain." Then Regan, the second daughter, taking heed of her sister's example and hoping to insinuate her way into her father's good graces, answered him with many oaths, swearing that she could by no means express how much she loved him, except to say that she loved him above all other creatures. Thus gulled, her father granted her the same dignity as her sister and promised to find her a husband and give her another third of his kingdom.

But when Cordelia, the youngest daughter, perceived that her father was content with her sisters' flattery, she thought she would test him and decided to answer him quite differently. "Is there, my father," she asked, "a daughter anywhere who can presume to love her father more than is fitting? I do not think that there is any daughter who would dare to confess this, unless she is seeking to conceal the truth with empty words. Indeed, I have always loved you as my father and even now my feelings do not waver. And if you insist on wrenching any more out of me, remember the constancy of the love I have held for you and cease your questioning. You truly have as much of my love as you are worth: that's how much I love you." Then her father grew exceedingly angry and indignant about this answer that she had given from the bottom of her heart. He did not delay in expressing himself thus: "Because you hold your aged father in such contempt and do not deign to love me as your sisters do, I refuse to let you share any part of this realm with your sisters. Since you are my daughter, however, I am not saying that I wouldn't marry you off to some foreigner if Fortune should permit it. But I assure you that I shall never seek to marry you with the same honour that I showed your sisters. Of course, while I had loved you until today more than your sisters, you have in fact loved me far less than they do."

Without delay, Leir followed the advice of his noble counsellors and married his two oldest daughters to the Duke of Cornwall and the Duke of Alban, along with half the island to rule between them as long as he lived. After his death, they would possess sovereignty over all of Britain.

Then it happened that Aganippus, the king of the Franks, having heard great tidings of Cordelia's beauty, sent messengers to the king asking for his daughter's hand in marriage. Her father, steadfast in his anger, answered that he would give her to him freely, but without land or dowry, for he had already partitioned his kingdom, along with all his gold and silver, to his daughters Goneril and Regan. When this settlement was announced to Aganippus, he was even more greatly inflamed with love for the girl. He sent again to Leir, saying that he had gold and silver and lands enough, for he possessed a third of Gaul. So he obtained the girl in this way in order to produce heirs with her. When the agreement was reached, Cordelia was sent to Gaul and married off to Aganippus.

After a long space of time, old age began to wear Leir down, and the dukes to whom he had partitioned the kingdom and married his daughters rose up against him. They seized from him the kingdom and the sovereign power that he had hitherto wielded bravely and gloriously. They avoided an all-out civil war, however, because one of his sons-in-law, Maglaurus the Duke of Alban, maintained Leir with one hundred forty knights so that the king would not appear dishonoured. When two years had passed with Leir in residence there, his daughter Goneril became impatient with the great crowd of her father's retainers because they made trouble with her own servants, always insisting on more sumptuous rations. Her husband therefore decided that her father should be content with a retinue of thirty, and he dismissed the remainder.

Leir became so indignant at this treatment that he left Maglaurus and sought out Henwin, the Duke of Cornwall, whom he had married to his second daughter, Regan. Although the duke welcomed him honourably, not a year had passed before there was again friction between the household and Leir's attendants. Regan became angry because of this and ordered her father to dismiss all of his men, except for five who should remain to serve him. Her father was then greatly anguished, and he went back to his first daughter to see if he could move her to pity and allow him to keep all of his retainers. But Goneril was not moved at all and rekindled her former hostility. She swore by the gods in heaven that he could not lodge with her unless he dismissed all his men and be content with a single retainer. She chided the old man, who now had nothing, for expecting to maintain such a following. Since she would in no way agree to anything he wanted, he yielded to her and dismissed the others and remained with one single servant.

But when Leir cast his memory back upon his former dignity, he began to detest the misery of his current state and thought about going to entreat his youngest daughter who lived across the ocean. He feared that she would not help him at all since he had married her off so ungraciously, yet he could tolerate his abjection no longer and set sail for Gaul. While crossing the sea, he noticed that he was accounted third among the princes there on the ship, and he lamented with crying and sobbing in these words: "O, you unbendable chain of Fate! you who keep to such an unswerving and narrow path! Why did you ever elevate me to an unstable happiness when it is a greater pain to revisit good times lost than to be oppressed by the sorrows to come? Indeed, the mere memory of that time when I was attended by a hundred thousand knights, when I was accustomed to cast down city walls and lay waste the lands of my enemies, grieves me more than the calamity of my present state. Fate has driven those who once lay beneath my feet to forsake me now in my weakness. O vengeful Fortune, will the day ever come when I will be able to repay those who have deserted me in my present state of poverty? O Cordelia, how true were those words you spoke when I asked what kind of love you bore me! You said 'I love you with as much of my love as you are worth.' While I was still able to give, I was worth much to them who were friends not to me but to my gifts. All the while they loved me but loved my riches more, for when the handouts went away so did they. But, dearest daughter, how will I dare to beg from you? Because of your words, I chose to marry you off more poorly than your sisters, who now, after receiving their inheritance, have reduced me to an exile and beggar."

Leir was saying these and similar things, and he came to Caritia where his daughter was dwelling. Waiting outside the city, he sent a messenger ahead to announce how he had fallen upon such hard times. And since Leir had neither food nor clothing, the messenger begged her to grant mercy upon the king. When her father was presented in this way, Cordelia was moved to bitter tears and she inquired as to how many men he had with him. He sent answer that he had only the one man who waited outside with him. At this, Cordelia seized all the gold and silver at hand and gave it to the messenger, instructing him to bring her father to a nearby city. There the messenger should treat the king as if he were ill, and he should provide Leir with baths, food, and shelter. Cordelia also arranged that her father retain forty well-dressed and fully-armed knights and that, after a time, he should send for King Aganippus and his own daughter.

When the messenger returned to King Leir, he brought him to another city and hid him there, carrying out all the things that Cordelia had commanded. As soon as Leir was arrayed in kingly attire and had established his new household, he sent messages to Aganippus and Cordelia, explaining that he had been cast out of Britain by his own sons-in-law and that he was coming now to seek their aid in recovering his realm. And so Aganippus and Cordelia came to him with their counsellors and retinue, and they treated him with great honour and restored him to the power and high dignity he had once commanded in his own kingdom. In the meantime, Aganippus sent messengers all throughout Gaul to muster every armed soldier for assistance in restoring the kingdom of Britain to his father-in-law. Once Aganippus had done this, Leir led Cordelia and the assembled host and fought against his sons-in-law and defeated them. Three years after he had regained all of his former power, he died. Aganippus, king of the Franks, had also died by then. So Leir's daughter Cordelia assumed the governance of the kingdom, and she buried her father in an underground chamber which she had had built beneath the River Soar downstream from Leicester. This crypt was built in honour of the two-faced god Janus. There, on the god's feast day, all the craftsmen of the city came to begin the first of the works that they would undertake for the entire year.

[32] After Cordelia had reigned tranquilly for fifteen years, the peace was broken by Margan and Cunedag, the sons of her two sisters who had been married to Maglaurus and Henwin. Both of these youths had an upstanding reputation. Maglaurus had fathered the younger of them, Margan, while Henwin had fathered Cunedag. Having succeeded after the deaths of their fathers to their respective duchies, these two grew outraged that Britain was now subject to a woman. Therefore, mustering their armies, they rebelled against the queen. They did not cease their hostilities until, having laid many provinces to waste, they finally met the queen in battle. At the last they captured her and cast her in prison, where, because of her grief at having lost the kingdom, she killed herself. Then the two men divided the island up between themselves: Margan received the part that extended from the River Humber towards Caithness, while Cunedag received the lands that stretch from the other side of the river towards the setting of the sun.

## Cap o' Rushes[1]

> The English folk tale on the "love like salt" theme, which strongly parallels the Lear story, has many variants, going back to the medieval period. One of the best known (now, as in the sixteenth and seventeenth centuries) is "Cap o' Rushes."

There was once a very rich gentleman, and he had three daughters, and he thought he'd see how fond they were of him. So he says to the first, "How much do you love me, my dear?"

"Why," says she, "as I love my life."

---

1   *Cap o' Rushes*   Written versions of this tale do not survive from Shakespeare's time; the text below has been slightly revised and modernized from that recorded by Joseph Jacobs in his compilation *English Fairy Tales* (1890).

"That's good," says he.

So he says to the second, "How much do *you* love me, my dear?"

"Why," says she, "better than all the world."

"That's good," says he.

So he says to the third, "How much do *you* love me, my dear?"

"Why, I love you as fresh meat loves salt," says she.

Well, but he was angry. "You don't love me at all," says he, "and in my house you stay no more." So he drove her out there and then, and shut the door in her face.

Well, she went away on and on till she came to a fen, and there she gathered a lot of rushes and made them into a kind of a cloak with a hood, to cover her from head to foot, and to hide her fine clothes. And then she went on and on till she came to a great house.

"Do you want a maid?" says she.

"No, we don't," said they.

"I haven't anywhere to go," says she, "and I ask no wages, and will do any sort of work," says she.

"Well," said they, "if you like to wash the pots and scrape the saucepans you may stay," said they.

So she stayed there and washed the pots and scraped the saucepans and did all the dirty work. And because she gave them no name they called her "Cap o' Rushes."

Well, one day there was to be a great dance a little way off, and the servants were allowed to go and look on at the grand people. Cap o' Rushes said she was too tired to go, so she stayed at home.

But when they were gone, she took off her cap o' rushes, and cleaned herself, and went to the dance. And no one there was so finely dressed as she.

Well, who should be there but her master's son, and what should he do but fall in love with her the minute he set eyes on her. He wouldn't dance with any one else.

But before the dance was done, Cap o' Rushes slipped off, and away she went home. And when the other maids came back, she was pretending to be asleep with her cap o' rushes on.

Well, next morning they said to her, "You did miss a sight, Cap o' Rushes!"

"What was that?" says she.

"Why, the beautifullest lady you ever see, dressed all bright and gay. The young master, he never took his eyes off her."

"Well, I should have liked to have seen her," says Cap o' Rushes.

"Well, there's to be another dance this evening, and perhaps she'll be there."

But, come the evening, Cap o' Rushes said she was too tired to go with them. Howsoever, when they were gone, she took off her cap o' rushes and cleaned herself, and away she went to the dance.

The master's son had been reckoning on seeing her, and he danced with no one else, and never took his eyes off her. But, before the dance was over, she slipped off, and home she went, and when the maids came back she pretended to be asleep with her cap o' rushes on.

Next day they said to her again, "Well, Cap o' Rushes, you should have been there to see the lady. There she was again, dressed all bright and gay, and the young master never took his eyes off her."

"Well there," says she, "I should have liked to have seen her."

"Well," says they, "there's a dance again this evening, and you must go with us, for she's sure to be there."

Well, come this evening, Cap o' Rushes said she was too tired to go, and do what they would she stayed home. But when they were gone, she took off her cap o' rushes and cleaned herself, and away she went to the dance.

The master's son was glad when he saw her. He danced with none but her and never took his eyes off her. When she wouldn't tell him her name, nor where she came from, he gave her a ring and told her if he didn't see her again he should die.

Well, before the dance was over, off she slipped, and home she went, and when the maids came home she was pretending to be asleep with her cap o' rushes on.

Well, next day they says to her, "There, Cap o' Rushes, you didn't come last night, and now you won't see the lady, for there are to be no more dances."

"Well, I should have greatly liked to have seen her," says she.

The master's son tried every way to find out where the lady was gone, but go where he might, and ask whom he might, he never heard anything about her. And he got worse and worse for the love of her till he had to keep his bed.

"Make some gruel for the young master," they said to the cook. "He's dying for the love of the lady." The cook set about making it when Cap o' Rushes came in.

"What are you a-doing of?" says she.

"I'm going to make some gruel for the young master," says the cook, "for he's dying of love of the lady."

"Let me make it," says Cap o' Rushes.

Well, the cook wouldn't at first, but at last she said yes, and Cap o' Rushes made the gruel. And when she had made it, she slipped the ring into it on the sly before the cook took it upstairs.

The young man drank it and then he saw the ring at the bottom.

"Send for the cook," says he.

So up she comes.

"Who made this gruel here?" says he.

"I did," said the cook, for she was frightened.

"No you didn't," says he. "Say who did it, and you shan't be harmed."

"Well, then, 'twas Cap o' Rushes," says she.

"Send Cap o' Rushes here," says he.

So Cap o' Rushes came.

"Did you make my gruel?" says he.

"Yes, I did," says she.

"Where did you get this ring?" says he.

"From him that gave it me," says she.

"Who are you, then?" says the young man.

"I'll show you," says she. And she took off her cap o' rushes, and there she was in her beautiful clothes.

Well, the master's son got well very soon, and they were to be married in a little time. It was to be a very grand wedding, and every one was asked far and near. And Cap o' Rushes's father was asked. But she never told anybody who she was.

Before the wedding, she went to the cook, and says she:

"I want you to dress every dish without a bit of salt."

"That'll taste nasty," says the cook.

"That doesn't matter," says she.

"Very well," says the cook.

Well, the wedding day came, and they were married. And after they were married, all the company sat down to the dinner. When they began to eat the meat, it was so tasteless they couldn't eat it. But Cap o' Rushes's father tried first one dish and then another, and then he burst out crying.

"What is the matter?" said the master's son to him.

"Oh!" says he, "I had a daughter. And I asked her how much she loved me. And she said 'As much as fresh meat loves salt.' And I turned her from my door, for I thought she didn't love me. And now I see she loved me best of all. And she may be dead for ought I know."

"No, father, here she is!" said Cap o' Rushes. And she goes up to him and puts her arms round him.

And so they were all happily ever after.

## from Anonymous, *The True Chronicle History of King Leir and his Three Daughters*[1] (1605)

This anonymous play was for Shakespeare an important source. The version that has come down to us (excerpts from which are included below) is that published in 1605 with the description "as it hath bene divers and sundry times lately acted."

### ACT 1, SCENE 1

*(Enter King Leir and Nobles.)*

LEIR.    Thus to our grief the obsequies[2] performed
    Of our (too late) deceast and dearest Queen,
    Whose soul I hope, possest of heavenly joys,
    Doth ride in triumph 'mongst the Cherubins;
    Let us request your grave advice, my Lords,
    For the disposing of our princely daughters,

---

1    *The True ... Daughters*    Spelling has been largely modernized for this edition by Laura Buzzard of Broadview Press. This text copyright Broadview Press, 2010.

2    *obsequies*    Acts of respect.

For whom our care is specially employed,
As nature bindeth to advance their states,
In royal marriage with some princely mates:
For wanting° now their mother's good advice,                    *lacking*
Under whose government they have received
A perfit° pattern of a virtuous life:                           *perfect*
Lest as it were a ship without a stern,
Or silly sheep without a Pastor's care;
Although our selves do dearly tender them,[1]
Yet are we ignorant of their affairs:
For fathers best do know to govern sons;
But daughters' steps the mother's counsel turns.
A son we want for to succeed our Crown,
And course of time hath cancellèd the date
Of further issue from our withered loins:
One foot already hangeth in the grave,
And age hath made deep furrows in my face:
The world of me, I of the world am weary,
And I would fain resign these earthly cares,
And think upon the welfare of my soul:
Which by no better means may be effected,
Than by resigning up[2] the Crown from me,
In equal dowry to my daughters three.

SKALLIGER.   A worthy care, my Liege, which well declares,
The zeal you bear unto our *quondam*[3] Queen:
And since your Grace hath licensed me to speak,
I censure° thus; Your Majesty knowing well,    *assess the matter*
What several suitors your princely daughters have,
To make them each a Joynter° more or less,              *joint heir*
As is their worth, to them that love profess.

LEIR.   No more, no less, but even all alike,
My zeal is fixt, all fashioned in one mold:
Wherefore unpartial shall my censure° be               *judgement*
Both old and young shall have alike for me.

---

1   *tender them*   Feel tenderly towards them.
2   *resigning up*   I.e., giving up.
3   *quondam*   Latin: former.

NOBLE.   My gracious Lord, I heartily do wish,
    That God had lent you an heir indubitate,°       *undisputed*
    Which might have set upon your royàl throne,
    When fates should loose the prison of your life,
    By whose succession all this doubt might cease;
    And as by you, by him we might have peace.
    But after-wishes ever come too late,
    And nothing can revoke the course of fate:
    Wherefore, my Liege, my censure deems it best,
    To match them with some of your neighbour Kings,
    Bord'ring within the bounds of Albion,
    By whose united friendship, this our state
    May be protected 'gainst all foreign hate.
LEIR.   Herein, my Lords, your wishes sort° with mine,     *agree*
    And mine (I hope) do sort with heavenly powers:
    For at this instant two near neighbouring Kings
    Of Cornwall and of Cambria, motion love
    To my two daughters, Gonorill and Ragan.
    My youngest daughter, fair Cordella, vows
    No liking to a Monarch, unless love allows.
    She is solicited by diverse Peers;
    But none of them her partial fancy hears.
    Yet, if my policy may her beguile,
    I'll match her to some king within this Isle,
    And so establish such a perfit peace,
    As fortune's force shall ne'er prevail to cease.
PERILLUS.   Of us & ours, your gracious care, my Lord,
    Deserves an everlasting memory,
    To be enrolled in Chronicles of fame,
    By never-dying perpetuity:
    Yet to become so provident a Prince,
    Lose not the title of a loving father:
    Do not force love, where fancy cannot dwell,
    Lest streams, being stopt, above the banks do swell.
LEIR.   I am resolved, and even now my mind
    Doth meditate a sudden stratagem,
    To try° which of my daughters loves me best:     *test*
    Which till I know, I cannot be in rest.

This granted, when they jointly shall contend,
Each to exceed the other in their love:
Then at the vantage¹ will I take Cordella,
Even as she doth protest she loves me best,
I'll say, "Then daughter, grant me one request,
To show thou lovest me as thy sisters do,
Accept a husband, whom my self will woo."
This said, she cannot well deny my suit,°                    request
Although (poor soul) her senses will be mute:
Then I will triumph in my policy,
And match her with a King of Brittany.
SKALLIGER.   I'll to them before, and bewray your secrecy.²
PERILLUS.   Thus fathers think their children to beguile,
And oftentimes themselves do first repent,
When heavenly powers do frustrate their intent.

(*Exeunt.*)

## ACT 1, SCENE 3

(*Enter Leir and Perillus.*)

LEIR.   Perillus, go seek my daughters,
Will them immediately come and speak with me.
PERILLUS.   I will, my gracious lord.

(*Exit.*)

LEIR.   Oh, what a combat feels my panting heart,
'Twixt children's love, and care of Common weale!³
How dear my daughters are unto my soul,
None knows, but he that knows my thoughts & secret
      deeds.
Ah, little do they know the dear regard,

---

1   *at the vantage* From a position of advantage.
2   *bewray your secrecy* I.e., divulge to them what you want to ask.
3   *Common weale* The prosperity of the state.

Wherein I hold their future state to come:
When they securely sleep on beds of down,
These agèd eyes do watch for° their behalf:                    *on*
While they like wantons sport in youthful toys,
This throbbing heart is pierced with dire annoys.°   *disturbances*
As doth the sun exceed the smallest star,
So much the father's love exceeds the child's.
Yet my complaints are causeless for the world
Affords not children more conformable:
And yet, me thinks, my mind presageth° still  *has presentiments*
I know not what; and yet I fear some ill.

(*Enter Perillus, with the three daughters.*)

Well, here my daughters come: I have found out
A present means to rid me of this doubt.
GONORILL.   Our royal Lord and father, in all duty,
We come to know the tenor of your will,
Why you so hastily have sent for us?
LEIR.   Dear Gonorill, kind Ragan, sweet Cordella,
Ye flourishing branches of a kingly stock,
Sprung from a tree that once did flourish green,
Whose blossoms now are nipt with Winter's frost,
And pale grim death doth wait upon my steps,
and summons me unto his next Assizes.[1]
Therefore, dear daughters, as ye tender the safety
Of him that was the cause of your first being,
Resolve a doubt which much molests my mind,
Which of you three to me would prove most kind;
Which loves me most, and which at my request
Will soonest yield unto their father's hest.°             *bidding*
GONORILL.   I hope, my gracious father makes no doubt
Of any of his daughters' love to him:
Yet for my part, to show my zeal to you,
Which cannot be in windy words rehearst,
I prize° my love to you at such a rate,                       *value*

---

1   *Assizes*   I.e., court of judgement.

I think my life inferior to my love.
Should you enjoin me for to tie a millstone
About my neck, and leap into the Sea,
At your command I willingly would do it:
Yea, for to do you good, I would ascend
The highest turret in all Brittany,
And from the top leap headlong to the ground:
Nay, more, should you appoint me for to marry
The meanest vassal in the spacious world,
Without reply° I would accomplish it:                         *question*
In brief, command what ever you desire,
And if I fail, no favour I require.

LEIR.   Oh, how thy words revive my dying soul!

CORDELLA.   Oh, how I do abhor this flattery!

LEIR.   But what sayeth Ragan to her father's will?

RAGAN.   O, that my simple utterance could suffice,
To tell the true intention of my heart,
Which burns in zeal of duty to your grace,
And never can be quench'd, but° by desire                     *except*
To show the same in outward forwardness.
Oh, that there were some other maid that durst°              *dared*
But make a challenge of her love with me;
I'd make her soon confess she never loved
Her father half so well as I do you.
I then, my deeds should prove in plainer case,
How much my zeal aboundeth to your grace:
But for them all, let this one mean° suffice,                *way*
To ratify my love before your eyes:
I have right noble suitors to my love,
No worse than Kings, and happ'ly I love one:
Yet, would you have me make my choice anew,
I'd bridle fancy,¹ and be ruled by you.

LEIR.   Did never Philomel² sing so sweet a note.

CORDELLA.   Did never flatterer tell so false a tale.

---

1   *bridle fancy*   Restrain [my own] impulses.
2   *Philomel*   A figure of Greek mythology who, in many versions of her story, was trans-
     formed into a nightingale.

LEIR.   Speak now, Cordella, make my joys at full,
    And drop down nectar from thy honey lips.
CORDELLA.   I cannot paint my duty forth in words,
    I hope my deeds shall make report for me:
    But look what love the child doth owe the father,
    The same to you I bear, my gracious Lord.
GONORILL.   Here is an answer answerless indeed:
    Were you my daughter, I should scarcely brook° it.    *tolerate*
RAGAN.   Dost thou not blush, proud Peacock as thou art,
    To make our father such a slight reply?
LEIR.   Why how now, Minion, are you grown so proud?
    Doth our dear love make you thus peremptory?
    What, is your love become so small to us,
    As that you scorn to tell us what it is?
    Do you love us, as every child doth love
    Their father? True indeed, as some
    Who by disobedience short° their fathers' day    *shorten*
    And so would you; some are so father-sick,
    That they make means to rid them from the world;
    And so would you: some are indifferent,
    Whether their aged parents live or die;
    And so are you. But, didst thou know, proud girl,
    What care I had to foster thee to this,
    Ah, then thou wouldst say as thy sisters do:
    "Our life is less than love we owe to you."
CORDELLA.   Dear father, do not so mistake my words,
    Nor my plain meaning be misconstrued;
    My tongue was never used to flattery.
GONORILL.   You were not best say I flatter: if you do,
    My deeds shall show, I flatter not with you.
    I love my father better than thou canst.
CORDELLA.   The praise were great, spoke from another's mouth:
    But it should seem your neighbours dwell far off.
RAGAN.   Nay, here is one, that will confirm as much
    As she hath said, both for myself and her.
    I say, thou dost not wish my father's good.
CORDELLA.   Dear father—
LEIR.   Peace, bastard Imp, no issue° of King Leir,    *offspring*

I will not hear thee speak one tittle more.
Call not me father, if thou love thy life,
Nor these thy sisters once presume to name:
Look for no help henceforth from me or mine;
Shift as thou wilt, and trust unto thy self:
My Kingdom will I equally divide
'Twixt thy two sisters to their royàl dower,
And will bestow them worthy their desèrts:[1]
This done, because thou shalt not have the hope,
To have a child's part in the time to come,
I presently will dispossess my self,
And set up these upon my princely throne.
GONORILL.    I ever thought that pride would have a fall.
RAGAN.    Plain dealing, sister: your beauty is so sheen,°    *bright*
You need no dowry, to make you be a Queen.

(*Exeunt Leir, Gonorill, Ragan.*)


CORDELLA.    Now whither, poor forsaken, shall I go,
When mine own sisters triumph in my woe?
But unto him which doth protect the just,
In him will poor Cordella put her trust.
These hands shall labour, for to get my
spending,°                                                                *earn a living*
And so I'll live until my days have ending.
PERILLUS.    Oh, how I grieve, to see my lord thus fond,°    *foolish*
To dote so much upon vain flattering words.
Ah, if he but with good advice had weighed,
The hidden tenure of her humble speech,
Reason to rage should not have given place,
Nor poor Cordella suffer such disgrace.

(*Exit.*)

---

1    *their desèrts*    What they deserve.

## ACT 5, Scene 32

(*Alarms and excursions, then sound victory.*)

(*Enter Leir, Perillus, King, Cordella, and Mumford.*)

KING.    Thanks be to God, your foes are overcome,
And you again possessèd of your right.
LEIR.    First to the heavens, next, thanks to you, my son,
By whose good means I repossess the same:[1]
Which if it please you to accept your self,
With all my heart I will resign to you:
For it is yours by right, and none of mine.
First, have you raised, at your own charge, a power
Of valiant soldiers; (this comes all from you)
Next have you ventured your own person's scathe.[2]
And lastly, (worthy Gallia never stand)
My kingly title I by thee have gained.
KING.    Thank heavens, not me, my zeal to you is such,
Command my utmost, I will never grutch.[3]
CORDELLA.    He that with all kind love entreats his Queen,
Will not be to her father unkind seen.
LEIR.    Ah, my Cordella, now I call to mind,
The modest answer, which I took unkind:
But now I see, I am not whit beguiled,
Thou lovedst me dearly, and as ought a child.
And thou (Perillus) partner once in woe,
Thee to requite, the best I can, I'll do.
Yet all I can, I, were it ne'er so much,
Were not sufficient, thy true love is such.
Thanks (worthy, Mumford) to thee last of all,
Not greeted last, 'cause thy desèrt was small;
No, thou hast lion-like laid on° today,          *fought*
Chasing the Cornwall King and Cambria;

---

1    *the same*  I.e., the right to kingship.
2    *ventured ... scathe*  Put yourself at risk of harm.
3    *Command ... grutch*  However much you demand of me, I will not complain.

Who with my daughters, daughters did I say?
To save their lives, the fugitives did play.
Come, son and daughter, who did me advance,
Repose with me awhile, and then for France.

(*Sound drums and trumpets. Exeunt.*)

## from Raphael Holinshed, *The Chronicles of England, Scotland, and Ireland*[1] (1577, 1587)

Holinshed's *Chronicles* was the result of an ambitious project to survey the history of the British Isles in more breadth and detail than any other work available at the time. In addition to writing the history of England portion himself, Holinshed acted as general editor, compiling the work of several contributors drawing from a wide range of earlier sources. The resulting text included, according to modern critical standards, legitimate history alongside unsubstantiated folklore; the *Chronicles* remained useful as a source of ideas for writers and artists long after it was no longer considered factually accurate.

Shakespeare used Holinshed's *Chronicles* as a reference in writing his English history plays, and it provided inspiration for *Macbeth*, *Cymbeline*, and, of course, *King Lear*. The following selection is from the revised and expanded 1587 edition, which is probably the version that Shakespeare read.

from THE FIFTH CHAPTER

Leir the son of Baldud was admitted ruler over the Britons, in the year of the world 3105,[2] at what time Joas reigned in Judea. This Leir was a prince of right noble demeanour, governing his land and subjects in great wealth. He made the town of Caerlier now called Leicester, which standeth upon the river of Sore. It is written that he had by his wife three daughters without other

---

1   *The Chronicles ... Ireland*   Spelling has been largely modernized for this edition by Laura Buzzard of Broadview Press; this modernized text is copyright Broadview Press, 2010.

2   *year ... 3105*   3105 years since creation, c. 872 BCE.

issue, whose names were Gonorilla, Regan, and Cordeilla, which daughters he greatly loved, but specially Cordeilla the youngest far above the two elder. When this Leir therefore was come to great years, & began to wax unwieldy through age, he thought to understand the affections of his daughters towards him, and prefer her whom he best loved, to the succession over the kingdom. Whereupon he first asked Gonorilla the eldest, how well she loved him: who calling her gods to record, protested that she "loved him more than her own life, which by right and reason should be most dear unto her." With which answer the father being well pleased, turned to the second, and demanded of her how well she loved him: who answered (confirming her sayings with great oaths) that she loved him "more than tongue could express, and far above all other creatures of the world."

Then he called his youngest daughter Cordeilla before him, and asked of her what account she made of him, unto whom she made this answer as followeth: "Knowing the great love and fatherly zeal that you have always borne towards me (for the which I may not answereth you otherwise than I think and as my conscience leadeth me) I protest unto you, that I have loved you ever, and will continually (while I live) love you as my natural father. And if you would more understand of the love I bear you, ascertain your self, that so much as you have, so much you are worth, and so much I love you, and no more." The father being nothing content with this answer, married his two eldest daughters, the one unto Henninus the duke of Cornewall, and the other unto Maglanus the duke of Albania,[1] betwixt whom he willed and ordained that his land should be divided after his death, and the one half thereof immediately should be assigned to them in hand: but for the third daughter Cordeilla he reserved nothing.

Nevertheless it fortuned[2] that one of the princes of Gallia (which now is called France) whose name was Aganippus, hearing of the beauty, womanhood, and good conditions of the said Cordeilla, desired to have her in marriage, and sent over to her father, requiring that he might have her to wife: to whom answer

---

1   *Albania* Albany.
2   *fortuned* Came by chance.

was made that he might have his daughter, but as for any dower he could have none, for all was promised and assured to her other sisters already. Aganippus notwithstanding this answer of denial to receive any thing by way of dower with Cordeilla, took her to wife, only moved thereto (I say) for respect of her person and amiable virtues. This Aganippus was one of the twelve kings that ruled Gallia in those days, as in the British history it is recorded. But to proceed.

After that Leir was fallen into age, the two dukes that had married his two eldest daughters, thinking it long yer[1] the government of the land did come to their hands, arose against him in armour, and reft[2] from him the governance of the land, upon conditions to be continued for term of life: by the which he was put to his portion, that is to live after a rate assigned to him for the maintenance of his estate, which in process of time[3] was diminished as well by Maglanus as by Henninus. But the greatest grief that Leir took, was to see the unkindness of his daughters, which seemed to think that all was too much which their father had, the same being never so little: in so much that going from the one to the other, he was brought to that misery, that scarcely would they allow him one servant to wait upon him.

In the end, such was the unkindness, or (as I may say) the unnaturalness which he found in his two daughters, notwithstanding their fair and pleasant words uttered in time past, that being constrained of necessity, he fled the land, & sailed into Gallia, there to seek some comfort of his youngest daughter Cordeilla, whom before time he hated. The lady Cordeilla hearing that he was arrived in poor estate, she first sent to him privily[4] a certain sum of money to apparel himself withal, and to retain a certain number of servants that might wait on him in honourable wise, as appertained to the estate which he had borne: and then so accompanied, she appointed him to come to the court, which he did, and was so joyfully, honourably, and lovingly received, both by his son in law Aganippus, and also by his daughter Cordeilla,

---

1  *thinking ... yer*  I.e., considering it too long to wait until.
2  *reft*  Took by force.
3  *in process of time*  As time passed.
4  *privily*  Secretly.

that his heart was greatly comforted: for he was no less honoured, than if he had been king of the whole country himself.

Now when he had informed his son in law and his daughter in what sort he had been used by his other daughters, Aganippus caused a mighty army to be put in readiness, and likewise a great navy of ships to be rigged, to pass over into Britaine with Leir his father in law, to see him again restored to his kingdom. It was accorded, that Cordeilla should also go with him to take possession of the land, the which he promised to leave unto her, as the rightful inheritor after his decease, notwithstanding any former grant made to her sisters or their husbands in any manner of wise.

Hereupon, when this army and navy of ships were ready, Leir and his daughter Cordeilla with her husband took the sea, and arriving in Britaine, fought with their enemies, and discomfited[1] them in battle, in the which Maglanus and Henninus were slain: and then was Leir restored to his kingdom, which he ruled after this by the space of two years, and then died, forty years after he first began to reign. His body was buried at Leicester in a vault under the channel of the river of Sore beneath the town.

from THE SIXTH CHAPTER

*The gynarchy[2] of queen Cordeilla, how she was vanquished, of her imprisonment and self-murder: the contention between Cunedag and Margan nephews for government, and the evil end thereof.*

Cordeilla the youngest daughter of Leir was admitted Q. and supreme governess of Britaine, in the year of the world 3155, before the building of Rome 54,[3] Uzia then reigning in Juda, and Jeroboam over Israell. This Cordeilla after her father's decease ruled the land of Britaine right worthily during the space of five years, in which mean time her husband died, and then about the end of those five years, her two nephews Margan and Cunedag, sons to her aforesaid sisters, disdaining to be under the government

---

1   *discomfited*   Overthrew.
2   *gynarchy*   Government by a woman.
3   *before ... 54*   54 years before the building of Rome, c. 822 BCE.

of a woman, levied war against her, and destroyed a great part of the land, and finally took her prisoner, and laid her fast in ward,[1] wherewith she took such grief, being a woman of manly courage, and despairing to recover liberty, there she slew herself, when she had reigned (as before is mentioned) the term of five years.

## from Edmund Spenser, *The Faerie Queene* (1590)

Shakespeare was certainly familiar with the work of Edmund Spenser (1552-99), and he borrows details from Spenser's interpretation of the Lear story, such as Cordelia's death by hanging, that are not present in other contemporary versions. This story is a small detail in Spenser's lengthy Protestant epic *The Faerie Queene*, which allegorizes the reign of Elizabeth I and explores the nature of the virtues. Spenser completed six of the twelve books he originally intended, and each book focuses on a single virtue personified by a heroic knight; in Book 2, the featured hero is Sir Guyon, Knight of Temperance. Canto 10 of Book 2, from which the following excerpt is taken, digresses from the plot of Sir Guyon's adventures to recount what Prince Arthur reads in a volume of British history.

from BOOK 2, CANTO 10

27

Next him[2] king Leyr in happie peace long raind,
  But had no issue male° him to succeed,             *sons*
  But three faire daughters, which were well
    uptraind,°                             *brought up*
In all that seemed fit for kingly seed:
Mongst whom his realme he equally decreed
To have divided. Tho when feeble age
Nigh to his utmost date[3] he saw proceed,
  He cald his daughters; and with speeches sage
Inquyrd, which of them most did love her parentage.

---

1  *fast ... ward*  Securely in prison.
2  *him*  King Bladud, the subject of the previous stanza.
3  *his utmost date*  The end of his lifespan.

## 28

The eldest Gonorill gan° to protest,                                    *began*
    That she much more then° her owne life him lov'd:         *than*
    And Regan greater love to him profest,
    Then all the world, when ever it were proov'd;[1]
    But Cordeill said she lov'd him, as behoov'd:
Whose simple answere, wanting colours faire
    To paint it forth, him to displeasance° moov'd,         *displeasure*
    That in his crowne he counted her no haire,°                 *heir*
But twixt the other twaine his kingdome whole did shaire.

## 29

So wedded th'one to Maglan king of Scots,
    And th'other to the king of Cambria,
    And twixt them shayrd his realme by equall lots:
    But without dowre° the wise Cordelia                              *dowry*
    Was sent to Aganip of Celtica.[2]
Their aged Syre, thus eased of his crowne,
    A private life led in Albania,°                                        *Albany*
    With Gonorill, long had in great renowne,
That nought him griev'd to bene from rule deposed downe.[3]

But true it is, that when the oyle is spent,
    The light goes out, and weeke° is throwne away;         *wick*
    So when he had resigned his regiment,
    His daughter gan° despise his drouping day,              *began to*
    And wearie waxe of his continuall stay.
Tho° to his daughter Rigan he repayrd,                              *So*
    Who him at first well used every way;
    But when of his departure she despayrd,°               *lost hope*
Her bountie she abated, and his cheare empayrd.

---

1   *when ... proov'd*   As would be seen if it were put to the test.
2   *Aganip of Celtica*   I.e., in France.
3   *long ... downe*   I.e., having possessed the crown for a long time, he was not upset to no longer rule.

The wretched man gan then avise[1] too late,
  That love is not, where most it is profest,
  Too truely tryde in his extreamest state;
  At last resolv'd likewise to prove the rest,[2]
  He to Cordelia him selfe addrest,
  Who with entire affection him receav'd,
  As for her Syre and king her° seemed best;                    *to her*
  And after all an army strong she leav'd,°                      *levied*
To war on those, which him had of his realme bereav'd.

## 32

So to his crowne she him restor'd againe,
  In which he dyde, made ripe for death by eld,°               *old age*
  And after wild,° it should to her remaine:                   *willed*
  Who peaceably the same long time did weld:[3]
  And all men's harts in dew obedience held:
  Till that her sisters children, woxen° strong                *grown*
  Through proud ambition, against her rebeld,
  And overcommen kept[4] in prison long,
Till wearie of that wretched life, her selfe she hong.°        *hanged*

### The Annesley Case

This contemporary scandal paralleled the Lear story and likely
revived interest in it; we do not know the extent to which it may
have provided some imaginative spark for Shakespeare. The Annesley case was a dispute over the property and mental health of
the aging Brian Annesley, who, like Lear, had three daughters:
Grace, Christian, and—as a noteworthy coincidence—a youngest
daughter named Cordell, who was his favourite. Grace wanted
her father declared insane, arguing that he was too senile to care
for himself or manage his property. Cordell defended her father's
reputation against her sister and was successful; Annesley died

---

1  *gan then avise*  Came to perceive.
2  *prove the rest*  Test his remaining daughter.
3  *weld*  Wield [the crown].
4  *overcommen kept*  I.e., overcome, Cordelia was kept.

without being declared a lunatic, and his will, which left most of his estate to her, was upheld.

*Letter from Sir John Wildegos and others to Lord Cecil (18 October 1603)*

According to your letter of the 12<sup>th</sup> of this present, we repaired unto the house of Bryan Annesley, of Lee, in the county of Kent, and finding him fallen into such imperfection and distemperature of mind and memory, as we thought him thereby become altogether unfit to govern himself or his estate, we endeavoured to take a perfect inventory of such goods and chattels as he possessed in and about his house. But Mrs. Cordall, his daughter, who during the time of all his infirmity hath taken upon her government of him and his affairs, refuseth to suffer any inventory to be taken, until such time as she hath had conference with her friends, by reason whereof we could proceed no farther in the execution of your letter.

*Letter from Sir Thomas Walsingham and others to the Same (23 October 1603)*

According to the authority given us by your letters, we repaired to the house of Mr. Bryan Annesley, and there in the presence of his two daughters, Lady Wildgosse and Mrs. Cordell Annesley, have sealed up all such chests and trunks of evidence, and other things of value, as they showed us to be his. We are informed that he holdeth diverse things by lease, which for not payment of the rent might be in danger to be forfeited. We have therefore requested Sir James Croftes, whom your lordship hath associated to us in this business, to take care of the payment of such rents as are reserved upon any lease made to the said Mr. Annesley and also for the receipts of rents due to him. As touching the government of his person and family, though by nature his two daughters may seem fittest to perform this duty, yet respecting the absence of Sir John Wildgosse at this time, and the present emulation between the two gentlewomen we have referred the determination thereof to your lordship.

*Letter from Cordell Annesley to Lord Cecil (23 October 1603)*

I most humbly thank you for the sundry letters that it hath pleased you to direct unto gentlemen of worship in these parts, requesting them to take into their custodies the person and estate of my poor aged and daily dying father: But that course so honourable and good for all parties, intended by your Lo., will by no means satisfy Sr. John Willgosse, nor can any course else, unless he may have him begged for a Lunatic, whose many years service to our late dread Sovereign Mistress and native country deserved a better agnomination,[1] than at his last gasp to be recorded and registered a Lunatic, yet find no means to avoid so great an infamy and endless blemish to and our posterity, unless it shall please your Lo. of your honourable disposition, if he must needs be accompted[2] a Lunatic, to bestow him upon Sir James Croft, who out of the love he bare unto him in his more happier days, and for the good he wisheth unto us his children, is contented upon entreaty to undergo the burden and care of him and his estate, without intendment to make one penny benefit to himself by any goods of his, or ought that may descend to us his children, as also to prevent any record of Lunacy that may be procured hereafter.

*Epitaph from a slab let in the wall of what was formerly the tower of the church at Lee, Kent*

Here lieth buried the bodies of Byran Anslye Esquier, late of Lee in the county of Kent, and Audry his wife, the only daughter of Robert Turell, of Burbrocke in the county of Essex Esquier. He had issue by her one son and three daughters, Bryan who died without issue; Grace married to Sir John Wilgoose, Knight; Christian married to the Lord Sands; and Cordell married to Sir William Hervey, Knight. The said Bryan the father died on the 10th of July 1604; he served Queene Elizabeth as one of the band of Gentlemen Pensioners to her Majesty the space of 30 years. The said Awdry died on the 25th of November 1591. Cordell, the

---

1   *agnomination*   I.e., reputation.
2   *accompted*   Accounted.

youngest daughter, at her own proper cost and charges, in further testimony of her dutiful love unto her father and mother, caused this monument to be erected for the perpetual memory of their names against the ingrateful nature of oblivious time.

"*Nec primus, nec ultimus, multi ante,*
*Cesserunt, et omnes sequetitur.*"[1]

## from Samuel Harsnett, *A Declaration of Egregious Popish Impostures*[2] (1603)

In the eighteenth century Lewis Theobald noted the connection between Harsnett's *Declaration* and *King Lear*; since then it has been accepted that Harsnett's work is the source for the names of the devils mentioned by Poor Tom (Act 3, Scene 6), many of which are included in the following excerpt, and that Shakespeare probably also drew on it for the "exorcism" of Gloucester by Edgar in Act 4, Scene 1. A more general influence on Shakespeare's language is also evident; for instance, the discussion of Edgar's vices as embodied by animals in Act 3, Scene 4 echoes the description found below of a parade of vices exiting a victim of possession. Harsnett's work attacks religious superstition through the ironic portrayal of several exorcisms, all of which Harsnett claimed were based on real life accounts; Stephen Greenblatt has suggested that the tone of the text influenced Shakespeare's presentation in *Lear* of "ritual and beliefs that are no longer efficacious, that have been emptied out" (See Greenblatt's *Shakespeare and the Exorcists,* 1985).

Harsnett was chaplain to the Bishop of London at the time his book was published, and as licenser of books for printing he exercised considerable authority. Shortly after the appearance of his *Declaration*, he was appointed Archdeacon of Essex; he was later elected Archbishop of York.

---

1   *Nec ... sequetitur*   Latin: Neither the first nor the last [am I]; many before / Have ceased to exist, and all will follow.
2   *A Declaration ... Impostures*   Spelling and punctuation have been largely modernized for this edition by Laura Buzzard of Broadview Press. This text copyright Broadview Press, 2010.

... Hiaclito[1] may not be slipped over without your observation: for he scorning a great while (as the author[2] saith) to tell his name, at last he answered most proudly, "my name is Hiaclito, a prince & monarch of the world." And being asked by the exorcist what fellows he had with him, he said that he had no fellows, but two men, and an urchin boy. It was little beseeming[3] his state (I wis[4]) being so mighty a monarch, to come into our coasts so scurvily attended, except he came to see fashions[5] in England, and so made himself private till the exorcist revealed him: or else that he was of the new Court cut,[6] affecting no other train[7] than two crazy fellows, and an urchin butterfly boy....

Sara Williams had in her, at a bare word, all the devils in hell. The exorcist asks Maho, Sara's devil, what company he had with him, and the devil makes no bones, but tells him in flat terms, "all the devils in hell." Here was a goodly fat *otium*[8] this meanwhile in hell: the poor souls there had good leave to play: such a day was never seen since hell was hell: not a doorkeeper left, but all must go a-maying[9] to poor Sara's house. It was not kindly done of the devils, to leave the poor souls behind, especially going to make merry amongst their friends. But what if the souls had fallen a madding, or maying, as fast as the devils,[10] and had gone a roaming abroad amongst their good friends, had not this (trow[11] we) made a pretty piece of work in hell?

And if I miss not my marks, this *Dictator Modu*[12] saith, he had been in Sara by the space of two years, then so long hell was clear,

---

1  *Hiaclito*  One from a list of "puny spirits" mentioned in a previous passage.
2  *the author*  The writer of the account from which Harsnett claims to have taken his information.
3  *beseeming*  Fit for.
4  *wis*  Know.
5  *to see fashions*  To learn the customs.
6  *cut*  Style.
7  *affecting ... train*  Choosing to have no other attendants.
8  *otium*  Latin: time of leisure. The narrator is suggesting that all the devils have left hell to be inside Sara Williams, leaving the souls in hell free to do what they like.
9  *maying*  Celebration involving dancing or flower-gathering; associated with the pagan festivities of May Day. The devils are throwing a party inside Sara.
10  *fallen ... devils*  I.e., become overexcited or gone to celebrate like the devils did.
11  *trow*  Think.
12  *Dictator Modu*  Latin: Magistrate of Commotion.

and had not a devil to cast at a mad dog. And sooth, I cannot much blame the devils for staying so long abroad; they had taken up an inn much sweeter than hell, and a hostess that wanted neither wit, nor mirth, to give them kind welcome.

Here, if you please, you may take a survey of the whole regiment of hell: at least the chief leaders and officers, as we find them enrolled by their names....

Frateretto, Fliberdigibbet, Hoberdidance, Tocobatto were four devils of the round, or Morris,[1] whom Sara in her fits,[2] tuned together, in measure and sweet cadence. And lest you should conceive that the devils had no music in hell, especially that they would go a-maying without their music, the fiddler comes in with his tabor[3] & pipe, and a whole Morris[4] after him, with motley visards[5] for their better grace. These four had forty assistants under them, as themselves do confess....

[After much further discussion of the nature of the spirits and their effects on the possessed, "the admirable final act of expelling the devils" is described, as well as the forms the devils take as they leave their victims.]

The first devil that was disseised[6] was Smolkin, Trayford's spirit, whom Sara espied (saith the *Miraclist*[7]) to go out at Trayford's right ear in the form of a mouse, and it made the poor wench at the sight of the mouse almost out of her wits. The next devil dispossessed was Hilcho at Uxbridge, who appeared (saith our author) to the possessed parties at his going out like a flame of fire, and lay glowing in the fire at Trayford's sight, till he had a new charge.[8] The third was Hoberdidance, Sara's dancing devil, who appeared to the patient like a whirlwind, turning round like

---

1   *devils ... Morris*   Morris dancing devils; Morris dancing was an important part of May Day celebrations.
2   *whom ... fits*   Who fit inside Sara.
3   *tabor*   A small drum used to accompany oneself when playing a pipe.
4   *Morris*   Troupe of Morris dancers.
5   *visards*   Disguises.
6   *disseised*   Ousted.
7   *the Miraclist*   Book of Miracles from which Harsnett presumably drew his account.
8   *till ... charge*   I.e., until he found someone else to possess.

a flame of fire, & his voice was heard by a cook as he flew over the larder. Captain Filpot went his way in the likeness of a smoke, turning round, and so took his way up into the chimney. Lusty Dick (as seems) did slip a button in one of his turns above ground, for he went out in a foul unsavory stench. Delicat and Lusty Jolly Jenkin went out, one whirling like a snake, the other in a vapor not very sweet. Lusty Huffcappe went out in the likeness of a cat. Killico, Hob, and the third Anonymous, all Captains, went out in a wind. Purre went out in a little whirlwind, Frateretto in a smoke.

Master Maynie had in him (as you have heard) the Master-devils of the seven deadly sins, and therefore his devils went out in the form of those creatures that have nearest resemblance unto those sins: the spirit of Pride went out in the form of a peacock (forsooth); the spirit of Sloth in the likeness of an ass; the spirit of Envy in the similitude of a dog; the spirit of Gluttony in the form of a wolf....

# King Lear on Stage in the Seventeenth Century

## from Richard Johnson, "The Ballad of King Lear and his Three Daughters" (1620)

The following ballad was first printed in *The Golden Garland of Princely Pleasures and Delicate Delights*, a miscellany compiled by Richard Johnson and dated 1620. It was long thought to have been one of Shakespeare's sources. That notion has now been discredited; far more likely is that the ballad draws on recollections of the play in performance. In passages such as the descriptions of Lear's madness (particularly that found in the Quarto version) and of his death, the ballad follows the play where the play differs from other versions of the Lear story; it is thus plausible that the ballad describes how Richard Burbage played the role of Lear in early performances.

King Lear once rulèd in this land
    With princely power and peace;
And had all things with heart's content,
    That might his joys increase.
Amongst those gifts that nature gave,
    Three daughters fair had he,
So princely-seeming beautiful,
    As fairer could not be.

So on a time it pleased the king
    A question thus to move,
Which of his daughters to his grace
    Could show the dearest love:
"For to my age you bring content,"
    Quoth he, "then let me hear,
Which of you three in plighted troth[1]
    The kindest will appear."

---

1   *plighted troth*  Promised faithfulness.

To whom the eldest thus began;
    "Dear father mine," quoth she,
"Before your face, to do you good,
    My blood shall tendered be.
And for your sake my bleeding heart
    Shall here be cut in twain,
Ere that I see your rev'rend age
    The smallest grief sustain."

"And so will I," the second said;
    "Dear father, for your sake
The worst of all extremities
    I'll gently undertake,
And serve your highness night and day
    With diligence and love,
That sweet content and quietness
    Discomforts may remove."

"In doing so, you glad° my soul,"        *gladden*
    The agèd king replied;
"But what sayst thou, my youngest girl,
    How is thy love allied?"
"My love," quoth young Cordela then,
    "Which to your grace I owe,
Shall be the duty of a child,
    And that is all I'll show."

"And wilt thou show no more," quoth he,
    "Than doth thy duty bind?
I well perceive thy love is small,
    Whenas° no more I find.        *inasmuch as*
Henceforth I banish thee my court,
    Thou art no child of mine;
Nor any part of this my realm
    By favour shall be thine."

"Thy elder sisters' loves are more
　　Than well I can demand,
To whom I equally bestow
　　My kingdom and my land,
My pompal° state and all my goods,　　　　　　　　*splendid*
　　That lovingly I may
With those thy sisters be maintained
　　Until my dying day."

Thus flatt'ring speeches won renown
　　By these two sisters here;
The third had causeless banishment,
　　Yet was her love more dear:
For poor Cordela patiently
　　Went wand'ring up and down,
Unhelped, unpitied, gentle maid,
　　Through many an English town,

Until at last in famous France
　　She gentler fortunes found;
Though poor and bare,° yet she was deemed　　*without retainers*
　　The fairest on the ground:
Where when the king her virtues heard,
　　And this fair lady seen,
With full consent of all his court
　　He made his wife and queen.

Her father, old king Lear, this while,
　　With his two daughters stayed.
Forgetful of their promised loves,
　　Full soon the same denayed;°　　　　　　　　　*gave up*
And living in queen Ragan's court,
　　The elder of the twain,°　　　　　　　　　　　*two*
She took from him his chiefest means,
　　And most of all, his train.°　　　　　　　　　*attendants*

For whereas twenty men were wont
    To wait[1] with bended knee:
She gave allowance but to ten,
    And after scarce to three.
Nay, one she thought too much for him,
    So took she all away,
In hope that in her court, good king,
    He would no longer stay.

"Am I rewarded thus," quoth he,
    "In giving all I have
Unto my children, and to beg
    For what I lately gave?
I'll go unto my Gonorel;
    My second child, I know,
Will be more kind and pitiful
    And will relieve my woe."

Full fast he hies° then to her court;              *hastens*
    Where when she heard his moan
Returned him answer that she grieved
    That all his means were gone:
But no way could relieve his wants,
    Yet if that he would stay
Within her kitchen, he should have
    What scullions gave away.

When he had heard with bitter tears,
    He made his answer then,
"In what I did let me be made
    Example to all men.
I will return again," quoth he,
    "Unto my Ragan's court;
She will not use me thus, I hope,
    But in a kinder sort."[2]

---

1   *were ... wait*  Used to wait on him.
2   *She ... sort*  I.e., I hope that she will treat me better than Gonorel has.

Where when he came, she gave command
    To drive him thence away.
When he was well within her court
    She said he could not stay.
Then back again to Gonorel
    The woeful king did hie,
That in her kitchen he might have
    What scullion boys set by.

But there of that he was denied,
    Which she had promised late;
For once refusing, he should not
    Come after to her gate.
Thus twixt his daughters, for relief
    He wandered up and down;
Being glad to feed on beggars' food,
    That lately wore a crown.

And calling to remembrance then
    His youngest daughter's words,
That said the duty of a child
    Had all that love affords,
But doubting° to repair to her,                         *reluctant*
    Whom he had banished so,
Grew frantic mad, for in his mind
    He bore the wounds of woe:

Which made him rend his milk-white locks,
    And tresses from his head,
And all with blood bestain his cheeks,
    With age and honour spread.
To hills and woods and wat'ry founts
    He made his hourly moan,
Till hills and woods and senseless things,
    Did seem to sigh and groan.

E'en thus possessed with discontents,
    He passèd o'er to France,

In hope from fair Cordela there,
　　To find some gentler chance.
Most virtuous dame, where when she heard,
　　Of this her father's grief,
As duty bound, she quickly sent
　　Him comfort and relief.

And by a train of noble peers,
　　In brave and gallant sort,
She gave in charge he should be brought
　　To Aganippus'[1] court;
Her royàl king, whose noble mind
　　So freely gave consent
To muster up his knights at arms,
　　To fame and courage bent.

And so to England came with speed,
　　To repossess king Lear,
And drive his daughters from their thrones
　　By his Cordela dear.
Where she, true-hearted noble queen,
　　Was in the battle slain,
Yet he, good king, in his old days,
　　Possessed his crown again.

But when he heard Cordela dead,
　　Who died indeed for love
Of her dear father, in whose cause
　　She did this battle move,
He swooning fell upon her breast,
　　From whence he never parted,
But on her bosom left his life,
　　That° was so truly-hearted.　　　　　　　　*she who*

---

1 *Aganippus* The king of France is given this name in Holinshed and some other
　versions.

The lords and nobles when they saw
    The end of these events,
The other sisters unto death
    They doomèd by consents;°                      *consensus*
And being dead, their crowns were left
    Unto the next of kin.
Thus have you seen the fall of pride,
    And disobedient sin.

## from Nahum Tate, *The History of King Lear* (1681)

In 1642, during the English Civil War, the Puritan faction gained control of London and closed its theaters. In 1660, when the monarchy was restored to power and the theaters were reopened, London enjoyed a resurgence of interest in English drama, adapted to the tastes of the new period. Innovations in performance—including elaborate movable scenery, the use of the proscenium arch, and the casting of women instead of boys in the female roles—changed the theatergoing experience. The texts themselves were also altered; in addition to new plays, updated versions of old plays were popular, and writers assumed a free hand in reshaping the originals. One of the era's most popular productions was Poet Laureate Nahum Tate's version of *King Lear*, which held the stage for 150 years after its first performance in 1681, after the original had twice been revived unsuccessfully. The excerpts from Tate's *Lear* reprinted here give a sense of Tate's intentions and the ways in which he changed the original text. While in the parallel scene in Shakespeare's *Lear*, Cordelia is executed after she and Lear are captured, and Lear then dies of grief, here both characters live and see their kingdom restored. Tate also removed the role of the Fool from the play entirely and undercut the character of Cordelia by having her fall in love with Edgar at the opening of the action, so that she has less to lose in defying her father, and acts largely in the interests of her future husband. Tate's *Lear* affirms that, even in the face of enormous adversity, "truth and virtue shall succeed at last."

Sir,

You have a natural right to this piece, since by your advice I attempted the revival of it with alterations. Nothing but the power of your persuasions, and my zeal for all the remains of Shakespeare could have wrought me so bold an undertaking. I found that the new-modelling of this story would force me sometimes on the difficult task of making the chiefest persons speak something like their character, on matter whereof I had no ground in my author. Lear's real and Edgar's pretended madness have so much of extravagant nature (I know not how else to express it), as could never have started but from our Shakespeare's creating fancy. The images and language are so odd and surprising, and yet so agreeable and proper, that whilst we grant that none but Shakespeare could have formed such conceptions; yet we are satisfied that they were the only things in the world that ought to be said on those occasions. I found the whole to answer your account of it, a heap of jewels, unstrung, and unpolished; yet so dazzling in their disorder, that soon I perceived I had seized a treasure. 'Twas my good fortune to light on one expedient to rectify what was wanting in the regularity and probability of the tale, which was to run through the whole, as love betwixt Edgar and Cordelia, that never changed a word with each other in the original. This renders Cordelia's indifference, and her father's passion in the first scene, probable. It likewise gives countenance to Edgar's disguise, making that a generous design that was before a poor shift to save his life. The distress of the story is evidently heightened by it; and it particularly gave occasion of a new scene or two, of more success (perhaps) than merit. This method necessarily threw me on making the tale conclude in a success to the innocent distressed persons: otherwise I must have encumbered the stage with dead bodies, which conduct makes many tragedies conclude with unseasonable jests. Yet was I wracked with no small fears for so bold a change, till I found it well received by my audience; and if this will not satisfy the reader, I can produce an authority that questionless will. Neither is it of so trivial an undertaking to make a tragedy end happily, for 'tis more difficult to save than 'tis to kill:

the dagger and cup of poison are always in readiness; but to bring the action to the last extremity, and then by probable means to recover all, will require the art and judgement of a writer, and cost him many a pang in the performance.

I have one more thing to apologize for, which is that I have used less quaintness of expression even in the newest parts of this play. I confess, 'twas design in me, partly to comply with my author's style, to make the scenes of a piece, and partly to give it some resemblance of the time and persons here represented. This, Sir, I submit wholly to you, who are both a judge and master of style. Nature had exempted you before you went abroad from the morose saturnine[1] humour of our country, and you brought home the refinedness of travel without the affectation. Many faults I see in the following pages, and question not but you will discover more; yet I will presume so far on your friendship as to make the whole a present to you, and subscribe myself

Your obliged friend and humble servant,
N. Tate

## Prologue

Since by mistakes your best delights are made
(For e'en your wives can please in masquerade),
'Twere worth our while, to have drawn you in this day
By a new name to our old honest play;
But he that did this evening's treat prepare
Bluntly resolved before hand to declare
Your entertainment should be most old fare.
Yet hopes since in rich Shakespeare's soil it grew
'Twill relish yet, with those whose tastes are true,
And his ambition is to please a few.
If then this heap of flow'rs shall chance to wear
Fresh beauty in the order they now bear,
Even this Shakespeare's praise; each rustic knows
'Mongst plenteous flow'rs a garland to compose
Which strung by this coarse hand may fairer show

---

1 *saturnine* Gloomy.

But 'twas a power divine first made 'em grow,
Why should these scenes lie hid, in which we find
What may at once divert and teach the mind;
Morals were always proper for the stage,
But are ev'n necessary in this age.
Poets must take the churches' teaching trade,
Since priests their province of intrigue invade;
But we the worst in this exchange have got;
In vain our poets preach, whilst churchmen plot.

from ACT 5

(*Scene, a prison.*)

[...]

(*Kent brought in.*)

LEAR.   Who are you?
My eyes are none o' th' best, I'll tell you straight;
Oh Albany! Well, sir, we are your captives,
And you are come to see death pass upon us.
Why this delay? Or is 't your Highness' pleasure
To give us first the torture? Say ye so?
Why here's old Kent and I, as tough a pair
As e'er bore tyrant's stroke—but my Cordelia,
My poor Cordelia here, O pity!
ALBANY.   Take off their chains. Though injured Majesty,
The Wheel of Fortune now has made her circle,
and blessings yet stand 'twixt thy grave and thee.
LEAR.   Com'st though, inhumane Lord, to sooth us back
To a fool's paradise of hope, to make
Our doom more wretched? Go to,[1] we are too well
Acquainted with misfortune to be gulled°                      *deceived*
With lying hope; no, we will hope no more.
ALBANY.   I have a tale t'unfold so full of wonder

---

1  *Go to*  Come on.

As cannot meet an easy faith;
But by that Royal injured head 'tis true.
KENT.   What would your Highness?
ALBANY.   Know the noble Edgar
  Impeacht Lord Edmund since the fight, of treason,
  And dared him for the proof to fight combat,
  In which the gods confirmed his charge by conquest;
  I left ev'n now the traitor wounded mortally.
LEAR.   And whither ends this story?
ALBANY.   E'er they fought
  Lord Edgar gave into my hands this paper,
  A blacker scroll of treason, and of lust,
  Than can be found in the records of Hell;
  There, sacred sir, behold the characters
  Of Goneril, the worst of daughters, but
  More vicious wife.
CORDELIA.   Could there be yet addition to their guilt?
  What will not they that wrong a father do?
ALBANY.   Since then my injuries, Lear, fall in with thine:
  I have resolved the same redress for both.
KENT.   What says my Lord?
CORDELIA.   Speak, for me thought I heard
  The charming voice of a descending god.
ALBANY.   The troops by Edmund raised, I have disbanded;
  Those that remain are under my command.
  What comfort may be brought to cheer your age
  And heal your savage wrongs, shall be applied;
  For to your Majesty we do resign
  Your kingdom, save what part yourself conferred
  On us in marriage.
KENT.   Hear you that, my liege?
CORDELIA.   Then there are gods, and virtue is their care.
LEAR.   Is't possible?
  Let the spheres stop their course, the sun make halt,
  The winds be husht, the seas and fountains rest;
  All nature pause, and listen to the change.
  Where is my Kent, my Cajus?
KENT.   Here, my liege.

LEAR.    Why, I have news that will recall thy youth;
Ha! Didst thou hear't, or did th'inspiring gods
Whisper to me alone? Old Lear shall be
A king again.
KENT.    The Prince, that like a god has power, has said it.
LEAR.    Cordelia then shall be a queen, mark that:
Cordelia shall be queen; winds catch the sound
And bear it on your rosy wings to heaven.
Cordelia is a queen.


(*Re-enter Edgar with Gloucester.*)


ALBANY.    Look, Sir, where pious Edgar comes
Leading his eye-less father: O my liege!
His wondrous story will deserve your leisure:
What he has done and suffered for your sake,
What for the fair Cordelia's.
GLOUCESTER.    Where is my liege? Conduct me to his knees to
    hail
His second birth of empire; my dear Edgar
Has, with himself, revealed the King's blest restoration.
LEAR.    My poor dark Gloucester.
GLOUCESTER.    O let me kiss that once more sceptred hand!
LEAR.    Hold, thou mistak'st the Majesty, kneel here;
Cordelia has our pow'r, Cordelia's queen.
Speak, is not that the noble suff'ring Edgar?
GLOUCESTER.    My pious son, more dear than my lost eyes.
LEAR.    I wronged him too, but here's the fair amends.
EDGAR.    Your leave, my liege, for an unwelcome message.
Edmund (but that's a trifle) is expired;
What more will touch you, your imperious daughters
Goneril and haughty Regan, both are dead,
Each by the other poisoned at a banquet;
This, dying, they confest.
CORDELIA.    O fatal period of ill-governed life!
LEAR.    Ingrateful as they were, my heart feels yet
A pang of nature for their wretched fall—
But, Edgar, I defer thy joys too long:

Thou serv'dst distrest Cordelia; take her crowned:
Th'imperial grace fresh blooming on her brow;
Nay, Gloucester, thou hast here a father's right;
Thy helping hand t'heap blessings on their head.

KENT.    Old Kent throws in his hearty wishes too.

EDGAR.    The gods and you too largely recompense
What I have done; the gift strikes merit dumb.

CORDELIA.    Nor do I blush to own my self o'er-paid
For all my suff'rings past.

GLOUCESTER.    Now, gentle gods, give Gloucester his discharge.

LEAR.    No, Gloucester, thou hast business yet for life;
Thou, Kent, and I, retired to some cool cell
Will gently pass our short reserves of time
In calm reflections on our fortunes past,
Cheered with relation of the prosperous reign
Of this celestial pair; thus our remains
Shall in an even course of thought be past,
Enjoy the present hour, nor fear the last.

EDGAR.    Our drooping country now erects her head,
Peace spreads her balmy wings, and plenty blooms.
Divine Cordelia, all the gods can witness
How much thy love to Empire I prefer!
Thy bright example shall convince the world
(Whatever storms of fortune are decreed)
That truth and virtue shall at last succeed.

(*Exeunt Omnes.*)

CPSIA information can be obtained
at www.ICGtesting.com
Printed in the USA
LVHW080345230822
726640LV00013B/463

9 781551 119670